"With characteristic robustness, M̶̶̶̶̶̶̶̶̶̶̶̶
seven sacraments of the mediaev
support that people received from the cɇ̶ɇ̶ɯ̶ᴜ̶..
confirmation, marriage, ordination, and even extreme unction. He ᴅᴇᴠɪꜱᴇᴅ
ways of capturing the beneficial purpose of each rite while insisting on the
absolute priority of faith as the way of salvation. In *Martin Luther and the
Seven Sacraments*, Brian Brewer reviews Luther's teaching in this field, com-
pares it with the opinions of subsequent reformers, and recommends methods
of reviving the legitimate purposes of the seven sacraments in Protestantism
today. This book is a model of the use of historical theology as a resource for
the contemporary church."

—**David Bebbington**, University of Stirling, Scotland; Baylor University

"This excellent volume by Brian Brewer is an important exploration of Luther's sacramental theology. Brewer not only offers a convincing historical
portrayal of how Luther reframed the sacraments but also probes possibilities
for enriching contemporary Protestant practices. For those seeking greater
understanding of the Lutheran Reformation and for those involved in contemporary ecclesial life in an ecumenical context, this stimulating study is
essential reading."

—**Ian Randall**, Spurgeon's College, London; International Baptist
Theological Study Centre, Amsterdam

"*Martin Luther and the Seven Sacraments* is both a historical review and a
practical retrieval—a must read for anyone interested in how the sacraments
and rituals of the church have been and are to be understood. In leading us
through the remains of medieval Catholic and early Protestant church towers,
Brewer not only offers us a banister with which to steady ourselves but may
have even got hold of the bell rope."

—**David Wilhite**, George W. Truett Theological Seminary, Baylor University

"In this searching and carefully researched book, Brian Brewer wears his
considerable learning lightly. His thorough—but thoroughly Protestant—
appreciation of Christian practices thought by Roman Catholics to be sacraments reveals their value even for Protestants. That marriage is not a sacrament
does not mean it is trivial; that ordination is not a sacrament must not hide its
importance. Brewer's work is ecumenical in the best sense of the word. Rather
than pretending that no differences remain among Christian communions,
it mines the depths of our traditions for nuggets of wisdom and insight. As
the church observes five hundred years of Reformation, this book will help
us remember what must be retained and what can be let go."

—**Derek Nelson**, Wabash College

Martin Luther
and the Seven
Sacraments

Martin Luther and the Seven Sacraments

A Contemporary Protestant Reappraisal

BRIAN C. BREWER

Baker Academic

a division of Baker Publishing Group
Grand Rapids, Michigan

© 2017 by Brian C. Brewer

Published by Baker Academic
a division of Baker Publishing Group
PO Box 6287, Grand Rapids, MI 49516-6287
www.bakeracademic.com

Printed in the United States of America

Library of Congress Cataloging-in-Publication Data
Names: Brewer, Brian C., author.
Title: Martin Luther and the seven sacraments : a contemporary Protestant reappraisal / Brian C.
    Brewer.
Description: Grand Rapids : Baker Academic, 2017. | Includes bibliographical references and index.
Identifiers: LCCN 2016059365 | ISBN 9780801049477 (pbk.)
Subjects: LCSH: Luther, Martin, 1483–1546. | Sacraments—History of doctrines—16th century. |
    Reformed Church—Doctrines.
Classification: LCC BR333.5.S33 B74 2017 | DDC 265—dc23
LC record available at https://lccn.loc.gov/2016059365

Special thanks to Yale University Press for permission to reproduce a passage from Heiko A. Oberman, *Luther: Man between God and the Devil* (New Haven: Yale University Press, 2006), in chapter 5 below.

17 18 19 20 21 22 23   7 6 5 4 3 2 1

Für Brittany,
die meine Liebe für Luther teilt

*It is dangerous
to remember the past only*

*for its own sake, dangerous
to deliver a message
that you did not get.*

                        Wendell Berry

Contents

Preface

The title of this book may strike some as curious and others as absurd. The vast majority of Protestants through history have believed there to be only two sacraments or ordinances: baptism and the Lord's Supper. Since the reforms of Martin Luther in the early Reformation period of the sixteenth century, this has consistently been the case. On the other hand, Roman Catholicism has historically avowed seven sacraments of the church—adding confirmation, holy orders (ordination), penance (reconciliation), matrimony, and extreme unction (or anointing of the sick) to baptism and the Lord's Supper—originating from its medieval practice, and it later reaffirmed this number in response to the development of Protestantism. Protestants thus believe in two sacraments, Catholics in seven. Hence this book may seem to be mistitled.

Yet this summation belies the whole picture. Even though Luther and his Reformation successors reduced the number of sacraments, they never intended to diminish most of the sacraments' material practice in the Christian faith. Their diminution, and even abandonment in some circles, has nevertheless become the unfortunate outcome within most Protestant congregations. Now, for centuries, Christians from the Protestant tradition have ignored important traditional and often biblical disciplines in their faith because of their misunderstanding of Luther's intentions. This book will review the thoughts of Martin Luther and many of the other Protestant Reformers in the sixteenth century to see how they actually attempted to shape their Christian followers regarding the sacraments and practices of the Christian faith.

To be clear, the book will not recommend a recovery of the seven sacraments for Protestant practice. Luther, Zwingli, Calvin, and the Anabaptists, the great leaders who shaped Protestantism as we inherit it today, though differing from one another in a number of important areas, all interpreted through Scripture that God granted only two sacraments for the church.[1] This book will not challenge their numbering. Yet often overlooked is that the Reformers also sought to reorder and reframe several other long-held practices within the Christian tradition. This book intends to underscore both the importance of the two Protestant sacraments and a robust understanding of other Christian practices that help to strengthen a Christian's faith in Christ.

In my years of teaching the history and theology of the Reformation period, I have found that most Protestant students do not fully comprehend the importance of sacramental theology within the nascent Reformation movement, within their own theological traditions, and in the life and worship of the church today. This book intends to rectify this void for all those who wish to study theology for their own edification and for the inexorable reshaping of the Christian church, as we observe and reflect upon the witness of five centuries of Protestant Christianity in the world.

---

1. Although Luther, Melanchthon, and early Lutheran confessions periodically also included penance as a third sacrament, or at least as a practice closely associated with the other two sacraments.

Acknowledgments

This book has been a long time coming. As one raised as a Presbyterian, trained at Baptist, Presbyterian, and Methodist schools, and now teaching at a Baptist institution, I am intrigued at how Protestant traditions share and yet differ in their church practices. As a student of historical theology in seminary and graduate school, I have always had a strong interest in how the church and its varying traditions have understood and practiced the sacraments in particular. As a pastor of two fine congregations and interim pastor of several more, I have been fascinated at how different churches appropriate and practice the ordinances in their own local communities. But I suppose it was at my prospectus defense at the commencement of my dissertation stage of graduate school that I was forced to reckon with something of the topic at hand as my liturgy professor, James F. White, recommended that I expand my dissertation on Balthasar Hubmaier's theology of baptism to a study of Hubmaier's sacramental theology in general. "That would be a much more interesting question," he said. And, of course, he was right.

Through that study, I recognized just how foundational Martin Luther's reinterpretation of the sacraments became for subsequent Protestant sacramental theology and how many Reformers, though differing in their own perspectives, used Luther's nascent thoughts as their initial point of reference. Although much work has been done on Luther's view of various sacraments or practices, a volume reviewing Luther's interaction with and reform of the entire medieval sacramental system curiously seems to be much neglected. I am delighted that this volume is timed to be released during the five hundredth anniversary of Luther's Ninety-Five Theses in 1517, the year historians have traditionally used to mark the beginnings of the Protestant Reformation. It is my hope that interest in the Reformation itself may serve as a catalyst for the continued reform of Protestant churches today, *Ecclesia semper reformanda est* (the church is always to be reformed), and that this book may help foster proper reflection on our accepted Protestant sacraments and other church practices.

This project could not have been accomplished without significant time, help, and encouragement from many people, institutions, and places. I am very grateful to my employer, Baylor University, for providing me a research leave in the spring of 2014 and a summer sabbatical in 2016 to give me designated time away from regular teaching and administrative responsibilities in order to write. On numerous days while working at a library or my own kitchen table as I researched and wrote, I reflected on what a privilege this work is—and how, perhaps as Luther would have understood it, I am provided this role as a theologian and historian of the church as one who is called to represent so many others in their own places of work and witness.

The book was written in several places beyond my office and the kitchen table. Perhaps my favorite location was a week spent at the aptly named Quiet House at Laity Lodge, an isolated cabin at an ecumenical retreat center in the beautiful Texas Hill Country setting near Leakey, Texas, where I wrote the chapter on penance between hikes in the woods and paddleboating in the Frio River with my wife.

I additionally want to thank my fine colleagues at Baylor University's George W. Truett Theological Seminary for their interest in and support of my work. I have had lengthy conversations with several of them on the themes taken up here, often drawing from the knowledge of their respective fields to help me grapple with various details or logjams in my research. I am privileged to work in a place of not only professional collegiality but also genuine friendships and shared callings in serving Christ's church.

I am appreciative of the editorial staff at Baker Academic for all their kindness and assistance in this work. Thanks especially to James Ernest, who procured my book proposal while he was still at Baker Academic and understood the original vision of the work. Thanks also to Dave Nelson, acquisitions editor and fellow sacramental theologian, for valuing the potential of this project; his kindness to me has been a source of encouragement. Finally, I want to express thanks to David Cramer, project editor and fellow Baylor Bear, and to his editorial team, for their careful work of improving the clarity and accuracy of these paragraphs.

I am grateful to my graduate assistant, Patrick Morrow, who was a tremendous help in research, initial editing of this volume, and compiling its bibliography. I have been honored to have worked alongside such a person of high integrity, work ethic, and detailed study as he has been. He is a teaching assistant who has gone above and beyond and is a fine scholar in his own right.

As always, I am especially thankful to have had the support of Amy, my dear wife of twenty-three years, who not only selflessly protected my time to research and write by taking up more than her fair share of parental responsibilities in this season, but also was the first set of eyes to proofread the original manuscript. And I will always remember the loving support of my two daughters, Brittany and Ashley, who were patient with my research schedule and encouraging of this endeavor. These three ladies are the most important persons in my life.

I remember my seminary theology professor, A. J. Conyers, once asking me, with his piercing eyes, an even more penetrating question about a previous, rather idiosyncratic project I had undertaken: "And how will this contribute to the kingdom of God?" I humbly pray that this book, through this broken instrument and especially God's abundant grace, might do just that.

Abbreviations

AD	anno Domini (in the year of our Lord)
ANF	*The Ante-Nicene Fathers*
art(s).	article(s)
BC	*Book of Concord*, ed. R. Kolb and T. J. Wengert (Minneapolis, 2000)
BCP	Book of Common Prayer
ca.	about, approximately (Latin *circa*)
CCCM	Corpus Christianorum: Continuatio Mediaevalis (Turnhout, 1966–)
CCSL	Corpus Christianorum: Series Latina (Turnhout, 1953–)
cf.	confer (compare with)
chap.	chapter
d.	died
Dillenberger	*Martin Luther: Selections from His Writings*, ed. John Dillenberger (New York, 1962)
DS	*Enchiridion symbolorum*, ed. H. Denzinger and A. Schönmetzer, 33rd ed. (Freiburg im Breisgau, 1965)
Inst.	*Institutes of the Christian Religion*, LCC 20–21 (Philadelphia, 1960)
LCC	Library of Christian Classics
Lull	*Martin Luther's Basic Theological Writings*, ed. Timothy F. Lull, 2nd ed. (Minneapolis, 1989)
LW	Luther's Works, American Edition
LXX	Septuagint
n(.)	note
no(s).	number(s)
NPNF[1]	*The Nicene and Post-Nicene Fathers*, First Series
NPNF[2]	*The Nicene and Post-Nicene Fathers*, Second Series
PL	Patrologia Latina, ed. J.-P. Migne (Paris, 1844–64)
q.	question
r.	reigned
Sacr.	*De sacramentis*, by Hugh of Saint Victor
trans.	translator, translated by

UK	United Kingdom of Great Britain and Northern Ireland
v(vv).	verse(s)
vol(s).	volume(s)
Vulg.	Latin Vulgate
WA	Weimarer Ausgabe: *D. Martin Luthers Werke*, Kritische Gesammtausgabe (Weimar, 1883–2009)
WA Br	Briefwechsel (Letters)
WA Tr	Tischreden (Table Talk)

Introduction

I am not saying this because I condemn the seven sacraments as usages, but because I deny that it can be proved from Scripture that these usages are sacraments.

Martin Luther

Five centuries ago, an Augustinian monk in a backwater town in Saxony rocked the known world with his writings calling for religious reform. Historians and theologians have rightly noted that Martin Luther's works eventually underscored the now familiar *solas* of Christian Protestantism: *sola scriptura* (Scripture alone), *sola fide* (faith alone), *sola gratia* (grace alone).[1] Luther separated justification, as an act solely of God, from sanctification, the fruits of God's work, effectively disentangling the assurance of salvation from the motivation for Christian practice. Such a development did not come about because Luther intended, from the outset, to be a Catholic contrarian. To the contrary, one might view Luther's initial absolute compliance with the doctrines and ethics of the Scholastic theology in which he was trained and the strict discipline of the monastic order to which he had dedicated himself as creating a personal crisis for the young monk. Luther's aim in his life was to find peace with God. On October 27, 1527, Luther wrote his colleague Philip Melanchthon with the request: "Pray for me, miserable and despised worm that I am, . . . for I seek and thirst only for a gracious God."[2]

Unfortunately, the anxious cleric had initially understood God as an unappeasable deity who was perpetually angry at humans for their iniquity. Luther was keenly aware of his own daily shortcomings, thus making his pursuit of

1. Some scholars also include *Solus Christus* ("Christ alone") and *Soli Deo gloria* ("glory to God alone") in Luther's lists of solas.
2. WA Br 4, no. 1162, 272.27–32.

1

grace, like Sisyphus's rock, unremitting. But in his persistent search, Luther ultimately found a gracious God in the gospel, the message of "the incarnate Son of God, given to us without any merit on our part for salvation and peace, a word of comfort, a word of joy."[3] Grace, he concluded, was not found in appeasing God with good works or even in the quality of one's soul. Luther ultimately eschewed such medieval concepts and, through his fresh reading of Scripture, came to posit that grace was, instead, God's way of relating to humanity. The gospel story reveals that God is not wrathful but forgiving, not angry but merciful and loving. In the Word, Luther found a gracious God. And humans could discover this gracious God through simple faith. "Therefore it is clear," Luther celebrated, "that, as the soul needs only the Word of God for its life and righteousness, so it is justified by faith alone and not any works."[4]

Thus the young monk set out to reframe much of the religious tradition he interpreted as inconsistent with this view of God. Luther's aim was to give to those who would ultimately follow his reforms a sense of promise of salvation as a divine gift and peace of assurance of one's salvation by faith alone. A derivative of such efforts was Luther's challenge to the authority and structures of the clerical hierarchy of Western Christianity, which the Reformer saw as guarding against this view of salvation. Much of the medieval church's tradition had placed the priest in the roles of intercessor between God and the people and warden over the church's divine authority. The clerical hierarchy had become the means by which a person understood God, the Scriptures, and the traditions and ceremonies of the church and the authority for how best to decipher the Bible and determine how a person is to live as a faithful Christian. By denouncing the hierarch's sole jurisdiction to interpret the Scriptures and appropriate the church's tradition, Luther ushered in a new regime, which practiced a more egalitarian "priesthood of all believers." Laypeople were granted the authority to read the Bible for themselves in their own language, confess and minister to one another, and ostensibly, when appropriate, even to baptize and grant absolution from sins for each other. All Christians were declared to be priests and seen to be ordained in their baptisms. Such reforms, which mitigated priestly authority and quashed priestly hegemony, went too far for most in the leadership of Western Christendom. Luther was excommunicated by Rome, and the Protestant Church in Germany (the Lutheran Church) was born. Other Protestant traditions emerged from Luther's Reformation fount throughout Europe and diverge from one another with their varying theological emphases, while still maintaining much of Luther's

3. LW 31:231.
4. LW 31:346.

focus on justification by grace alone through faith alone. While maintaining a clergy class to function on behalf of the congregation in worship, Protestants agreed that God's saving work was fully accomplished by Christ on the cross and was not contingent upon sacerdotal prerogative. Grace alone through faith alone remains today the keystone of Protestantism.

As astounding as Luther's reforms were at the time, what is often overlooked today regarding Luther's attempts to reform the church of Western Christianity and what became hallmark to his bourgeoning Protestantism is the theological shift he and his Reformation successors made regarding the sacraments of the church. As Ernst Walter Zeeden has observed regarding the father of the Reformation, after arriving at his theological conclusions regarding grace alone, Luther found that "everything—polity, worship, and law—had to be transformed or reshaped in such a way that it was consonant with the new doctrine or at least did not contradict it."[5] Salvation by faith alone would prove to transform sacramental theology to the point that one might even posit that the Reformation was born out of sacramental disagreements. The question of the degree to which the elements of Christian ritual transmitted saving grace to the believer and by what authority this was accomplished became the framework for theological debates about grace, the role of clergy, and a person's "meritorious works" during the Reformation period. "To be right about the sacraments," declared one Reformation scholar, "was to be right about God and salvation."[6] A significant apportionment of the Protestant Reformation then was sacramental reform. "The Reformation was in this sense fundamentally a ritual process," writes another scholar.[7] "Because Christians in the sixteenth century considered the correct understanding of the sacraments to be essential for ecclesial life and salvation, to be wrong about the sacraments was not merely to hold a mistaken idea, but not to be a Christian at all," observed a third scholar.[8] The faithful then argued among themselves over the role, nature, number, and power of the sacraments in the life of the church and the individual believer. Protestants disagreed strongly with the teaching that grace flowed through the elements in a mechanical sense or by virtue of the properly ordained priest officiating the rite. Instead, they maintained that salvation came solely through faith

5. Ernst Walter Zeeden, *Faith and Act: The Survival of Medieval Ceremonies in the Lutheran Reformation* (St. Louis: Concordia, 2012), 1.

6. Carter Lindberg, "Sacraments," in *The Oxford Encyclopedia of the Reformation*, ed. Hans J. Hillerbrand (New York: Oxford University Press, 1996), 3:463.

7. Robert W. Scribner, *Popular Culture and Popular Movements in Reformation Germany* (London: Hambledon, 1987), 122.

8. Gregory J. Miller, "Sacraments," in *The Westminster Handbook to the Theologies of the Reformation*, ed. R. Ward Holder (Louisville: Westminster John Knox, 2010), 141–42.

in Christ. And while they disagreed among each other on the significance of the sacraments, Protestants were united on the centrality of faith for receiving the sacraments and comprehending what meaning they were intended to convey. Only by understanding the sacraments rightly, they thought, could one understand God and salvation rightly, too. The sacraments were seen as inextricably related to God's redeeming work in the world. One cannot appreciate Protestant theology and what Luther and the succeeding Reformers proposed without reference then to these ordinances of the church.

Yet one of the great ironies of contemporary Christianity is that most Christians within Protestantism today do not give much consideration to sacramental theology at all. While new denominational worship books are now abundant, and many more liturgically minded congregations have made a recent concerted effort to recover a stronger sense of the sacraments in worship and Christian practice, it is disturbing that this movement seems to be an aberration from the norm. An increasing number of churches in the Protestant tradition today have only further deemphasized both sacramental theology and even the observance of the sacraments themselves in the pursuit of seeking "relevance" for people's lives. Such attempts are ironic along two lines: First, as previously stated, the initial impulse within Protestantism was to give greater focus and clarity to the sacraments; and, second, for centuries the sacraments were intended to become touchstones to daily life, rites of passage for the various stages of one's spiritual journey, and the means to a relevant faith. As one scholar summarizes, "One's entire life from cradle to grave was ministered to by the sacraments. They formed the basis of pastoral care and provided resources for each stage of life passages as well as for the day-in and day-out journey."[9] In the minds and hearts of early Christians, the rites of the church were part and parcel of practical, relevant faith.

The Meaning and Development of "Sacrament" in Early and Medieval Christian Tradition

The origin and development of sacramental theology in the early church was gradual, informal, and subtle. Kendig B. Cully observes that "in the beginning no one merely invented the sacraments; nor did a small group of people conjure them up out of the imagination. The early Christians did not sit down one day and just decide to choose this, that or the other thing to do in their worship. Rather, their worship grew out of certain given factors in

9. James F. White, *The Sacraments in Protestant Practice and Faith* (Nashville: Abingdon, 1999), 14.

their common life."[10] In fact, the earliest Christians appear to have established practices for the faith without a fully developed definition of "sacrament." The New Testament describes the early church as initiating new members through the waters of baptism, breaking bread in its fellowship, preaching in its worship gatherings, and having the elders anoint the sick—all as ministries and patterns of ritual for the nascent church without any apparent formalized classification of "sacrament." The *Didache*, an early Christian writing dating anywhere from the late first to early second century, gave simple and practical instructions for performing baptism, eucharistic thanksgiving, and prayer, along with instructions regarding appointing church leaders and exercising church discipline. As the years ensued, fathers of the church began to observe that many of these rites contained physical symbols that represented or conveyed God's gift of grace. Underscoring the incarnation as the archetype for God's recapitulation with humanity, Irenaeus, in the second century, stressed God's intentional use of the physical with the spiritual as reflecting divine reconciliation with fallen humanity:

> True, the Lord could have provided the wedding guests with wine and filled the hungry with food without using any pre-existing created thing. But that is not what He did. . . . He changed the water into wine, satisfying those reclining at table and quenching the thirst of those invited to the wedding. By doing so, He showed that the God who made the earth and commanded it to bear fruit, who established the waters and brought forth fountains, has in these last times granted [hu]mankind . . . the Incomprehensible through the Comprehensible, the Invisible through the Visible.[11]

While he was specifically developing an early eucharistic understanding for the church against gnostic claims for a spiritual hegemony of reality, the connection that Irenaeus made between spirit and created matter is also significant christologically. The second Adam "repeats the whole natural development of [the hu]man at the higher level of divine reality," not just replicating but actually uniting sinful and mortal humanity with an eternal and uncorrupted God.[12] And through God's use and gift of appointed physical matter, humanity's perishable flesh shall one day put on the imperishable.[13]

10. Kendig Brubaker Cully, *Sacraments: A Language of Faith* (Philadelphia: Christian Education Press, 1961), 4.

11. Irenaeus, *Against Heresies* 3.11.5; via Hans Urs von Balthasar, ed., *The Scandal of the Incarnation: Irenaeus against the Heresies* (San Francisco: Ignatius, 1990), 90.

12. Balthasar, *Scandal of the Incarnation*, 53.

13. Says Irenaeus in *Against Heresies* 5.2.2–3: "Our bodies, having been nourished by the Eucharist, having been laid to rest in the earth, and having there dissolved, will rise again at

A century later, the Latin father Tertullian gave further shape to the meaning of these gifts or rites:

> No soul whatever is able to obtain salvation unless it has believed while it was
> in the flesh. Indeed, the flesh is the hinge of salvation. . . . The flesh, then, is
> washed [baptism] so that the soul may be made clean. The flesh is anointed
> so that the soul may be dedicated to holiness. The flesh is signed so that the
> soul may be fortified. The flesh is shaded by the imposition of hands [confir-
> mation] so that the soul may be illuminated by the Spirit. The flesh feeds on
> the body and blood of Christ [the Eucharist] so that the soul too may feed on
> God. They cannot, then, be separated in their reward, when they are united
> in their works.[14]

Tertullian was giving theological insight into certain rituals that Christians
had already observed for three centuries. The established liturgical practice
among Christians gave rise to the theological drive to understand, define,
and classify these rites, not the other way around. Many of these rites made
use of physical elements to connect the body to the spirit in order to help the
believer perceive the spiritually abstract through palpable signs. All evidence
then points to these rituals as being practiced by Christian communities long
before the church had developed a comprehensive theology for these customs
and especially before theologians had given any "sacramental" category for
them.

Gradually, the Western fathers of the early and medieval church developed
the notion of sacrament from the Greek word *mystērion* (mystery), which
they rendered in Latin as *sacramentum*, a term originally derived from the
associated Latin words *sacro* (consecrate, hallow) and *sacer* (sacred, holy).
In 384, as he translated the four Gospels into Latin, Jerome rendered the
Latin word from this Greek term. In classical Latin, *sacramentum* has its
etymology in a conventional military context. A *sacramentum militare* was
a soldier's oath of alliance to the king or military commander, often accompanied by the visible sign of a tattoo. Tertullian intentionally used this
militaristic term, referring to the baptism of water as one's initiation into
the *militia Christi*. Roman contract law eventually broadened the term to a
formal *stipulatio*, a formula for oath-making between parties, which may
have given rise to a formal catechetical question to and answer by baptismal
candidates to serve as a public "binding or solemn obligation" (*sacramentum*)

---

their appointed time, for the Word of God will grant them resurrection 'to the glory of God
the Father.'"
14. Tertullian, *Resurrection of the Flesh* 8.2–3; cf. ANF 3:551.

of believers within the community of faith.[15] As Christian catechesis developed for those preparing for baptism and, to a lesser degree, for the Lord's Supper, these ceremonies began to incorporate formal oaths or promises by the participants individually and sometimes the entire congregation, when appropriate. But this act of pledging oneself to God was not to be viewed as a merely human action. As these ceremonies utilized signs described and even commissioned in Scripture, early Christians saw the sacraments as God's gifts to the church and to each believer. Just as the early church fathers had contended against the Donatist and Pelagian heresies by arguing that faith is received, not achieved, so too were the church's rites often understood primarily as God's own promise of faith, salvation, and spiritual renewal, a truly divine *sacramentum*.

However, the church apparently made use of the signs and ceremonies in worship and practice before developing a fully orbed theology of them, and no particular number of sacraments was codified by church authorities during these formative centuries. A treatise titled *On the Sacraments*, whose date and authorship is unknown, though attributed to Ambrose, consists of six sermons apparently addressed to the newly baptized in Easter week. Interestingly, the "sacraments" noted include baptism, confirmation, the Eucharist, the Lord's Prayer, and the practice of prayer.[16] Theologians as early as Augustine (d. 430) believed that God dispensed an indelible spiritual mark or character (*character indelebilis*) on the soul through the rites of baptism, confirmation, and ordination. As permanent marks, the character remains regardless of subsequent sin committed by the recipient. Thus Christians are to receive these three rites only once. Yet Augustine also emphasized that sacraments were not objectively operative without the genuine subjective belief of the participant(s). In describing the effective power of baptism, for instance, Augustine wrote:

> Why does He not say: you are clean because of the baptism with which you were washed, but says: "because of the word that I have spoken to you" [John 15:3], unless the reason is that even in water it is the word that cleanses? Take away the word and what is water but water? The word is joined to the element and the result is a sacrament, itself becoming, in a sense, a visible word as well. . . . Whence this power of water so exalted as to bathe the body and cleanse the soul, if it is not through the action of the word; not because it is spoken, but because it is believed? . . . All this takes place through the word, concerning

15. Maxwell E. Johnson, *The Rites of Christian Initiation*, rev., expanded ed. (Collegeville, MN: Liturgical Press, 2007), 85.
16. PL 16.435–82.

which the Lord says: "You are already clean because of the word that I have spoken to you."[17]

With water baptism as his example, what Augustine seemed to be arguing is that a sacrament is not merely made effective by the performance of the ceremony itself, nor by any power found inherently in the object itself, but by the word of God believed by the recipient. At the same time, Augustine emphasized that God's objective work was still established through the sacrament, regardless of any impurity of the administrator or the timing of the recipient's heartfelt belief:

> When baptism is given in the words of the gospel, no matter how great the perverseness of either the minister or the recipient, the sacrament is inherently holy on His account whose sacrament it is. And if any one receives baptism from a misguided man, he does not on that account receive the perversity of the minister, but only the holiness of the mystery, and if he is intimately united to the Church in good faith and hope and charity, he receives the remission of his sins. . . . But if the recipient himself is perverse, that which is given is of no profit while he remains in his perversity; and yet that which is received does remain holy within him, nor is the sacrament repeated when he has been corrected.[18]

Augustine then referred to baptism and other sacraments as "visible signs" and "visible words" through which God would sanctify "by invisible grace through the Holy Spirit."[19] The Spirit of God was said to "give fruit to the visible sacraments."[20] And those sacraments Augustine saw described in the New Testament "give salvation"[21] to the believer. "In no religion, whether true or whether false," Augustine wrote, "can men be held in association, unless they are gathered together with a common share in some

17. Augustine, *Treatise on the Gospel of John* 80.3 (ca. 416); via Paul F. Palmer, ed., *Sacraments and Worship: Liturgy and Doctrinal Development of Baptism, Confirmation, and Eucharist*, vol. 1 of *Sources of Christian Theology* (London: Darton, Longman & Todd, 1957), 127–28; see also James F. White, *Documents of Christian Worship: Descriptive and Interpretive Sources* (Louisville: Westminster John Knox, 1992), 119–210; Maxwell E. Johnson, ed., *Sacraments and Worship: The Sources of Christian Theology* (Louisville: Westminster John Knox, 2012), 2.

18. Augustine, *Baptism* 4.11.18 (ca. 400); via Palmer, *Sacraments and Worship*, 123. See also White, *Documents*, 121; Johnson, *Sacraments and Worship*, 3.

19. Augustine, *Questions on the Heptateuch* 3.84 (ca. 410); via Bernard Leeming, trans., *Principles of Sacramental Theology*, 2nd ed. (London: Longmans, Green, 1960), 563; see also White, *Documents*, 120.

20. Ibid.

21. Augustine, *Commentary on the Psalms* 73.2 (ca. 416); via Palmer, *Sacraments and Worship*, 128–29; see also White, *Documents*, 120.

visible signs or sacraments; and the power of these sacraments is inexpressibly effective."[22] Suggesting several dozen such visible words as examples,[23] Augustine defined a sacrament somewhat ambiguously and inconsistently. One may sense that Augustine was attempting to explain a mystery that can only be described by analogy and definitions that all fall short of that which is symbolized. Importantly, however, he explained what a sacrament is by positing, "The signs of divine things are, it is true, things visible, but . . . invisible things themselves are also honored in them,"[24] leading later church scholars to utilize his key phrases of "visible things" and "invisible reality" to paraphrase his definition as "the visible form of an [inward and] invisible grace [or reality]."

Leo I, who followed Augustine in the fifth century, also explained something of the essence of the sacraments in general. In his work on the ascension of the Lord, Leo described how both the resurrection and the ascension of Christ were visible works in the time of the apostles to "keep our faith firm, our hope confident, and our love ardent," even as historical and present works. But while the disciples' hearts were awakened by the visible work of Christ from the grave and to the heavens, the people of today must have great faith to believe that which is invisible. Nevertheless, God understood the need for those now removed from the incarnation also to have access to the visible in the present age. At this point, Leo famously wrote: "Therefore, what was visible in our Redeemer when on earth has become operative in sacramental signs."[25] While these signs will only go so far to encourage and sustain faith, as the disciples often failed to see and be encouraged even with Christ physically present, like Christ's incarnate work these "sacramental signs" become God's operative means to strengthen faith.[26] Thus, while Augustine and Leo I helped develop the early church's understanding of the sacraments as a classification, medieval theologians would debate and give greater clarity to their meaning, work, and precise number in the ensuing centuries.

22. Augustine, *Against Faustus the Manichaean* 19.11 (ca. 398); via Leeming, *Sacramental Theology*, 562–63. See also White, *Documents*, 120.
23. Augustine, e.g., even suggested that the Christian commemoration of Easter was a "sacrament" in a sense in that "it signifies something that is to be taken in a holy manner," in *Letter 55 to Januarius* 1.2; via Raniero Cantalamessa, ed., *Easter in the Early Church: An Anthology of Jewish and Early Christian Texts* (Collegeville, MN: Liturgical Press, 1993), 108–9; see also Johnson, *Sacraments and Worship*, 3–4.
24. Augustine, *Catechizing the Uninstructed* 26.50; NPNF[1] 3:312.
25. *Quod itaque Redemptoris nostri conspicuum fuit, in sacramenta transivit.*
26. All cited passages of Leo I are from his *De Ascensione Domini* 2, in *Benedictine Daily Prayer: A Short Breviary*, ed. Maxwell E. Johnson (Collegeville, MN: Liturgical Press, 2005), 300–301.

Medieval Sacramental Development

Saying that early Christianity was unclear about the sacraments and thus that these rites needed subsequent elucidation and precision lets the modern mind place a value judgment on the theological framework of early to medieval Christians. Perhaps these Christians were not theologically unrefined and primordial, their thought needing to be further enlightened or developed. Unlike modern Westerners, the church fathers were apparently much more comfortable abiding in divine mystery. The sacraments were a specimen of many aspects of theological praxis for maintaining such ambiguity. This is an important note for the contemporary reader: the evolution of increased clarity regarding the sacraments and the evolution of the church's sacramental system are products of the modern Western mind, particularly at the advent of Scholasticism. Medieval theologians attempted to perceive, understand, and at times control that which the church's forebears simply accepted as an enigmatic, unexplainable, and celestial gift. Regardless, as the sacraments began to mark the rites of passage from birth, adolescence, marriage, daily practice of faith, and ultimately to death, theologians began to explore not only the meaning of each singular ritual performed through the Christian's life but also what these ceremonies mean collectively and how God uses particular rites to mediate divine grace.

Through the Middle Ages, Augustine's definition of the sacraments as a "visible form [or sign] of an invisible grace" and Leo's description of the rites as "operative sacramental signs" of Christ's work were foundational for subsequent thought. Sacraments became known as signs of holy things, which several medieval theologians attempted to enumerate, often varying widely from one another in content and number. For instance, in the eleventh century, the Benedictine monk and Gregorian reformer Peter Damian (d. 1072) counted twelve ceremonial observances as sacraments: baptism, confirmation, anointing of the sick, consecration of bishops, anointing of kings, consecration of churches, confession, marriage, and the consecration of canonists, monks, hermits, and nuns. Interestingly missing from this list were two of the original three sacraments listed by the fathers: penance and the Lord's Supper.[27]

By the twelfth century, Peter Abelard (d. 1142) counted only five sacraments: baptism, chrismation (confirmation), Eucharist, anointing, and matrimony. Bernard of Clairvaux (d. 1153) settled somewhere between Damian and Abelard, deciding upon eleven rites as sacraments, a list that even included

27. Lindberg, "Sacraments," 463.

footwashing. However, perhaps no notable theologian enumerated as many sacraments as Hugh of Saint Victor (an abbot; d. 1141). Hugh, a Saxon canon regular in the twelfth century, wrote a significant work on the sacraments, giving greater clarity to the definition of and qualification for a rite to be seen as "sacrament." Hugh's great work *De sacramentis* was, as one scholar explained, "one of the first attempts to identify and standardize the major sacraments—here baptism, confirmation, communion, marriage, penance, and extreme unction—and give these special prominence."[28] Hugh was comfortable to a point with a simple Augustinian definition of sacrament as a "sign of a sacred reality," which is to imply that visible and tangible material objects can embody and impart invisible and spiritual grace.[29] However, he ultimately felt that Augustine's definition was too broad and needed greater refinement leading to a stricter definition. A holy sign was a genuine sacrament if it met three qualifications, he argued: "A sacrament is a corporeal or material element set before the senses without, representing by similitude and signifying by institution and containing by sanctification some invisible and spiritual grace."[30] In other words, a sacrament is constituted through three basic components: element, grace, and institution. Hugh proudly evaluated his threefold definition as "so fitting and perfect that it is found to befit every sacrament and a sacrament alone. For every thing that has these three is a sacrament, and every thing that lacks these three cannot be properly called a sacrament."[31] Hugh of Saint Victor's sacramental development here has been referenced by subsequent theologians for centuries. For Hugh, a sacrament "ought to have a kind of similitude to the thing itself of which it is a sacrament, according to which it is capable of representing the same thing." For instance, water, often used to cleanse the body, would have appropriate "similitude" with the symbol for baptism, which was seen as cleansing the soul; food that nourishes the body fittingly represents that which nourishes the soul.[32]

At the same time, Hugh used the term "sacrament" broadly beyond these widely accepted sacramental practices to expand their number to as many as thirty, including the dedication of churches, monastic vows, and death and

28. Margot Fassler, *Gothic Song: Victorine Sequences and Augustinian Reform in Twelfth-Century Paris* (Cambridge: Cambridge University Press, 1993), 288.

29. Hugh of Saint Victor, *Sacr.* 1.9.2; PL 176:317B–C; via *On the Sacraments of the Christian Faith*, trans. Roy J. Deferrari (Cambridge, MA: Medieval Academy of America, 1951), 154; Boyd Taylor Coolman, *The Theology of Hugh of St. Victor: An Interpretation* (Cambridge: Cambridge University Press, 2010), 117.

30. Hugh, *Sacr.* 1.9; via Deferrari, 155; see also White, *Documents*, 121.

31. Hugh, *Sacr.* 1.9.2; PL 176:318A–B; Deferrari, 155; cf. as excerpted in White, *Documents*, 121; and Johnson, *Sacraments and Worship*, 5.

32. Coolman, *Theology of Hugh*, 118.

judgment. Many of these ceremonies had their own inner logic to justify their sacramental status. For instance, he saw the ritual of dedicating a church building as a sacrament because the edifice would house the sacramental baptisms of individual neophytes. The connection Hugh made between corporate and individual, and even between building structure and each worshiper within, must not be missed. "Regeneration is first symbolized in the dedication of a church," he opined. "Then it is exhibited in the sanctification of a faithful soul. For what is expressed visibly in a figure in this house is exhibited entirely through invisible truth in the faithful soul."[33] Although expanding their number, Hugh also categorized the sacraments into classes. While these holy things all had a "sanctifying effect"[34] in a sense, Hugh categorized certain rites as "sacraments of salvation"—namely, baptism and Eucharist; some as nonsalvific but still transmitting a "fuller grace," such as "the water of aspersion and the reception of ashes"; and yet other sacraments of "preparation" or "administration," including ordination, clerical orders, sacramental vessels, liturgical vestments, and church buildings. Many of these tertiary-level sacraments served to bolster and promote the primary and secondary-level sacraments.[35]

Hugh was aware that he had added much more explanation and commentary to rituals that had been observed with a sense of simplicity in previous centuries. He rationalized this development as a progressive revelation wherein "with the progress of time the signs of the spiritual graces would be made ever more and more evident and declarative so that with the effect of salvation would grow the knowledge of truth."[36] In other words, the sacramental effect of the sacraments would be sharpened and strengthened by design. Just as the fall occurred because of humanity's misappropriation of physical elements, so humanity would be redeemed by the work of the physical, too—first through the incarnation and second through the sacraments. Christ Jesus instituted certain material things as signs of sacred reality to communicate his grace. Over time the more acutely aware humanity became of these ordained objects, the more effective and intensely the sacraments would communicate divine grace.[37]

---

33. Hugh, *Sacr*. 2.5.1; PL 176.439B–C; Deferrari, 279; here via Coolman, *Theology of Hugh*, 110. Coolman even outlines how Hugh would include an extensive liturgy for this sacramental dedication, directing the bishop to process across the floor from the eastern left corner to the western right corner while inscribing the Greek alphabet to trace lines so as to symbolize "the form of the cross which is impressed upon the minds of the people by the faith of the evangelical preaching." See *Sacr*. 2.5.3; PL 176.441B; Deferrari, 281.

34. *Sacr*. 1.9.6; PL 176.326B–327A; Deferrari, 163–64.

35. Coolman, *Theology of Hugh*, 118.

36. Hugh, *Sacr.* 2.6.3; PL 176.448D; Deferrari, 289.

37. Coolman, *Theology of Hugh*, 118.

Influenced both by Hugh of Saint Victor and by Augustine, Peter Lombard (d. 1160), the Scholastic theologian and onetime bishop of Paris, wrote later that century (in 1152) what became the "standard theological textbook" for the Middle Ages.[38] In his *Four Books of Sentences*, Lombard built upon Augustine's and Hugh's definitions of sacrament by describing this category of Christian practices this way: "Something is properly called a sacrament because it is a sign of God's grace, and is such an image of invisible grace that it bears its likeness and exists as its cause. Sacraments were instituted, therefore, for the sake, not only of signifying, but also of sanctifying."[39] Therefore sacraments were designed both to closely resemble the grace they each represent and to be causal for the grace's communication. Citing Augustine, Lombard explained: "'A sacrament is a sign of a sacred thing.' However, a sacrament is also called a sacred secret just as it is called a sacrament of the deity, so that a sacrament both signifies something sacred and is something sacred signified."[40]

With these stated stipulations in mind, after elucidating the institution and efficacy of these rites, Lombard streamlined previous lists of sacramental practices and reduced their number to what would ultimately become the traditional number of seven for Roman Catholicism: "Now let us approach the sacraments of the new law, which are [these]: baptism, confirmation, the bread of blessing, that is the eucharist, penance, extreme unction, orders, marriage. Of these, some provide a remedy against sin and confer assisting grace, such as baptism; others are only a remedy, such as marriage; others strengthen us with grace and power, such as the eucharist and orders."[41] That the sacraments now totaled a sacred number was no coincidence. Lombard gave much authority to biblical numerology. In detailing the sacrament of sacred orders (ordination), for instance, he argued that "there are seven degrees or orders of spiritual function," that "there are seven on account of the sevenfold grace of the Holy Spirit," and that "in the sacrament of the sevenfold Spirit there are seven ecclesiastical degrees."[42] Thus for Western Christianity, Lombard's reasoning had the added attraction of appearing to have a holy aggregate.

Moreover, for these practices to be viewed as sacraments, Lombard insisted that they must also be specifically ordained by God. At the same time—perhaps not a contradiction in his own mind—Lombard allowed for extreme unction

38. James F. White used this apt descriptor, although Carter Lindberg similarly called it the "standard textbook in theology in the Middle Ages." See White, *Sacraments*, 16; Lindberg, "Sacraments," 463.
39. Lombard, *The Four Books of Sentences* 4, *Distinction* 1.2–7; via Owen R. Ott, trans., LCC 10:338–41.
40. Ibid.
41. Lombard, *Sentences* 4, *Distinction* 2.1; via LCC 10:344–45.
42. Lombard, *Sentences* 4, *Distinction* 24.1–3; via LCC 10:349.

as a sacrament, though he admitted that "this sacrament of the unction for the sick is said to have been instituted by the apostles" in James 5 and not directly by God himself.[43] Regardless, since extreme unction is found in the New Testament, he reasoned that all seven of his named Christian rites then qualified as the only legitimate sacraments for the church. Another possible discrepancy was Lombard's attempt to systematize these seven rites as coming from Christ as a means of grace after the fall. Here again, Lombard conceded that "marriage, however, was certainly not instituted before sin as a remedy, but as a sacrament and a duty," which now serves as a remedy against subsequent sins of concupiscence.[44] Written in 1150, Lombard's *Sentences* was highly influential through the ensuing centuries, ultimately both shaping Aquinas's sacramental thought and laying the foundation for codifying these seven practices as the official Catholic sacraments by the Second Council of Lyons in 1274, the Council of Florence in 1439, and the Council of Trent (1545–63) following the Protestant Reformation.

To be clear, though Lombard was important to subsequent generations of theologians and councils, his own writing did not determine and fix all varying theories and numbers of sacraments for Western Christianity. A generation following Lombard's death, the Third Lateran Council alluded to the "enthronement of ecclesiastical persons or the institution of priests, . . . [and] the burying of the dead" also as sacraments.[45] It took Aquinas's *Summa theologiae* and ultimately two subsequent councils to side with Lombard for his work to be cemented as the church's tradition.

Much can be said of the thirteenth-century Dominican friar and priest Thomas Aquinas, who became the most influential Scholastic philosopher and theologian. Aside from Augustine, perhaps no theologian has affected the Western church as much as Thomas Aquinas. His *Summa* is perhaps the best example of the commitments of the Scholastic method in theology and the Scholastics' desire to use reason and the fathers to systematize Christian knowledge. Regarding the sacraments, on the one hand, Aquinas answered many of the burning questions regarding the salvific effects, the proper officiant, and even whether both the priest and the recipient needed to believe in order for the sacrament to be effective. It was in keeping with the Scholastic theology of the time to ponder hypothetical questions regarding the mysteries of God. Joseph Martos well describes this culture of inquiry regarding the sacraments:

<del>43.</del> 43. Lombard, *Sentences* 4, *Distinction* 23.3; via Elizabeth Frances Rogers, trans., *Peter Lombard and the Sacramental System* (Oakland: University of California Libraries, 1917), 221.
44. Lombard, *Sentences* 2.1; via LCC 10:345.
45. See Norman Paul Tanner, *Decrees of the Ecumenical Councils: From Nicaea I to Vatican II* (Washington, DC: Georgetown University Press, 1990), 1:315; via White, *Sacraments*, 16.

Early in the thirteenth century, theologians had wrestled with this question, and the main objections to saying that the sacramental effects did not depend at all on the minister or recipient came from those who envisioned cases where the rite might be performed in jest or in ignorance. Suppose, for example, that a child playfully poured water over an unbaptized friend's head and said the words of baptism; would the friend be baptized? Or suppose that a priest were teaching students how to say Mass and said the words of consecration over an unnoticed piece of bread; would it automatically become the body of Christ?[46]

Keenly aware of these questions, Aquinas determined that both the officiant and the recipient of any sacrament must intend to participate in the rite, but that the sacramental effectiveness was contingent upon the sacramental action itself.[47] Thus Aquinas made popular the phrase *ex opere operato* (Latin for "from the work worked"), meaning that the action of the rite is what conveys grace, not the sacerdotal power of the priest or the state of mind of the recipient: "If we hold that a sacrament is an instrumental cause of grace, we must needs allow that there is in the sacraments a certain instrumental power of bringing about the sacramental effects."[48] Aquinas also answered other Scholastic queries ranging from the practical to what moderns may see as ridiculous. The "validity of a sacrament does not require that the minister should have charity, and even sinners can confer sacraments, . . . so neither is it necessary that he should have faith, and even an unbeliever can confer a true sacrament, provided the other essentials are there." Even a "wicked" priest could confer the sacraments. On the other hand, the sacraments, he argued, must be performed by a human: "It belongs to men, not to angels, to dispense the sacraments and to take part in their administration."[49]

A summary of Aquinas's sacramental thoughts would not be complete without some mention of the influence of Aristotle on Thomas's theology. Much of this is probably related to the rediscovery of recent editions and translations of the Greek philosopher in the twelfth and thirteenth centuries, just as Aquinas undertook his magnum opus. Aristotle perceived all reality as composed of "matter" and "form," or "substance" and "accidents." Aquinas

46. Joseph Martos, *Doors to the Sacred* (Liguori, MO: Liguori Publications, 2001), 64.
47. Liam Kelly, *Sacraments Revisited: What Do They Mean Today?* (London: Darton, Longman & Todd, 1998), 13.
48. See art. 4, "Whether There Be in the Sacraments a Power of Causing Grace," in *Summa theologica*, part 3, q.62; via Aquinas, *The "Summa theologica" of St. Thomas Aquinas*, trans. Fathers of the English Dominican Province, part 3 (London: Burns, Oates & Washbourne, 1914), 63–65.
49. Thomas Aquinas, *Summa theologica*, part 3, q. 64, a. 7, 125. See also a. 5 and a. 9 of the same question, 115–19 and 129–33, respectively.

applied this dualism to explain the sacraments. This discussion will be further
developed in chapter 7, on the Lord's Supper, since Aquinas used Aristotle's
distinction logically to explain the mystery of transubstantiation of the host.
Here the Dominican priest found a helpful clarification for how the elements
appeared to remain bread and wine while a worshiper still received Christ's
actual body and blood. This interpretation also served to quash the insurgent
theory that Christ was merely spiritually present among the physical elements.[50]

Aquinas also posited that three of the sacraments of the church imprinted
a character into the recipient. Baptism, confirmation, and ordination all on-
tologically altered the person's character by virtue of their dispensation.[51]
This point became especially contentious during the Reformation, since both
Lombard and Aquinas had maintained what ultimately became Catholic tradition that "the episcopate is a dignity rather than an order."[52] In other words,
ordination brought the intrinsic power to officiate a wedding, preside at the
Eucharist, hear confession, anoint the sick, and bury the dead. As James F.
White observed, "Much of the medieval church finances centered to a large
extent on the power to say mass. Mass stipends supported large numbers of
priests,"[53] leading ultimately to perceived abuses of the Eucharist and other
sacraments that Luther and other Reformers maligned and abandoned.

Ironically, while he is noted for shaping the sacramental thought of Roman
Catholicism for the ensuing centuries,[54] much of Aquinas's sacramental
theology was, in fact, unoriginal but mostly a grand homogenization of the
disparate thought of previous theologians. First, like Hugh of Saint Victor, Aquinas affirmed that the sacraments are necessary to salvation because
humanity requires tangible, physical elements and because humanity fell by
way of the same. Second, he agreed with Lombard that God alone, and no
tradition untethered to God's institution, may establish a sacramental practice. This part of Aquinas's sacramental qualification, that "God alone can
institute the sacraments,"[55] became an important flashpoint for Protestant
theology, a notion the Reformers took very seriously.[56] Finally, and perhaps
most importantly, Aquinas concurred with Lombard on both the number

50. Kelly, *Sacraments Revisited*, 11–12.
51. See, e.g., Thomas Aquinas, *Summa theologica*, part 3, q. 63, a. 6, 95–99; via Kelly, 13.
52. Thomas Aquinas, "De articulis fidei et ecclesiae sacramentis," in *Opuscula theologica*
(Turin: Marietti, 1954), 1:151; via White, *Sacraments*, 132.
53. White, *Sacraments*, 132.
54. One Catholic scholar opines: "His importance cannot be underestimated, for he gathered
together the thoughts and experiences of twelve centuries of sacramental life." Kelly, *Sacraments Revisited*, 13.
55. Thomas Aquinas, *Summa theologica*, part 3, q. 64, art. 2; via ibid., 61.
56. White, *Sacraments*, 16.

and the substance of the sacraments. What Aquinas uniquely added to Lombard's completed list, reflectively, is that these seven sacraments exemplified the stages of life and were rites of passage for each period: baptism related to birth, confirmation to maturity, Eucharist to food or nourishment, penance to alienation, marriage to human love and procreation, ordination to vocation, and extreme unction to sickness and dying. Noted one observer of Aquinas's point: "In this way, it could be seen that through the sacraments Jesus was touching the most basic aspects of human life."[57] All of life was in connection with Christ's salvific and restorative work.

With Aquinas and the hegemony of Scholastic thought in the Western church, the desire for theological resolution was amplified as the liberty to interpret the number and definition of the sacraments was curtailed. In 1274, the year of Aquinas's death, the church seemed to be in harmony with Aquinas's sacramental numbering and reasoning. At the Second Council of Lyons, the church declared: "Furthermore, the same holy Roman Church holds and teaches that there are seven sacraments of the Church."[58] In its Decree for the Armenians, the Council of Florence in 1439 accepted Lombard's list of sacraments, less likely because Lombard said it and more likely because Aquinas had already concurred with the list. The council also observed that of the seven sacraments,

> five pertain to the spiritual perfecting of individuals; the other two are ordained to the governing and increase of the Church. Through baptism we are spiritually reborn; through confirmation we are made to grow in grace and are strengthened in faith. When we have been reborn and strengthened, we are sustained by the divine nourishment of the eucharist. But if through sin we incur sickness of the soul, through penance we are made healthy; we are healed, spiritually and physically according as the soul needs, through extreme unction. Through ordination the Church is governed and increased spiritually, through marriage it grows physically.[59]

The council additionally stipulated that these sacraments were made authentic by three things: "things or matter, words or form, and the person of the minister performing the sacrament with the intention of doing what the Church does." Absent any one element, the sacrament would be "incomplete."[60]

57. Kelly, *Sacraments Revisited*, 13.
58. See "The Second Council of Lyons (1274)," here via John F. Clarkson, SJ, et al., eds., *The Church Teaches: Documents of the Church in English Translation* (St. Louis: B. Herder, 1955), 260.
59. Decree for the Armenians, in DS 332–33.
60. Ibid., 333.

If Aquinas and Florence were the synthesis and determinative voices of medieval Christianity, then the church found itself in an awkward position regarding the sacraments at the advent of the Reformation. As James F. White amusingly observed:

> The scholastics, in trying to fit all seven sacraments into a procrustean bed of form (words), matter (physical elements), and minister had imposed on them definitions which were not intrinsic to them. What is the matter of marriage except the conjugal act, which was rather difficult for the church to perform? And if each sacrament had to have a precise form, does that not render actions and prayers essentially indifferent? The way was open to a sacramental minimalism in which baptism could be valid even if performed with a medicine dropper. The sign value of the acts and matter was basically indifferent.[61]

Another vexing quandary is that medieval Christianity had reversed the experience of the early church, where practice led to theological reflection. To understand and systematize, the Western mind had made believing shape praying, and not the other way around.[62] By the turn of the sixteenth century (1509), the humanist Desiderius Erasmus was mocking the Scholastic mindset along these lines:

> They are so closely hedged in by rows of magistral definitions, conclusions, corollaries, explicit and implicit propositions, they have so many "holes they can run to," that Vulcan himself couldn't net them tightly enough to keep them from escaping by means of distinctions. . . . Moreover, they explicate sacred mysteries just as arbitrarily as they please, explaining . . . how accidents subsist in the Eucharist without any domicile. . . . In all of these there is so much erudition, so much difficulty, that I think the apostles themselves would need to be inspired by a different spirit if they were forced to match wits on such points with this new breed of theologians.[63]

If the Western instinct to question and theologize mysterious rites had created the new state of sacramentalism, even the sound reflection of the West's greatest thinkers was so muddled with the unrealistic and pedantic speculation of their contemporaries that those seeking clarity ultimately elicited calls for theological, ecclesial, and sacramental reform.

61. White, *Sacraments*, 16.
62. Ibid.
63. Desiderius Erasmus, *In Praise of Folly*, trans. C. H. Miller (New Haven: Yale University Press, 1979), 87–89.

The original form of this perceived melioration was the *devotio moderna*, beginning at the end of the fourteenth century. While not invalidating the seven sacraments, the movement emphasized the greater importance of the inner life of the person, with spiritual confrontation with and growth in Christ. The Christian was to devote life to prayer, penance, and service. The *devotio moderna* and other alternative approaches to Scholastic theology, combined with "the proliferation of miraculous stories of bleeding hosts, kneeling donkeys, and Jews converted by the consecrated host,"[64] increasingly led to a corporate sentiment against pedantic theologizing and represented a longing for spiritual change by many, both within the ecclesial hierarchy and among the church's faithful.

At the advent of the sixteenth century, White reports, the "public worship life of Christian laity in the West was almost monopolized by the sacraments."[65] Life stages all seemed to be represented in ritual as the life of many Europeans was largely centered on the church. One is welcomed into the world and prepared for death through sacraments. Between these cradle-to-grave sacramental bookends, the daily life was spiritually maintained through penance and Eucharist, and special occasions were marked through confirmation, marriage for the majority, and ordination for a minority (perhaps 10 percent). Collectively, the sacraments provided the system for appropriating the spiritual life for late medieval Christians.[66]

Luther and the Redefinition and Numbering of the Sacraments

Those with a cursory knowledge of Reformation history may view Luther as a giant bull bursting into the proverbial shop of fragile china, the late medieval theological system. Such superficiality fails to understand that Luther was no outsider to the Western church, its theologians, councils, and traditions, but was a product of the same system. And his critiques of this system did, ironically, still utilize the logic of his medieval theological ancestors. Regardless of whether he was seen as a black sheep at the close of the Middle Ages and the beginning of a new era, Luther was a descendant of the same theological flock.

Luther was born to a faithful Catholic family in 1483, just five years before Gabriel Biel wrote his prodigious *Exposition of the Canon of the Mass*, which the student Luther no doubt carefully studied. The day after he was born,

64. White, *Sacraments*, 15.
65. Ibid., 14.
66. Ibid., 14–15.

Martin was baptized and named for the appointed saint of the day, Martin of Tours. He surely participated in all the sacraments appropriate to a child in the Holy Roman Empire. Though pressed by his father to study law, the young Luther found the questions and tradition of theology to be more satisfying. He graduated from the University of Erfurt 1502 and again with his master's degree in 1505, where he read the works of Augustine, Lombard, and the contradictory decrees of the Third and Fourth Lateran Councils, the Second Council of Lyons, and finally the decision of the Council of Florence. Noted Denis Janz, "He studied assiduously the tradition of sacramental theology, in all its complexity and ambiguity."[67] In 1506 he took his monastic vows in the Augustinian order and on April 3, 1507, was ordained as a priest, thus becoming an officiant over the sacraments, baptizing the newly born, presiding at the Table, hearing confession of the penitent, anointing the dying. Though fragile in its provenance, the medieval sacramental system now unwaveringly maintained that the sacraments of the church were the means by which a person was saved; they were, as Aquinas had articulated, the "cause of grace" (by virtue of the divine principal agent) and maintained the "instrumental power of bringing about sacramental effects." No wonder the newly ordained German priest was known to quake while consecrating the host (and was visibly distressed when officiating his first Eucharist) when reflecting on the potency of such an act.

And yet, despite being, or perhaps because he was, a product of this ascendant tradition, Luther questioned the religious rules that caused him such personal anguish. It was not that Luther did not take the sacramental system seriously as a young monk, but quite the opposite. He participated in the Mass daily at the cloister. Luther took the penitential disciplines at their most rigid and disciplined himself for his sinfulness to the utmost. As biographers have reported, the young priest nearly died from such self-inflicted punishment to tame his flesh and regulate his spirit. Luther himself later wrote of the poor condition of his body because of his youthful self-torture. If it is appropriate for modern scholars of psychology to wonder about his mental health[68] and Catholic scholars to question the interpretation of his own sacramental exercises, at the very least the young Luther could not be accused of rejecting the medieval sacramental system. He was a son of the church.

Nor should Luther be seen as abruptly snapping in some rebellious act in 1517 of nailing ninety-five recalcitrant theses to the cathedral door of the

67. Denis R. Janz, "Sacraments (General)," in *The Westminster Handbook to Martin Luther* (Louisville: Westminster John Knox, 2010), 119.

68. See, most notably, Erik H. Erikson, *Young Man Luther: A Study in Psychoanalysis and History* (New York: Norton, 1958).

Wittenberg Castle Church as a sudden and final repudiation of the church's sacramental system and tradition. Luther was actually relatively measured and reflective in his early uncertainty regarding some of the church's sacramental theology and practices. In his first exegetical lectures on the Psalms in 1513–15, Luther surprisingly mentioned little about the sacraments, perhaps demonstrating some reserve in challenging much of the medieval system, save for his continued connection between Word and sacrament and his reliance upon earlier Augustinian ideas.[69] By the time he lectured on Romans and Hebrews, the young theology professor seemed more at ease while addressing the sacraments. While exposing Romans 6 and 7, Luther showed continued reliance on Augustine by arguing that baptism remits the character of guilt for one's sins but that a bent toward evil persists after the rite. Regarding the Lord's Supper in the Romans lecture, Luther was even more conservative: it is still a sacrifice and purifies actual sin. But Luther manifested the greatest novelty concerning penance. A Christian is never finished praying for forgiveness in the Our Father.[70] While baptism serves as the onetime act of receiving grace, repentance becomes the inexorable exercise of that grace "for the humbling of pride, for the repression of presumptuousness."[71] It is just this point that Luther made in his opening thesis on All Hallows' Eve, 1517: "When our Lord and Master Jesus Christ said, 'Repent' [Matt. 4:17], he willed the entire life of believers to be one of repentance." Thus, Luther contended, the later papal invention of indulgences did not seem as spiritually valuable as the long-held practice of the third sacrament. "Any truly repentant Christian," Luther argued in thesis 36, "has a right to full remission of penalty and guilt, even without indulgence letters." And in thesis 48, he opined: "Christians are to be taught that the pope, in granting indulgences, needs and thus desires their devout prayer more than their money."[72] What Luther seemed to exhibit in his notable theses was a rigorous defense of the sacrament of penance, its purpose out of human need, more than a denunciation of Catholic tradition. From a broader viewpoint, Luther could be seen as defending the church's sacramental system against more recent innovations, especially when its leaders appeared to sacrifice the heartfelt spiritual practice to expiate sin on the altar of short-term monetary gain. If the Reformation began, as is often believed, as a consequence of Luther's Theses, then the tipping point of Protestantism developed, ironically, in defense of long-held sacramental customs.

69. Bernhard Lohse, *Martin Luther's Theology: Its Historical and Systematic Development* (Minneapolis: Fortress, 2011), 57–58.
   70. Ibid., 78–79.
   71. LW 25:339.
   72. LW 31:25, 29.

Understandably, it was probably after 1517 that Martin Luther began to formulate much of what is known today as Protestant theology, particularly his foundational understanding of justification by grace through faith.[73] Only after the posting of the theses does Luther seem to write definitively about the assurance one may experience of salvation, which seems to be a logical outcome of and benefit to an objective divine justification as predicated in Protestant theology. If this is the case, then it is likely that Luther's robust critique of traditional Catholic theology came after his first foray with Catholic authorities regarding the abuse of indulgences and their negative effect on the sacrament of penance.[74] In other words, in the context of endorsing traditional sacramental practices and in the crucible of defending himself from a somewhat surprising[75] backlash regarding the long-held Catholic customs of penance and absolution, Luther apprehended a conviction regarding the forgiveness of sins: that God comes to earth as fulfillment for human iniquity and justifies each person by faith alone. Observed Dorothea Sattler: "In particular, abuses in indulgences and in penitential and eucharistic practice provided the occasion for fresh Reformation thinking on the issue of the sacraments."[76]

Following this transformational insight, Luther began to question the theological underpinnings of the entire medieval sacramental system. If God objectively justifies by the condition of faith alone, then the rationale and human motivation for observing these practices is considerably altered. The sacraments become the means for recognizing God's saving Word and promise to us, not made effective by the officiant or by the exercise of the sacrament but by faith alone. God's promise of salvation and forgiveness are received in the sacrament when the participant trusts in God's strong Word. Faith is what makes the sacrament effective.

While he seemed not altogether clear about this in his 1517 Theses, Luther suddenly had much greater theological clarity on this point as he wrote his

73. Yet some historians place his "tower experience" before the Ninety-Five Theses, in 1514–15. At the same time, given his conservative statements in his early work, and especially his lack of assurance of salvation until 1518, a date following the Ninety-Five Theses seems more reliable for Luther's soteriological transformation. See Lohse, *Luther's Theology*, 85–88, for a concise discussion of theories about the date of Luther's "Reformation discovery."

74. As Lohse observes: "But if the late date [1518] is chosen, then the unavoidable consequence is that[,] respecting the core of his theology[,] conflict with the ancient church was decisive" (ibid., 86–87).

75. It is "somewhat surprising" in that Luther's "Disputation against Scholastic Theology," published earlier that year, went mostly unnoticed, though it was arguably more provocative.

76. Dorothea Sattler, "Sacrament," in *The Encyclopedia of Christianity*, ed. Erwin Fahlbusch et al. (Grand Rapids: Eerdmans, 2005), 4:795.

Explanations of the Ninety-Five Theses in August of the following year. Now Luther confidently declared: "It is a heresy to hold that the sacraments . . . give grace to those who place no obstacle in the way. . . . It is not the sacrament, but the faith in the sacrament, that justifies."[77] The centrality of faith in Luther's sacramental theology was both a repudiation of Aquinas's ex opere operato and, at least in the eyes of some of his would-be opponents, a move from the objective working of the rites to a subjective appropriation, thus displacing God's unconditional action of dispensing grace. Indeed, at the Augsburg hearing later that year, Cardinal Cajetan refuted Luther's interpretation as an innovation.[78] But at Augsburg, Luther presented Cajetan with a formal statement to be passed on to the pope, which repudiated papal infallibility, positing instead conciliar superiority over the papacy and pressing the notion that any sacraments absent faith could convey no grace but that justification by faith was instead supported by much of the Scriptures. Harold Grimm states that "although Cajetan agreed to send the statement on to the pope with a refutation, it irritated him so much that he lost his self-control and asked Luther to revoke [his position] or never again come into his presence."[79]

Not to be dissuaded, Luther continued to formulate his sacramental ideas. In November of 1519, Luther gives us a window into his sacramental development through a sermon written to bring encouragement to a man fearful of death: "A Sermon on Preparing to Die." Amid his advice for the living to prepare for the inevitable by drafting a will, forgiving those who have slighted them, and making full and genuine confession of sin, Luther also advised: "We must earnestly, diligently, and highly esteem the holy sacraments, hold them in honor, freely and cheerfully rely on them, and so balance them against sin, death, and hell that they will outweigh these by far." However, Luther made plain how Christians rightly honor the sacraments, by receiving "what the sacraments signify and all that God declares and indicates in them." Thus "God himself here speaks and acts through the priest," and the Christian can only affirm with Mary, "Let it be to me according to your words and signs" (Luke 1:38). When the dying then look upon the sacrament in the hour of death, they recognize that the sign "points to Christ and his image, enabling you to say when faced by the image of death, sin, and hell, 'God promised and in his sacraments he gave me a sure sign of his grace that Christ's life overcame my death in his death, that his obedience blotted out my sin in his suffering, that his love destroyed my hell in his forsakenness.'"[80] The reliance

77. LW 31:106–7.
78. LW 31:261.
79. See Grimm's introduction to the "Proceedings at Augsburg, 1518," LW 31:257.
80. Luther, "A Sermon on Preparing to Die," LW 42:101.

upon the sacraments in faith grants the dying an assurance of their election in God's salvation. But faith, Luther maintained, is what makes these signs effective. "The sacraments will be completely fruitless [if] you do not believe the things which are indicated, given and promised there to you."[81] Faith in the sacraments is one's strongest ally, doubt one's vilest sin.

In the last two months of 1519, Luther penned a series of sermons directly addressing the sacraments. Conspicuously, he only wrote on three of the seven: "The Sacrament of Penance," "The Holy and Blessed Sacrament of Baptism," and "The Blessed Sacrament of the Holy and True Body of Christ." Only from his letter to George Spalatin, court chaplain and secretary to the Elector of Saxony, in that December do we get Luther's rationale for curtailing the series: he would not be writing on the other four because, at this juncture, Luther did not consider them to be sacraments. Luther explained to his friend: "Neither you nor anyone else should look for or expect a word from me on other sacraments, till I discover under what condition I can accept them. For no other sacrament is left to me, since there is no sacrament except where a divine promise is expressly given and evokes faith, and since apart from the word of promise and the faith that receives it there could be nothing of our dealing with God."[82] Although at this point he still did not seem completely convinced that he should never consider the other four rites as sacraments, Luther wrote only on what he could proclaim. These three sacraments, he said, are a means of grace and a vehicle to strengthen faith.

What makes these three sermons especially important is that here Luther developed his own working definition of "sacrament" that had been suggested in his *Explanations*, a definition that drew from the thought of medieval theologians but that also made a unique claim. In each sermon, Luther described the necessity of a sign and its significance for conveying a promise, but he additionally described the necessity of faith's presence in the recipient of the rite if the sacrament is to be effective. This latter qualification, Bernhard Lohse declares, is "without precedent in all the [Christian] tradition."[83] For Luther, faith is a necessary constituent of the sacrament. Without the reception in faith, for Luther, the promise that the sacrament conveys is inoperative. What makes the sacrament of penance effective for the believer is when the penitent hears the words of absolution from the priest and believes "that the absolution and words of the priest are true, by the power of Christ's words, 'Whatever you loose . . . shall be loosed, etc.'"[84] What became especially controversial

81. LW 42:109.
82. WA Br 1, no. 231.19–24; via Lohse, *Luther's Theology*, 128n3.
83. Lohse, *Luther's Theology*, 128.
84. LW 35:11.

was that the power of the sacrament did not reside in the elements or in the officiant but in the words of Christ and the faith of the participant. Therefore, if the role of the priest does not affect the communication of the sacrament, Luther proactively concluded, then any person might convey the same words of promise: "Indeed, where there is no priest, each individual Christian, even a woman or child does as much."[85]

Hence, Luther introduced the concept of the priesthood of all believers, that every Christian might minister to every other, as a priest and servant to the other. In the same way, faith plays a significant role in both baptism and the Lord's Supper. In baptism, there must be the sign of water, combined with the pronunciation of the divine promise of God's presence with the recipient through death and new life, and, finally and importantly, one's faith: "Faith means that one firmly believes all this: that the sacrament not only signifies death and resurrection at the Last Day, . . . but also that it assuredly begins and achieves this."[86] Likewise, through the signs of bread and wine in the Supper, God conveys the promise of the forgiveness of sins. The Eucharist serves as a strengthening sacrament if one receives this divine promise with faith. Through these three sermons, Luther solidified his definition of sacrament as a sign of God's promise received by faith.

By 1520, disturbed by the commotion in Germany, Pope Leo X issued a papal bull, *Exsurge Domine*, denouncing some forty-one statements of Martin Luther as "heretical, scandalous, erroneous, offensive to pious ears, misleading to simple minds, and contradictory to Catholic teaching."[87] The edict from Rome gave Luther sixty days to recant from his offensive theology or be excommunicated. The controversial nature of Luther's sacramental views is indicated by the fact that, among the points enumerated by the pope against Luther's Reformation ideas, the first sixteen pertained to the sacraments, each declaring one of Luther's views on them heretical.

After receiving the papal bull of warning in August of 1520, Luther spent the next several months producing what were later regarded as some of the greatest classics in defense of Protestant theology. Among these works was a treatise officially titled *The Pagan Servitude of the Church*, which quickly became known as *The Babylonian Captivity of the Church*, an obvious biblical reference that had also been revived to describe the controversial period of the Avignon papacy in Catholicism's recent past (1309–77). This time Luther reprised the epithet to assert that the Eucharist and much of the remaining

85. LW 35:12.
86. LW 35:35.
87. See Leo X, *Exsurge Domine* (1520); here via Denis R. Janz, ed., *A Reformation Reader*, 2nd ed. (Minneapolis: Fortress, 2008), 381.

sacramental system of the church had been held captive by the church's hierarchy through poor doctrine, tradition, and practice.[88] Scholars have rightly
stated that this treatise is undoubtedly the most important document to shape
Protestant sacramental theology.[89] It was in Luther's *Babylonian Captivity*
where the Reformer, building on his previous sermons, fully formulated his
understanding of a sacrament as a promise of God, conveyed in Scripture
and represented by a sign. Thus, Luther concluded, "To begin with, I must
deny that there are seven sacraments, and for the present maintain that there
are but three: baptism, penance, and the bread. All three have been subjected
to a miserable captivity by the Roman curia, and the church has been robbed
of all her liberty."[90]

Much of the substance of this present book will be to reevaluate Luther's
sacramental conclusions, drawn mainly from this treatise. However, this 1520
work, perhaps more than any other place in Luther's theology, portrays a
Reformer who was not static but was perpetually reconsidering and altering
his views. For, while already having reduced the sacraments from seven to
three at the outset of his treatise, Luther reduces the number again to two,
ultimately concluding:

> Nevertheless, it has seemed proper to restrict the name of sacrament to those
> promises which have signs attached to them. The remainder, not being bound
> to signs, are bare promises. Hence there are, strictly speaking, but two sacra-
> ments in the church of God—baptism and the bread. For only in these two
> do we find both the divinely instituted sign and the promise of forgiveness of
> sins. The sacrament of penance, which I added to these two, lacks the divinely
> instituted visible sign.[91]

Luther here not only rejected Lombard and Aquinas's numbering of the sacraments, repudiating the (then widely accepted) sacramental system, but he also
rejected Aquinas's concept of the sacraments' *ex opere operato* effectiveness.
Instead, as has already been established, Luther intended to frame the sacraments around the faith of the one who receives the divine promise. Only if
these rites are divine promises found in Scripture with associated signs might
they be numbered among the sacraments. Thus even penance, a rite of which
Luther was especially appreciative, does not qualify on his accounting, but
only baptism and the Supper.

88. Luther, *Babylonian Captivity*, LW 36:11–126.
89. See, e.g., White, *Sacraments*, 17.
90. LW 36:18.
91. LW 36:124.

While the Reformer did nuance these principles in later polemical writings, his sacramental framework was now established.[92] If and only when a person believed one's own sins were forgiven by God's grace alone, mediated through these two sacraments, would the supplicant receive through the elements the grace promised. Former requisite contingencies of a properly ordained priest officiating or the ontic power of the elements were superfluous. In opposition to medieval formulations, Luther countered:

> It cannot be true, therefore, that there is contained in the sacraments a power efficacious for justification, or that they are "effective signs" of grace. All such things are said to the detriment of faith, and out of ignorance of the divine promise. . . . For if the sacrament confers grace on me because I receive it, then indeed I receive grace by virtue of my work, and not by faith; and I gain not the promise in the sacrament but only the sign instituted and commanded by God. Thus you see clearly how completely the sacraments have been misunderstood by the theologians of the *Sentences*. . . . Thus . . . they have not only taken the sacraments captive, but have completely destroyed them, as far as they were able.[93]

Luther's concern, what he termed as the new "Babylonian Captivity," was that the church not invent new means of grace to make Christians dependent on the hierarchy instead of dependent on God.[94] Scripturally based sacramental signs were effective by faith alone, with Luther placing the hope of salvation on the latter, not on the officiant or the element itself. When speaking very technically, Luther even reduced the sacraments to one—namely, Christ; the others he kept as "sacramental signs."[95] Such was Luther's "full-blown assault on the traditional sacramental system."[96]

At this juncture Luther is often misunderstood by his detractors. Luther did not see the sacraments as even necessary for salvation, since sola fide was the overriding principle. He wrote in *The Babylonian Captivity*: "Faith is such a necessary part of the sacrament that it can save even without the sacrament."[97] The gospel of grace and God's forgiveness can be mediated through preaching, teaching the Word, and through penance. Yet Luther later

---

92. Janz, "Sacraments (General)," 120.
93. LW 36:66–67.
94. Hans-Martin Barth, *The Theology of Martin Luther: A Critical Assessment* (Minneapolis: Fortress, 2013), 224.
95. Luther would interpret 1 Tim. 3:16 as Christ himself being the *sacramentum*, as translated in the Vulgate. See LW 36:18.
96. Janz, "Sacraments (General)," 120.
97. LW 36:67.

needed to clarify the importance of the sacraments when he encountered those spiritualists[98] who completely discounted the use of physical elements. The Large Catechism cites his clarification: "What God institutes and commands cannot be useless."[99] The sacraments are God's chosen, normative mechanism for reaching individual Christians with the Word of promise. They are not unimportant but uniquely useful for receiving God's promised grace. But as physical elements, they are not, without the accompanying Word and faith, essential to salvation. One really only needs to receive the Word, according to Luther.

On the other hand, Luther felt compelled to ward off the Anabaptists, who made the work of the sacraments depend on previous faith. For instance, in his work *Concerning Rebaptism* in 1528, Luther clarified:

> True, one should add faith to baptism. But we are not to base baptism on faith. There is quite a difference between having faith, on the one hand, and depending on one's faith and making baptism depend on faith, on the other. Whoever allows himself to be baptized on the strength of his faith, is not only uncertain, but also an idolater who denies Christ. For he trusts in and builds on something of his own, namely, on a gift which he has from God, and not on God's Word alone.[100]

The Word or promise then was central to Luther's sacramentology. "For I can enjoy the sacrament in the mass every day if only I keep before my eyes the testament, that is, the words and promise of Christ, and feed and strengthen my faith on them."[101] If one observed a sacrament without the words and promise of God, one would have an empty ceremony devoid of meaning and effect, "like a body without a soul, a cask without wine, a purse without money, a type without a fulfillment, a letter without the spirit, a sheath without a knife, and the like."[102] Conversely, if the Christian received the sacrament with faith in the promised forgiveness from God, then the ritual was used rightly and was indeed effective.[103]

Finally, since he reformed the notion of church from the clerical hierarchy to be one composed of all God's people, Luther saw the entire church as

98. Particularly Thomas Müntzer and Caspar Schwenckfeld.
99. The Large Catechism via Robert Kolb and Timothy Wengert, eds., *The Book of Concord: The Confessions of the Evangelical Lutheran Church* [hereafter *BC*] (Minneapolis: Fortress, 2000), 457.
100. Luther, "Concerning Rebaptism," LW 40:252.
101. Luther, *A Treatise on the New Testament, That Is, the Holy Mass*, LW 35:91.
102. Ibid.
103. H.-M. Barth, *Theology of Martin Luther*, 228.

also having a share in its priesthood. The early Luther[104] believed any Christian could preach, baptize, and pray, and all should at times, especially in emergencies, but normatively the selected minister(s) should carry out these rites and perform these functions publicly on behalf of the other "priests" so that everything might "be done . . . in order" (1 Cor. 14:40). Those chosen for this specific function should be called "ministers, deacons, stewards, [or] presbyters," and not "priests," for again, all Christians are priests.[105] Yet the sacraments are not gifts of the church (i.e., the hierarchy) to the masses (i.e., the laity), a function controlled by an elite clerical class, but now are to be seen as gifts of God to the church—that is, to all God's people—exercised by and for one another.

The Sacramental Interpretations of Other Reformers

By the 1520s, Luther was being read widely throughout Europe, and the ripple effects of his Reformation went beyond Germany to the far reaches of the continent. In Germany, Lutheran churches swelled from township to township, principality to principality. By 1525, George of Polentz, the first Lutheran bishop of Samland and Pomesania in the Duchy of Prussia, issued a reform program for the churches under his jurisdiction. As a sign of the priority of sola fide vis-à-vis (and as framing) sacramental theology in the Lutheran reforms, the first enumerated reform by George stated: "Hitherto you have held seven sacraments, but not rightly. Henceforward faith must be before all things the foundation of your salvation, and you must have no more sacraments than Christ ordained, namely, Holy Communion and Holy Baptism."[106]

Switzerland, too, had undergone its own reform movement under the influence of Ulrich Zwingli, the lead priest at the cathedral church, the Grossmünster, in Zurich. Like Luther, Zwingli began to focus on Scripture as the authority over church tradition and preached exclusively from the Scriptures, *lectio continua*, by 1521. Although Zwingli himself claimed his own originality in his reforming ideas, his similarities to Luther are often uncanny. However, Zwingli's understanding of the role of faith in reference to the sacraments went beyond Luther's. For Zwingli, the sacraments are "signs or ceremonials" to serve as one's public proclamation of faith. The signs are still important,

---

104. Following the German Peasants' War in 1525, Luther became more distrustful of the laypeople's abilities.

105. LW 40:34–35.

106. See "Programme of Reforms of the Bishop of Pomesania, 1 January 1525"; here via *Documents Illustrative of the Continental Reformation*, ed. B. J. Kidd (Oxford: Clarendon, 1911), 189.

but they are symbols only. After he abolished the Mass in 1525, he wrote
a brief systematic theological treatise that, among other major theological
ideas, explained his view of the symbolic nature of the sacraments to cor-
roborate one's faith:

> If your faith is not so perfect as not to need a ceremonial sign to confirm it, it is
> not faith. For faith is that by which we rely on the mercy of God unwaveringly,
> firmly, and singleheartedly, as Paul shows us in many passages.
>
> So much for the meaning of the name. Christ left us two sacraments and
> no more, Baptism and The Lord's Supper. By these we are initiated, giving the
> name with the one, and showing by the other that we are mindful of Christ's
> victory and are members of His Church. . . . The other sacraments are rather
> ceremonials, for they have no initiatory function in the Church of God. Hence
> it is not improper to exclude them; for they were not instituted by God to help
> us initiate anything in the Church.[107]

There is much to be observed in Zwingli's statement. While more details
of Zwingli's sacramental theology will be developed in chapters 6 and 7 on
baptism and the Lord's Supper, respectively, a focus here is made on Zwingli's
concept of "sign." Zwingli understood the physical elements of the sacraments
to symbolize the promise and presence of Christ, but they did not transmit
grace or convey Christ except in commemoration. Thus the two remaining
sacraments were powerful signs of the historic work of Christ on the cross
and of the individual and congregation's present participation in the faith.
Eventually Luther and Zwingli had their own rancorous debate on this issue
at Marburg, in the fall of 1529.

A group of more radical Christians, some of whom were originally disciples
of Zwingli in Zurich, received Luther's principle of faith's importance to make
a sacrament effective and applied it to what seemed its logical conclusion: they
baptized only adult believers and restricted the observance of the Supper to
only those like-minded and dedicated within their own baptized congregations.
This restriction seemed obvious. If Luther's sola fide and not the Catholic
ex opere operato doctrine is the operative principle for theological praxis,
then, they deductively concluded, only those who believe should participate
in the sacraments. Because they had been baptized originally as infants but
repeated the act once they had experienced faith, these brethren were called
"Anabaptists" (rebaptizers) by Catholics and other Protestants. The greatest
theologian of the first generation of Anabaptists was Balthasar Hubmaier, a

---

107. Zwingli, "On True and False Religion," trans. Samuel Macauley Jackson and Clarence
Nevin Heller (Durham, NC: Labyrinth, 1981), 184; via Johnson, *Sacraments and Worship*, 16–17.

former Catholic priest who received his doctorate at the University of Ingolstadt. Hubmaier, who had read much of Luther's Reformation writings, used Luther's own terminology to express Anabaptist sacramentalism. In framing the sacraments around sola fide, Luther had maintained: "For where there is the word of a promising God, there must necessarily be the faith of the accepting man. It is plain, therefore, that the beginning of our salvation is a faith which clings to the Word of the promising God. . . . With plain words, life and salvation are freely promised, and actually granted to those who believe in the promise."[108]

On this note, Hubmaier interpreted Luther as arguing that faith is a prerequisite for the sacraments. To this point, Luther himself had declared, "Nothing else is needed for a worthy holding of mass than a faith that relies confidently on this promise."[109] Thus, concluded the Anabaptist theologian, if faith must precede the sign, then only those who are capable of manifesting faith should participate in the sacraments. Hubmaier then used Luther's terminology but drew a very different conclusion.

He described the baptism of water, for instance, as

> an outward and public testimony of the inner baptism in the Spirit, which a person gives by receiving water, with which one confesses one's sins before all people, . . . before which church the person also publicly and orally vows [i.e., promises] to God and agrees in the strength of God the Father, the Son, and the Holy Spirit that he will henceforth believe and live according to his divine Word.[110]

What is fascinating is that Hubmaier, as a significant early Anabaptist, adopted Luther's nomenclature of "sign" and "promise" but altered the meaning of the latter. Luther intended the "promise" of a sacrament to refer to the divine promise of God as provided in the Scriptures. For Hubmaier, the promise was a human pledge of devotion to God, in response to God's gift of grace. Thus, while the Anabaptists understood and practiced the sacraments much differently from their Protestant counterparts, Luther's influence here is undeniable.[111]

108. LW 36:39–40.
109. LW 36:40.
110. Balthasar Hubmaier, "A Christian Catechism," here via *Balthasar Hubmaier: Theologian of Anabaptism*, ed. and trans. H. Wayne Pipkin and John H. Yoder (Scottdale, PA: Herald Press, 1989), 349.
111. For further development of these similarities, see Brian C. Brewer, "Radicalizing Luther: How Balthasar Hubmaier (Mis)Read the 'Father of the Reformation,'" *Mennonite Quarterly Review* 84, no. 1 (January 2010): 95–115; Brian C. Brewer, *A Pledge of Love: The Anabaptist Sacramental Theology of Balthasar Hubmaier* (Milton Keynes, UK: Paternoster, 2012), esp. 2–6, 20–23, 87–89.

A generation after Zwingli, John Calvin, the most significant magisterial Reformer of Switzerland, also accepted Luther's reduction of the sacraments but
defined their meaning differently from both Luther and his Swiss predecessor
while appropriating concepts from both Reformers. He defined "sacrament"
simply as "an outward sign by which the Lord seals on our consciences the
promises of his good will toward us in order to sustain the weakness of our
faith; and we in turn attest our piety toward him in the presence of the Lord
and of his angels and before men." Calvin also added that a sacrament was
"a testimony of divine grace toward us, confirmed by an outward sign, with
mutual attestation of our piety toward him."[112]

Through these definitions, Calvin found himself only building upon Augustine's simple definition of a "visible sign [or form] of an invisible grace."[113]
Calvin viewed the sacraments as divine gifts and as outward seals of the divine
promises, seals each believer needs because of human frailties and sinfulness.
Here God "condescends to lead us to himself even by these earthly elements,
and to set before us in the flesh a mirror of spiritual blessings." In this sense,
the sacraments do not awaken but instead substantiate faith. Yet the sacraments are empty signs without the working presence of the Holy Spirit, "by
whose power alone hearts are penetrated and affections moved and our souls
opened for the sacraments to enter in."[114] As in Luther, the efficacy of the
sacrament is not in the action but in the believing. Unlike in Luther, God's
action is not tied too closely to the outward signs: "They do not bestow any
grace of themselves, but announce and tell us, and (as they are guarantees and
tokens) ratify among us, those things given us by divine bounty."[115]

As to the number of sacraments, Calvin also followed Luther's lead and
ultimately settled on two, but he determined this number by his own means of
reduction. While observing the importance of the Old Testament sacraments
(circumcision, sacrifices, purifications, etc.) for their day, Calvin observed that
following the incarnation "two sacraments were instituted which the Christian church now uses, Baptism and the Lord's Supper." What is important in
Calvin's own determination of this number is that these two rites are for the
entire church. At the same time, Calvin seemed to contemplate the possibility
of a third sacrament: "I would not go against calling the laying on of hands,
by which ministers of the church are initiated into their office, a sacrament,

112. Both of Calvin's definitions appear in his *Institutes of the Christian Religion* [hereafter
Inst.] 4.14.1, ed. John T. McNeill, trans. Ford Lewis Battles, LCC (Philadelphia: Westminster,
1960), 21:1277; via Johnson, *Sacraments and Worship*, 17.
113. Calvin, *Inst.* 4.14.1–3; LCC 21:1277–78.
114. Calvin, *Inst.* 4.14.9; LCC 21:1284–85; via White, *Documents*, 133.
115. Calvin, *Inst.* 4.14.17; LCC 21:1293; via Johnson, *Sacraments and Worship*, 18.

but I do not include it among the ordinary sacraments";[116] and later, "I have not put it as number three among the sacraments because it is not ordinary or common with all believers, but is a special rite for a particular office."[117] Calvin then concluded that one qualification for a rite to be considered a sacrament was that all Christians might observe it.

By 1549, Calvin and Zwingli's successor, Heinrich Bullinger, drew up an agreement of Zurich in order to unify the Swiss Reformation. Regarding the purpose of the sacraments, the Consensus Tigurinus stated,

> They should be marks and badges of the Christian profession and fellowship or brotherhood, and . . . they should be incitements to thanksgiving and exercises of faith and godly living, indeed contracts binding us to this; . . . [that principally] by means of the sacraments God may testify, represent, and seal His grace to us. For . . . they call us to our remembrance of Christ's death for us and all its benefits, so that faith may be more fully exercised.[118]

Additionally, the Swiss Reformers agreed that sacraments did not confer grace except by faith and that the notion of the local presence of Christ in the elements should be "put away."[119]

In the decades to follow, the Churches of Scotland and England, respectively, also formulated statements on the meaning of the sacraments. Not surprisingly, the Kirk of Scotland generally affirmed Calvin's interpretation of the two sacraments as divinely ordained for God's people "to seal in their hearts the assurance of his promise, and of that most blessed conjunction, union, and society, which the elect have with their head *Christ Jesus*."[120] However, the Kirk was unwilling to reduce the sacraments to Zwingli's symbolism, affirming instead: "We utterly damn the vanity of they that affirm Sacraments to be nothing else but naked and bare signs." The sacraments actually effect what they signify, uniting the believer(s) with Christ.[121]

Despite its unique entry into the Reformation foray, the Church of England appropriated Lutheran ideas regarding sola fide and the Protestant numbering of the sacraments, stipulating in the Thirty-Nine Articles (1563) that "those commonly called sacraments, that is to say, confirmation, penance, orders,

---

116. Calvin, *Inst.* 4.14.20; LCC 21:1296; via White, *Sacraments*, 25.

117. Calvin, *Inst.* 4.19.28; LCC 21:1476; via White, *Sacraments*, 25.

118. See "The Consensus Tigurinus (August 1, 1549)"; here via Carter Lindberg, ed., *The European Reformations Sourcebook* (Oxford: Blackwell, 2000), 177.

119. Ibid.

120. See The Scotch Confession of Faith (1560), in Philip Schaff, trans., *The Creeds of Christendom* (Grand Rapids: Baker, 1969), 3:467.

121. White, *Sacraments*, 21.

matrimony, and extreme unction, are not to be counted for sacraments of the gospel,"[122] ambiguously observing their quasi-apocryphal origin: "Grown partly of the corrupt following of the apostles, [they] partly are states of life allowed in the Scriptures."[123] And echoing much of Calvin's sacramental interpretations, the articles reject the Zwinglian notion of being "only badges or tokens," but instead are "sure witnesses and effectual signs of grace toward us, by the which [God] doth work invisibly in us, and doth not only quicken, but also strengthens and confirms our faith in him." But, as they describe the effective work of the Supper in the lives of those who believe, the articles also conclude that "the wicked, and such as be void of a lively faith," are "in no wise" to be considered "partakers of Christ."[124]

Though these British Reformers, along with the continental Reformers Zwingli, Hubmaier, and Calvin, all came to somewhat contrasting sacramental theologies, it is interesting that they all still agreed with Luther on the number of the sacraments as expressed in Scripture as well as with Luther's general understanding of the sacraments, encapsulated by Berndt Hamm as "essential personal appropriations of the gospel for the assurance of faith."[125] What each meant by this idea was nuanced differently, but they were of one accord that faith was the sine qua non for sacramental effectiveness.

Although the Catholic Church had ultimately agreed on Lombard's and Aquinas's number of sacraments through its later councils, its own history to that point was in no way consistent. Observed one scholar regarding the sixteenth-century interpretations by Protestant theologians: "The challenging of the seven sacraments by the Reformation may well be due to a lack of clarity and uniformity among the Fathers in defining the term 'sacrament.'"[126] But while among themselves Augustine, Peter Damian, and Hugh of Saint Victor might all disagree on the nature and number of the sacraments (and also not match what eventually became the settled position of the church) without endangerment to their standing in the church, the Protestant Reformers lived in a different era, following Florence (1439), and they would not be accorded the same latitude since the church had already decreed the topic as decided and closed.

At the same time one might argue that Luther, Calvin, and the other Reformers were also products of their own age, not only in their challenging

122. From art. 25 in The Thirty-Nine Articles (1563); here via Janz, *Reformation Reader*, 373.
123. Ibid.
124. From art. 29; via ibid., 374.
125. Berndt Hamm, *The Early Luther: Stages in a Reformation Reorientation* (Grand Rapids: Eerdmans, 2014), 152.
126. Dorothea Sattler makes this claim, in "Sacrament," 792.

what they perceived as antiquated superstitions from a bygone time, but also in their unwitting adoption of much of the same framework of the very medieval Scholasticism they attempted to replace. For instance, James F. White has observed:

> In insisting on both institution by Christ and a visible sign, Luther is simply trapped by the thirteenth-century qualification that only God can institute sacraments. And that means for him a New Testament proof text, the so-called dominical injunction. Had the earlier freedom prevailed, with sacraments being instituted by apostles or subsequently (Ash Wednesday ashes, for example), Luther would not have felt compelled to restrict the number to two. Had he appealed to the freedom of an earlier age than the scholastics', there would have been no problem. But we are shaped by those who immediately precede us, and Luther followed the scholastics in demanding divine institution.[127]

Beyond White's point, one may observe that the Reformation was, in a sense, a continuation of the Western mind's desire to understand, categorize, and at times control what early Christians had accepted as mystery and pious practice. For both Catholic and Protestant leaders, the head at times led the heart. Mindful of that point, one may see much greater similarity between Protestant and Catholic sacramental developments and arguments than between either tradition and Eastern Orthodoxy. The former groups assumed the same cognitive and philosophical approach, and contemporary Westerners must acknowledge their inheritance of this same mind-set, for good or for ill. Now as products of postmodernism, contemporary Westerners may learn to perceive and advance ideas with a greater spirit of humility, respect for other Christian traditions, and understanding of the frailty and imperfections shared by all.

The Purpose of This Book

This book intends to outline each of Lombard's seven sacraments, which became traditional to Catholicism, to examine how Luther understood each practice, evaluate why it was or was not a sacrament, and explore how the rite might be properly understood and positively used in the Protestant tradition still today. The volume is especially contrived to help those who have inherited Luther's tradition in the broad family of Protestantism in order to assist in recovering a more robust understanding of the rites, ceremonies, and traditions

127. White, *Sacraments*, 24–25.

that are still in keeping with Protestant convictions and appropriate within Protestant worship practices. As James F. White rightly stated, "Denying that a rite or ceremony is a sacrament does not mean necessarily abolishing it."[128] While he did dispute the designation of five of the seven sacraments, Luther did not, in most cases, discredit their value and serviceableness as ongoing rites for the Christian church, a point that readers often miss in reviewing Luther's reinterpretation of the medieval sacramental development.

Luther's influence over what became the vast Protestant tradition has been powerful and persevering. It is fascinating that virtually all Protestant denominations have followed Luther's lead in accepting two sacraments or ordinances as those instituted by Christ in the New Testament. The redefinition and reduction of the sacraments have in many ways ushered in the kind of theological reform that Luther intended but also, unexpectedly, have affected the entire Protestant tradition of Christianity, both positively and negatively. Critics can compellingly argue that Luther's sacramental project may have overreached by diminishing necessary rituals and rites of passage that delineate the Christian pilgrimage throughout a believer's life and thereby leaving Protestantism bereft of important ceremonies.

Ironically, however, a closer reading of the father of the Reformation may suggest a way for recovering a proper and more biblical Christian understanding of those same practices to help the reclamation of the theology, liturgy, and worship of the church some five centuries after Luther's reforms. Even in his most rhetorically critical treatise on sacramental theology, where he accused the pope of withholding the sacraments from the people, referred to the papacy as Babylon, and finally declared there to be but two biblical sacraments—even here Luther exhibited a disciplined temperament and nuance regarding the sacraments themselves: "I am not saying this because I condemn the seven sacraments as usages, but because I deny that it can be proved from Scripture that these usages are sacraments."[129] Yet, for many Protestants today, these "usages" are no longer maintained and observed. Perhaps the theologian who might be blamed for causing this sacramental abatement, along with the Reformers who followed his lead, might also provide the church a means of reintroducing important rites for its ongoing practice and renewal. That idea is what this book attempts to address.

128. Ibid., 26.
129. LW 36:91.

Penance

The Once Third Protestant Sacrament

Repentance opens the heavens, takes us to Paradise, overcomes the devil. Have you sinned? Do not despair! If you sin every day, then offer repentance every day! When there are rotten parts in the old houses, we replace the parts with new ones, and we do not stop caring for the houses. In the same way, you should reason for yourself: if today you have defiled yourself with sin, immediately clean yourself with repentance.

John Chrysostom

Now wherever you see that sins are forgiven or reproved in some persons, be it publicly or privately, you may know that God's people are there.

Martin Luther

MOST READERS ARE KEENLY AWARE that the vast majority of Christians in the Protestant tradition observe two sacraments, baptism and the Lord's Supper, and not the seven sacraments held within Catholicism. One might begin a review of Protestant sacramentalism by outlining the two sacraments that Western Christians hold in common. But Martin Luther's Reformation project was not initiated by his interpretation of baptism or even the Lord's Supper, though he critiqued the abuses of the Mass early in his theological career. Instead, the movement that ultimately developed into Protestant Christianity began over a disagreement on another of the traditional seven sacraments—a rite that Luther, at least at first, wanted to retain as a sacrament for the church, a rite that he debated, sometimes with opponents, sometimes seemingly even with himself. It was Luther's initial Reformation design "to reform penance, not to abolish it."[1] Consequently, this book begins by outlining the history and development of confession and penance through the centuries and then sketches the reason why this ongoing practice for confession ultimately once became the third Protestant sacrament, an act that Luther initially retained as sacramental along with baptism and the Supper. Finally, as in each following chapter, this one addresses how the discussed discipline might be more properly understood and faithfully observed among Protestant Christians today.

Christian Confession in Scripture and the Origins of Penance

A man sits at his desk in the quietness of the midafternoon work week. Over lunch, feeling guilt for returning to an old habit, he silently prays to God for forgiveness and strength not to make that sin his way of life again. A woman slips down the nave of her parish, making her way to the wooden confessional, a kind of closet set to the side of the church pews, where she, weighed with remorse, speaks to her priest through a small, covered window, "Forgive me, Father, for I have sinned." It may come as a surprise to Protestants and Catholics alike that neither picture fully represents the ancient practice of Christian confession; both scenes contain elements faithful to their original respective traditions but are also products of streamlining the practice through the centuries.

What is clear is that, from the New Testament and other early Christian documents, Christians have always practiced the confession of sins, first upon initial profession of faith and subsequently through the life of discipleship. New believers repent of their iniquity while making their new beliefs public through baptism. Such a practice can be found even before Christ with the preaching of John the Baptist (Matt. 3:6), and repeated again in the early Christian tradition through the preaching of Peter: "Repent, and be baptized . . . in the name of Jesus Christ for the forgiveness of your sins" (Acts 2:38 NIV). Thus initial repentance was linked to one's initiation into the church through the waters of baptism. As Allan Fitzgerald observes: "At the beginning of Christianity, penance was not a set of procedures for remitting the serious sinner to the community. It was, first and foremost, part of a process

---

1. White, *Sacraments*, 121.

of conversion from a world described as 'perverse' (Acts 2:40 [NET]), learning how to be part of a holy people (Eph. 5:27), forgiven for past sins and thus capable of a different way of living (1 Pet. 2:12)."[2]

The message of repentance and reconciliation resounded throughout the New Testament. Perhaps the most prominent parable of Jesus is that of the reconciliation of a prodigal son to his father (Luke 15). Jesus's injunction to his disciples to forgive others "not seven times, but . . . seventy-seven times" (Matt. 18:22) demonstrates the abounding grace that Christians are to show to others. Echoing Psalm 14, Paul reminds the church of the universality of human fallenness, that "all have sinned and fall short of the glory of God" (Rom. 3:23), while 1 John promises Christians who acknowledge their iniquity: "If we say that we have no sin, we deceive ourselves and the truth is not in us. If we confess our sins, he who is faithful and just will forgive us our sins and cleanse us from all unrighteousness. If we say that we have not sinned, we make him a liar, and his word is not in us" (1:8–10).

Important to the development of repentance and reconciliation in Scripture is the communal accountability each believer bears. Jesus is recorded as admonishing the would-be Christian congregation:

> If another member of the church sins against you, go and point out the fault when the two of you are alone. If the member listens to you, you have regained that one. But if you are not listened to, take one or two others along with you, so that every word may be confirmed by the evidence of two or three witnesses. If the member refuses to listen to them, tell it to the church, and if the offender refuses to listen even to the church, let such a one be to you as a Gentile and a tax collector. (Matt. 18:15–17)

Jesus is recorded as establishing the principle of binding and loosing as a responsibility of the entire congregation for one another. "For where two or three are gathered in my name, I am there among them" (v. 20). The fact that in this passage Jesus established what became known as the church's "power of the keys" became a point of contention by the advent of the Reformation. For just two chapters earlier, Jesus appeared to commission Peter with the power of the keys, telling him, "Whatever you bind on earth will be bound in heaven, and whatever you loose on earth will be loosed in heaven" (Matt. 16:19). Whether one interprets this power as being vested in an individual "head" of the church or within the congregation came to affect ecclesiological differences between Catholics and Protestants. Regardless, what seems clear

---

2. Allan D. Fitzgerald, OSA, "Penance," in *The Oxford Handbook of Early Christian Studies*, ed. Susan Ashbrook Harvey and David G. Hunter (Oxford: Oxford University Press, 2008), 787.

is that the church is empowered in some capacity for fraternal admonition and church discipline regarding the management of sin and repentance. In his resurrected body, Jesus again gave this power by breathing on the disciples and saying: "Receive the Holy Spirit. If you forgive the sins of any, they are forgiven them; if you retain the sins of any, they are retained" (John 20:22–23). On this point, as Liam Kelly observes, these collective passages "are not proof that Jesus [and Paul] initiated some formal ritual celebration of forgiveness, but rather texts that demonstrate that the Church's subsequent development of the ritual was consistent with Jesus' attitude to forgiveness."[3] These passages, when taken together, reflect that the early church's practice of confession was a communal activity, particularly in the case of serious immorality. Such biblical injunctions of the New Testament also provide a framework for the future practice of confession, church discipline, and reconciliation. Regardless, Christian communities did not solidify a consistent ritual for confession within the church in its first two centuries.

The strong tie that several Scripture passages make between baptism and repentance elicited a particular quandary for early Christians: what to do about postbaptismal sin. As Jim Forest explains: "In the first generations of Christianity, conversion was so momentous an event, the community of believers so small, motivation so profound, and preparation for baptism so thorough, that it came as a shock to the community that any member, once baptized, would ever again commit a serious sin."[4] New converts sacrificed the safety of family and often governmentally approved religion to join this new way of living, undergoing an extensive catechesis period of preparation (often two to three years) and awaiting the full induction into the church through baptism, wherein a person ceremonially turned from the devil, renounced sinful living, and anticipated being raised in the newness of life through the baptismal waters. The new inductee was initiated into a disciplined community of converts, in which each person cared for, ministered to, and admonished the others through holy living. Conversion, and ultimately the baptismal ceremony representing it, was seen as fundamentally effecting change in the neophyte such that, through the church's teaching on discipline and the accountability of the community, the new convert seemed unlikely to wander into serious iniquity. "Baptism into the church, celebrated by the community, was a sign of reconciliation with God. Any sin after baptism alienated a person both from God and the community."[5] Because the early Christians expected the

3. Kelly, *Sacraments Revisited*, 99.
4. Jim Forest, *Confession: Doorway to Forgiveness* (Maryknoll, NY: Orbis Books, 2002), 22.
5. John C. Bauerschmidt, "The Godly Discipline of the Primitive Church," *Anglican Theological Review* 94, no. 4 (Fall 2012): 686–87.

imminent return of Christ, a baptized believer would have little opportunity or desire to sin before the second coming.[6]

It is only in the ensuing centuries that "the Christian community in the Roman Empire passed from being a despised and even persecuted minority to become a privileged and protected majority. The moral standards necessary to maintain the identity and promote the cohesion of the community, standards enforced by the rituals of penance, [were] changed with the social status of the Christians."[7] Until that time, the Christians' communal management for sin was simpler, inconsistently practiced from community to community, and enacted with little added ceremony and sacramental vocabulary.

While the responsibility of the "keys" of binding and loosing was seriously borne by the church, the perpetual question of the early church seems to have been what sins might be forgiven and what sins rise to the level of excommunication. The strictest of congregations, while more open to forgiving prebaptismal sins, did not see postbaptismal forgiveness as permissible. But over the course of time, it seems that most churches provided a simple form for remitting minor sins through prayer and the reception of communion, while they ultimately considered idolatry, adultery, abortion, murder, fornication, homosexuality, schism, and apostasy as graver sins, which required public confession, discernment, and serious discipline. In the second century, the *Shepherd of Hermas* admonished the rigorists, who refused to remit all serious postbaptismal sins, by arguing that such a view was an ideal but proved impractical and was without a spirit of charity. The ancient document recommended instead one more opportunity for such a sinner, provided that heartfelt repentance by the sinner and accountability to the congregation were also present. Here, even apostasy and adultery might be forgiven.[8] Tertullian, the father of Latin Christianity, in his work *On Repentance*, also reluctantly accepted this subsequent exception, opining, "It is irksome to append mention of a second—nay, in that case the last—hope; lest by treating of a remedial repenting yet in reserve, we seem to be pointing to a yet further space for sinning." Here Tertullian called on the sinner to "lie in sackcloth and ashes, to cover his body in mourning, to lay his spirit low in sorrows, to exchange for severe treatment the sins which he has committed; moreover, to know no food and drink," but instead "to feed prayers on fastings, to groan, to weep and make outcries unto the Lord

6. Kelly, *Sacraments Revisited*, 99.

7. J. Patout Burns Jr. and Robin M. Jensen, *Christianity in Roman Africa: The Development of Its Practices and Beliefs* (Grand Rapids: Eerdmans, 2014), 296.

8. Frank H. Hallock, "Third Century Teaching on Sin and Penance," *Anglican Theological Review* 4, no. 2 (October 1921): 129.

your God; to bow before the feet of the presbyters, and kneel to God's dear ones; to enjoin all the brethren to be ambassadors to bear his deprecatory supplication (before God)."[9]

By the early third century, Origen in Alexandria outlined seven stages for receiving forgiveness:

> First, we are baptized for the remission of sins. Second, there is the suffering of martyrdom. Third, there is the remission of sins given in return for works of mercy. Fourth, we obtain forgiveness through our forgiveness of others. Fifth, forgiveness is won when a man has converted a sinner from the error of his ways. Sixth, sins are remitted through an abundance of love. Finally there is a seventh way of forgiveness, hard and painful though it is, namely remission of sins through penitence, when the sinner washes his bed with tears, and tears are his bread day and night, and when he does not hold back in shame from declaring his sin to the priest of the Lord and asking for medicine.[10]

Eventually penance was more traditionally enumerated to have three integral parts. First, individuals must show proper contrition for their own sin through self-examination. Second, sinners must confess their sins (and at times this was customarily done before a priest). The priest would "absolve" the sin by declaring the promised forgiveness of and on behalf of God. Third, sinners must perform works of "satisfaction," demonstrating a change in their lives from selfishness to love for Christ and others (a task often assigned by the priest or other confessor). John Chrysostom, archbishop of Constantinople, wrote: "This is fruitful penance; that just as we offend God in three ways, that is, with the heart, the mouth, and the deed, so in three ways we make satisfaction."[11]

Protestants later critiqued this development of a multistage process of works to achieve forgiveness as originating in what they perceived as a mistranslation of *poenitentiam agite* in Matthew 3:2 in the Latin Vulgate as "do penance." Drawing heavily upon Erasmus,[12] Luther and subsequent Reformers held that

9. Tertullian, *On Penance* 203; trans. S. Thelwall, in *ANF* 3:662, 664.

10. Origen, *Homilies on Leviticus*; via Oscar D. Watkins, *A History of Penance* (New York: Burt Franklin, 1961), 1:136.

11. Chrysostom, here via Lombard, *Sentences* 4, in Rogers, *Peter Lombard and the Sacramental System*, 171. In 1439 the church codified these three movements to constitute penance in the Decree for the Armenians at the Council of Florence.

12. Erasmus repudiated the notion that Matt. 3:2 pertained to the work of satisfaction as the final stage of penance. The famous humanist would write: "Our people think that *poenitentiam agite* means to wash away one's sins with some prescribed penalty . . . yet *metanoia* is derived from *metanoein*, that is, to come to one's senses afterwards when someone who sinned, finally after the fact, recognizes his error." See Erika Rummel, *Erasmus's Annotations on the New*

such a rendering mistranslated the Greek word μετανοέω (*metanoeō*), which more rightly conveys a change (*meta*) of mind (*noos*). This idea implies "a coming to one's senses,"[13] that Christians would recognize the iniquity in their past actions and regret this course. Thus, as Protestants later argued, repentance was less a work and more a change of disposition. Because there was no corollary word in Latin for μετανοέω, Jerome selected the words *poenitentiam agite* in his translation of the Vulgate, calling for the performance of acts of reparation and mortification as conditions for forgiveness. The Vulgate translation of this Greek word in the New Testament was not a peripheral quodlibet but later proved to be a significant challenge to the foundations of the Catholic notion of penance.

Penance at the Advent of the Middle Ages

In the fourth to eighth centuries, as Christians increasingly sought out monastic spiritual guides for private counsel and eventually for absolution, private confession was ultimately made to the priest for minor sins, while grave sins (later named "deadly") were confessed publicly, before priest and congregation alike. After the fourth century, when Constantine's Edict of Milan recognized Christianity and Theodosius I declared Nicene Christianity as the official religion of the Roman Empire, Christian confession gradually became less communal and more a private and ambiguous expression. "The Constantinian evolution of Christianity, . . . as it became coextensive with society, strained the practicality of the old public discipline when applied rigorously to all sin."[14] That which was a public faith increasingly became private as reconciliation applied now to the individual's relationship with God and not as a repair to a breach with one's faith community. The proliferation of adherents to Christianity in the West appears to have necessitated the truncation of the period of catechesis before baptism from years to months or even weeks of preparation and teaching before initiation through baptism took place. At the same time, perhaps in part as a way to counteract the expanding privatization of the faith, entire congregations began joining the catechumens in prayer, fasting, and confession during the spring rite of passage before Easter baptisms, a practice named simply for the annual season of spring, "Lent." Repentance became an integral part of this important annual period of time in preparation for Easter.

Testament: From Philologist to Theologian (Toronto: University of Toronto Press, 1986), 152; via Timothy George, *Reading Scripture with the Reformers* (Downers Grove, IL: IVP, 2011), 99.

13. George, *Reading Scripture with the Reformers*, 98–99.
14. Bauerschmidt, "Godly Discipline," 687.

That the penitential season was now a perennial prepaschal observance following the fourth century also reflected an important shift in theological focus
for many Christians: a loss of focus on the imminent return of Christ and a
new focus on the memory of the Christ-event. Maxwell E. Johnson explains:

> Only in the late-fifth century and beyond when infant initiation comes to replace
> that of adult, thus effectively bringing about the extinction of the catechume-
> nate, and when the system of public penance is replaced by the form of repeat-
> able individual confession and absolution, do the forty days then take on the
> sole character of preparation of the faithful for the events of Holy Week and
> the celebration of Easter. Such a focus, extremely penitential and "passion of
> Jesus" oriented in character and piety with little attention given to its baptismal
> origins, has tended to shape the interpretation and practice of the "forty days"
> of Lent until the present day.[15]

And yet the discipline of penance was not merely to be observed season-
ally. Instead, what was once seen, as Jerome put it, as "the second plank
after shipwreck,"[16] as a onetime postbaptismal confession, was now (perhaps
again) a practice of ongoing repentance before God for one's recurring sins
throughout life.

The twelfth-century theologian Peter Lombard referred to penance as both
a "sacrament" and a "virtue of the mind," explaining, "For there is an inner
penance and an outer: the outer is the sacrament, the inner is the virtue of the
mind; and both are for the sake of salvation and justification."[17] Following
Lombard, the church increasingly labeled penance as a "sacrament." By the
thirteenth century, the Western church had seen the virtual disappearance of
public confession before a congregation; private confession before the priest
had now become standard. In 1215, the Fourth Lateran Council in Rome
determined that all Christians who had reached the "age of reason" were
required to confess at least once each year before Easter. Perhaps not a surprising result of this injunction, as James F. White observed, "The minimum
often became the norm."[18]

In the ensuing years of the Middle Ages, the traditional final stage of
the discipline of penance (i.e., the assigned works of satisfaction known as
"penances") underwent both restructuring and innovation. Initially works
of satisfaction were tied to the actual sin committed by the penitent. For

15. Johnson, *Rites of Christian Initiation*, 216.
16. Jerome, *Epistles* 84; PL 22:748. Before Jerome, Tertullian used similar language with
even the shipwreck metaphor in *Repentance* 7; here via White, *Documents*, 216.
17. Lombard, *Sentences* 4, in Rogers, *Peter Lombard and the Sacramental System*, 151.
18. White, *Sacraments*, 121.

instance, if a peasant had robbed a neighbor of a loaf of bread, the work of satisfaction would ideally have involved not only replacing the loaf but also baking several other loaves to give to the poor. As Christianity expanded, priests had increased difficulty in adjudicating all confessions such that the works of satisfaction were streamlined to set prayers, alms, fasts, and eventually paying money (tariff penances) contingent upon the type and severity of each trespass. Such developments occurred alongside the notion of purgatory, formally defined by the Councils of Lyons (1274) and Florence (1439) as a "third place" between heaven and hell, where individuals might, over time, be purged of their sins. The medieval Christian tradition understood that only the great saints of God, whose meritorious actions outweighed their iniquities, would be ushered directly to heaven. The vast majority of believers would require a period of preparation, probably hundreds or thousands of years, for their sins to be expurgated because most individuals' lives would undoubtedly fall short of the necessary merits to experience immediate heavenly bliss. Thus, for the majority of Christians, "penances performed in this life would be unlikely to pay off more than a portion of this necessary tariff: a spell in purgatory would secure the rest."[19]

Further innovation in penance came when the practice of indulgences became attached to the penances imposed by confessors. This action grew insidiously. First, over time, the church developed a practice of truncating works of satisfaction if those works were accompanied by donations or pilgrimages to venerate holy sites or relics of the church—a practice common by the tenth century. Such meritorious actions to mitigate traditional acts of penance were further developed when, in 1095, Pope Urban II declared a full plenary indulgence for all those who, out of genuine faith, joined the First Crusade to capture Jerusalem.

By around 1230, the Dominican Hugh of Saint-Cher is traditionally credited with being the first to develop the notion of a "treasury of merit,"[20] by which excess merits had been accumulated through the superabundant works of Christ, Mary, the apostles, and other saints of the church. The pope, as Christ's vicar, was then privileged to dispense these merits through indulgence certificates that testified to the reduction or plenary remission of sins by the

---

19. Peter Marshall, "Purgatory," in *The Westminster Handbook to Theologies of the Reformation*, ed. R. Ward Holder (Louisville: Westminster John Knox, 2010), 133.

20. Although Hugh of Saint-Cher is often credited with this idea, recent scholars observe he may not have "invented" it. Hugh's own writings on the subject have now been lost, but he and other early proponents of the "treasury" were undoubtedly influenced by Dan. 12:3, 2 Macc. 12:45, and 1 Cor. 3:12–15 as giving scriptural warrant for the concept. See Ane L. Bysted, *The Crusade Indulgence: Spiritual Rewards and the Theology of the Crusades, c. 1095–1216* (Leiden: Brill, 2015), 135–36.

penitent. Pope Clement VI approved of this practice in 1343, arguing for his role to dispense indulgences by authority of "the keys of heaven": "The purposes served should be proper and reasonable: sometimes total, sometimes partial remission for punishment due for temporal sins."[21] Albertus Magnus, Thomas Aquinas, and Bonaventure all affirmed this notion, and their aggregate works proposed a "union of charity" of these heavenly merits, wherein a living benefactor may vicariously make donations on behalf of another, living or deceased (the latter ostensibly suffering in purgatory). Ultimately Pope Sixtus IV allowed indulgences to be applied to those presently in purgatory.[22] Through the course of the high and late medieval periods, then, Western Christians increasingly saw penance as an antidote for weakness, reducing time in purgatory, and regarded indulgences, pilgrimages, and relics as recourses for the full, traditional works of satisfaction.

The more the medieval understanding of purgatory intensified, the more some church authorities stressed true penance[23] and other leaders accentuated the new alternatives to traditional meritorious actions. Thus, by the advent of the sixteenth century, the discipline of penance had undergone "two seemingly contradictory tracks. On the one hand, the sacrament was impossibly rigourous and tyrannical [one was required to repent of all his or her sins and in due course make proper satisfactions], and on the other hand, it was so lax [both in required frequency and often in priestly oversight] as to encourage sin."[24]

Luther's Reworking of the Sacrament of Penance

There are several entryways into the theology of Martin Luther. One scholar might highlight Luther's notion of justification by grace through faith alone (in contrast with the perceived necessity of works-righteousness in his late-medieval upbringing), a concept that challenged the soteriology of Western Christianity. Another academic might underscore Luther's focus on the *theologia crucis* instead of the *theologia gloriae* of Scholasticism as recentering

21. Clement VI, *Unigenitus*, here via Janz, *Reformation Reader*, 57.

22. Here Sixtus wrote: "It is then our will that plenary remission should avail by intercession for the said souls in purgatory, to win them relief from their punishments." *Salvator noster*; here via Janz, *Reformation Reader*, 57.

23. Thomas à Kempis, e.g., advised: "It is better now to purge out our sins and cut short our vices than to reserve them to be purged away in the future." *Imitation of Christ*, ed. Hal M. Helms and Robert J. Edmonson (Brewster, MA: Paraclete, 2008), 73.

24. R. Emmet McLaughlin, "Truth, Tradition, and History: The Historiography of High/ Late Medieval and Early Modern Penance," in *A New History of Penance*, ed. Abigail Firey (Leiden: Brill, 2008), 21.

Christian theology on Christ's work on behalf of all believers. Other researchers might call attention to Luther's rejection of ordination as a divine institution with its accompanying indelible character, sacerdotalism, power of the keys, and spiritual hierarchy. Here Luther replaced such inimitability with an egalitarian priesthood of all Christians so that all believers might read Scripture, pray, and minister to one another on behalf of the church; thus Luther was ushering in a new Protestant ecclesiology. Any one of these themes can be convincingly argued as the principal subject of Luther's Reformation project. However, one concept among and interconnected with these important overarching themes in Luther's work is his concentration on restructuring the theology and practice of repentance. No theologian, historian, or Christian can rightly understand Martin Luther's theology without engaging with his doctrine of penance.

Indeed, before he had fully developed much of the aforementioned commonly cited themes in his critique of the church's status quo, Luther penned the Ninety-Five Theses, which focused primarily on reforming Western Christianity's understanding and practice of confession. To that point, the very first thesis of the "great 95" read: "When our Lord and Master, Jesus Christ, said 'Repent,' He called for the entire life of believers to be one of penitence" or "of daily repentance."[25] While the presenting issue, of course, was the sale and abuse of indulgences, the underlying source of Luther's rage was that indulgences were "vitiating the [cure] of souls through penance."[26] The sale of indulgences, the imminent threat of purgatory, and the power of the papacy beyond one's earthly life are all challenged in this, his most famous publication, because he posited that they all undermined the proper understanding of the act of Christian repentance. Luther did not wish to abolish this practice but to reform it.[27] "Any truly repentant Christian," Luther wrote in thesis 36, "has a right to full remission of penalty and guilt, even without indulgence letters."[28]

In his *Explanation of the Ninety-Five Theses* the following year, Luther developed his original thoughts: "We pray throughout our whole life and we must pray 'forgive us our debts' [Matt. 6:12]; therefore, we repent throughout our whole life and are displeased with ourselves. . . . For the debts for which we are commanded to pray are real and not to be treated lightly."[29] Luther then indicated that the Christian is admonished and should want to confess daily.

25. Dillenburger, 490; cf. LW 31:25.
26. White, *Sacraments*, 121.
27. Ibid.
28. LW 31:28.
29. Luther, Thesis 1 in *Explanation of the Ninety-Five Theses*, LW 31:84–85.

The notion of daily repentance that Luther described in the Ninety-Five Theses, which was to replace sacramental penance, was both novel and radical.[30] For Luther, one who does not daily recognize his own depravity thus relies upon his works, which is, at bottom for Luther, the definition of sin (i.e., "Every good work is sin"). Hence, as one Lutheran scholar rightly concludes, for Luther "repentance and faith are synonymous" since faith is a reliance upon Christ's righteousness instead of one's own.[31] One year later Luther wrote in a famous sermon, "This righteousness, then, is given to men in baptism and whenever they are truly repentant."[32] Luther's new penance underscored the human condition of utter sinfulness, thus bringing reason for a doctrine of faith alone and confession as a welcomed practice of liberation from iniquity and guilt for the believer.

Additionally in 1519, Luther subtly demonstrated his rejection of Lombard's traditional seven sacraments by preaching an only three-part series on the sacraments of the church—on penance, baptism, and the Lord's Supper. On December 18 of that year, Luther wrote a letter to George Spalatin indicating that he would not be preparing sermons on the other four, since Luther did not regard those practices as sacraments.[33] A "sacrament," Luther went on to explain, exists only where a divine promise is expressly given. Thus penance was one such sacrament because of the scriptural word of promise it offers along with the requirement of faith for those who receive it.

Those who have read Luther cursorily may find it strange that he once deliberately categorized penance as among legitimate sacraments, given that the Reformer notoriously stripped this designation from the practice just one year later, in 1520, leaving only what are now seen as the traditional two Protestant sacraments, baptism and the Lord's Supper. However, a closer investigation into the development of his thought during this important period demonstrates that Luther did not wish to diminish confession in the life of the believer, but, quite to the contrary, he wished to enhance it by releasing this act from its medieval trappings of perceived works-righteousness.

The Vulgate's rendering of the words *poenitentiam agite* (found in John the Baptist's admonishment in Matt. 3:2 and similar passages) could arguably be translated as "repent" (that is, as referring to penitence) or "do penance," the latter of which became the traditional adaptation of medieval Christianity.

30. David Bagchi, "Luther and the Sacramentality of Penance," in *Retribution, Repentance, and Reconciliation: Papers Read at the 2002 Summer Meeting and the 2003 Winter Meeting of the Ecclesiastical History Society* (Woodbridge, Suffolk, UK: Boydell, 2004), 121.
31. Lohse, *Luther's Theology*, 102.
32. Luther, *Two Kinds of Righteousness*, LW 31:297.
33. Lohse, *Luther's Theology*, 127–28.

Over time, "doing penance" became a discipline composed of three acts: contrition (demonstrating genuine regret for one's iniquity), confession (to the priest), and satisfaction (that is, following the priestly instructions to right one's wrongs).[34] From Luther's earlier struggles as a monk, he believed that such an interpretation of penance led to the high potential of the priest to abuse the power of the keys and to play the role not of comforter but of torturer. Consequently, Luther abolished the need for contrition because he perceived it to be an unpredictable feeling, subjective, and a human work.[35] Satisfaction was also eliminated because it undermined the objective absolution of God in the crucified Christ.[36] The priest as persecutor was additionally eliminated by Luther, who argued instead for a therapeutic model for confession, wherein the priest was more the counselor who reminded the confessor of God's love and grace than a tormentor who coldly provided a "method" to remedy one's wrongs.[37] Doing penance, Luther concluded, disregarded the comforting promise of Christ and diminished God's work in Christ Jesus.

Luther translated *poenitentiam agite* instead as "repent," and in his 1519 sermon "The Sacrament of Penance" replaced the tripart medieval exercises with absolution, grace, and faith. Absolution is composed of the comforting words of the priest that the sinner is released from the burdens of individual sinfulness and is forgiven by the promise of Christ through the power of the keys granted to "the whole Christian Church." Grace is the actual forgiveness of God, which can serve as a balm to one's conscience, peace to one's spirit. And faith is the confidence the believer has in the words of both the priest and the scriptural promise of being loosed, which empowers the priest's absolution.[38] Thus, penance is a sacrament because of the divine promise it grants and the faith requisite for its reception. Referencing Augustine, Luther argued that "the sacrament removes sin, not because it takes place, but because it is believed."[39]

Luther's formulation of sola fide is then developed in connection with his sacramental project, initially with the sacrament of penance. While absolution and grace are granted to the genuine confessor, "everything, then," Luther

34. From E. Theodore Bachman's introduction to *The Sacrament of Penance*, LW 35:6.
35. See Jared Wicks, SJ, "Fides sacramenti—Fides specialis: Luther's Development in 1518," *Gregorianum* 65, no. 1 (Rome: Pontificia Universitas Gregoriana, 1984), 64.
36. Bagchi, "Sacramentality of Penance," 121–22.
37. Bachman's introduction, LW 35:7.
38. Luther, *The Sacrament of Penance*, LW 35:11.
39. Here Luther is undoubtedly referring to Augustine's *On the Gospel according to St. John*, wherein the church father writes: "Whence does water have such great power that it cleanses the body and purifies the heart, except from the word—not because it is spoken but because it is believed?" Augustine, *Tractates in the Gospel of John* 80.3; NPNF¹ 7:344.

wrote, "depends on this faith, which alone makes the sacraments accomplish
that which they signify, and [makes] everything that the priest says come true.
For as you believe, so it is done for you. Without this faith, all absolution and
all sacraments are in vain and indeed do more harm than good. . . . Not the
sacrament, but the faith that believes in the sacrament is what removes sin."[40]

Luther's significant rejection of ex opere operato sacramentalism, in favor
of underscoring the individual's appropriation of faith as effecting forgiveness,
divulges why the Wittenberg professor had written vehemently against not
only indulgences and pilgrimages but also the performance of good works,
"even fasting and straining," all of which were intended to make satisfaction
for the sinner's past failures. Wrote Luther, undoubtedly autobiographically:
"Some have ruined their bodies and gone out of their minds, thinking by virtue
of their works to do away with their sins and soothe their heart."[41] And it is
in reference to reforming repentance that Luther concluded: "They want to
do good works before their sins are forgiven, whereas on the contrary, sins
must be forgiven before good works can be done. For good works must be
done with joyful heart and good conscience toward God, that is, out of the
forgiveness of guilt."[42] Even here as early as 1519 and in reference to penance,
we find Luther decrying a works-based salvation when he wrote: "There is
no greater sin than to not believe this article of 'the forgiveness of sins' which
we pray daily in the Creed."[43]

It is not the priest but Christ through the priest who gives the reminding
words of grace through absolution.[44] While the believer must have faith in the
promise of God's forgiveness, the priestly declaration of this promise, "*Ego te
absolvo!*" (I absolve you!), is essential to the reception of this good news, not
because of its ex opere operato quality, traditionally understood, but solely
because it is believed by the repentant person. And since the effectiveness of
the sacrament is not contingent upon the officiant but only upon the faith of
the recipient, Luther "for the first time" made public "the Reformation view
of the universal priesthood of all the baptized."[45] Here Luther wrote:

> It follows in addition that in the sacrament of penance and forgiveness of guilt
> a pope or bishop does nothing more than the lowliest priest. Indeed where there
> is no priest, each individual Christian—even a woman or child—does as much.

40. LW 35:11.
41. LW 35:10.
42. Ibid.
43. LW 35:14.
44. See Wicks, "Fides sacramenti—Fides specialis," 63.
45. Lohse rightfully makes this claim in *Luther's Theology*, 129.

For any Christian can say to you, "God forgives you your sins, in the name," etc., and if you can accept that word with a confident faith, as though God were saying it to you, then in the same faith you are surely absolved.[46]

What made the act of penance a sacrament for Luther, then, was that the *signum* became the *res* itself, "the linguistic sign is already the matter itself."[47] Because God uses the declared word as the medium through which to distribute divine righteousness, the priest's declaration is effective not because he discerns that justification or absolution has already taken place in the inner life of the penitent but because, as Luther saw it, the speech act itself is God's means of communicating grace and through which the recipient receives confidence in God's promise, accomplished through God's Word. The speech act establishes communication of the promise of God and liberates the hearers from their sins. Luther's formulation of this doctrine of the power of the spoken Word of God, then, also was developed, at least in part, in the context of his modification of penance.

The fall of 1520 was the most prolific season of Luther's life. Among his notable works was Luther's consequential treatment of the traditional seven sacraments officially named *The Pagan Servitude of the Church*, but quickly nicknamed *The Babylonian Captivity of the Church*, because the Reformer equated Rome with Babylon by accusing the church of tyrannically and arbitrarily taking captive the means of grace from the laity. Unlike in his three sermons on the sacraments of baptism, the Supper, and penance in 1519, wherein he tacitly negated the genuine sacramentalism of the other four practices through passive omission, now for the first time Luther publicly and actively demoted the other four sacraments of the Western church, not counting them as genuine sacraments because they were, for various reasons, not divine promises accompanied by signs, designed to elicit faith.

The remaining three sacraments were held captive by the "regime of Nimrod." And as he broached the topic of the third sacrament, Luther argued that the captivity of penance was that "the sacrament itself has been made so utterly void that not a vestige of it remains."[48] But, like baptism and the Supper, it was intended to convey both the words of divine promise and Christian faith. He accused the church hierarchy of distorting the divine promise of the keys into a kind of power by which the clergy kept the laity in fear, in order to compel service from them.

46. LW 35:12.
47. Oswald Bayer, *Martin Luther's Theology: A Contemporary Interpretation*, trans. Thomas A. Trapp (Grand Rapids: Eerdmans, 2008), 52.
48. Luther, *Pagan Servitude*, in Dillenberger, 315; cf. LW 36:81.

While he again rejected the medieval tripartite understanding of the sacrament as contrition, confession, and satisfaction, Luther argued here that faith itself brings genuine contrition. With such faith, confession was necessary for the ongoing life of a believer. He observed that "secret confession" was "highly satisfactory" in that as "we lay bare to a brother what lies on our consciences, and in confidence unveil that which we have kept hidden, we receive, through the mouth of a brother, a comfort which God has spoken. When we accept this in faith, it gives us peace by the mercy of God through the words spoken to us by a brother." What Luther found as distorted was the assigning of "pilgrimages, the perverse worship of saints, the mendacious legends of saints, various beliefs in works and in the practice of ceremonies; by all of which, faith in God is lessened, while idolatry is fostered."[49]

What is further developed in this 1520 treatise concerning penance is the certainty that Luther exhibited regarding who can receive another Christian's confession. Utilizing Matthew 18, the Reformer observed that Christ instructed Christians to correct and reprove one another in private, and only in the case of continual stubbornness in sinfulness are the sinners to be brought before the church. Here Luther interpreted the Roman tradition as making the last resort the first requirement, concluding: "It is not necessary to tell it to the church, that is, as these babblers interpret it, to the prelate or priest."[50] Thus Luther's ecclesiology also developed in reference to this sacrament: the power of the keys and the work of the priesthood are shared by the entire congregation, one with the others; they are not a privilege reserved by the ordained cleric alone. Hence, "where two or three are gathered in my name, there am I in the midst of them" (Matt. 18:20 RSV).[51] Consequently, when individuals voluntarily confess in private to a fellow Christian, requesting reproof and pardon, their sins are forgiven. Priests, Luther argued, must release Christians to hear and minister to one another, confess to and forgive each other, and not take captive this sacrament through any "reservation" of this privilege to "ensnare consciences of the weak," to "establish their wicked despotism"[52] over the people, or to require superfluous satisfactions in order to drive "souls to despair."[53]

Having seen Luther make his case for the proper practice of penance as a sacrament of the church both in his 1519 sermon and then in his section on penance in the heart of *The Babylonian Captivity of the Church*, we may find it strange that Luther changed his categorizing of this act before he reached

49. Luther, *Pagan Servitude*, in Dillenberger, 320; cf. LW 36:86–87.
50. LW 36:87; cf. Dillenberger, 320.
51. Ibid.; cf. Dillenberger, 321.
52. LW 36:88.
53. LW 36:90.

the conclusion of this same 1520 treatise. Yet, in the final paragraphs of *The Babylonian Captivity*, Luther famously reduced his own list of sacraments from three to two, eliminating penance. Here he explained purely through logic: a sacrament must contain the promise of the forgiveness of sins in conjunction with a visible sign instituted by Christ. Since penance has no accompanying sign, it technically, according to his own definition, falls short of being a sacrament.[54] At this juncture Luther changed not only his numbering of the sacraments but also his working definition of "sign" from that which is proclaimed in Word to that which is visible and tangible.

It is at this juncture that historical and liturgical theologians have tended to refrain from further research of Luther's development of penance—and this diminution has undoubtedly affected any potential preservation of a robust theology and practice of confession, whether private or public, within most Protestant churches in contemporary Christianity. If Luther has dropped the act of penance from the list of scripturally sanctioned sacraments, one might reason, it should be heaped on the discard pile along with marriage, confirmation, and extreme unction. However, such a conclusion is not only an irresponsible amplification of one paragraph of Luther's early writing; it also fails both to take that paragraph in the context of its own treatise and, what is more important, to account for all that Luther wrote regarding the proper understanding and practice of this rite, both before the conclusion of *The Babylonian Captivity* and in all his writings that follow it. In a brief introductory article outlining strange facts about Luther's life, Herbert Jacobsen noticed an apparent paradox involving Luther: "Early on as a reformer, Luther publicly concluded that penance . . . wasn't a sacrament at all. Yet he continued to daily confess his sins to another person for most of his life."[55] While Luther's treatment of penance appears dialectical, a closer examination of the corpus of Luther's works demonstrates this not to be the case.

One may observe that, not only in *The Babylonian Captivity* but also in subsequent writings and confessions, the Reformer appears to vacillate about whether the act of penance itself is a sacrament.[56] While certainly he buries this designation from being applied to penance in *The Babylonian Captivity*,

54. Bagchi, "Sacramentality of Penance," 119. At the conclusion of *Babylonian Captivity*, Luther declares: "Nevertheless, it has seemed proper to restrict the name of sacrament to those promises which have signs attached to them. The remainder, not being bound to signs, are bare promises. Hence there are, strictly speaking, but two sacraments. . . . For only in these two do we find both the divinely instituted sign and the promise of forgiveness of sins. The sacrament of penance, which I added to these two, lacks the divinely instituted visible sign." LW 36:124.

55. Herbert K. Jacobsen, "Martin Luther's Early Years: Did You Know?," *Christian History* 9, no. 2 (April 1992): 2.

56. Bayer, *Luther's Theology*, 269.

Luther surprisingly resurrects the term shortly thereafter in his *Defense and Explanation of All the Articles Condemned by the Pope*. The sacramentality of penance was not a peripheral argument in this defense against the papal bull *Exsurge Domine* but was central to his rebuttal.[57] Additionally, it is also telling that Luther and early Lutheranism assigned the rite to a place alongside the other two sacraments in its practice in the new evangelical church. Luther continued to write about penance as that which "was instituted by Christ and conveys eschatological graces."[58] While it admittedly lacks a physical, representative sign, Luther seems inexact and undetermined as to its precise designation and placement. Oswald Bayer suggests that if the bread and wine are sign number one for Luther, and the water of baptism is sign number two, then, because of its relationship to baptism, "as a return to it—[penance is] what one might call 'sign number two and one-half,' as an evangelical sacrament."[59]

While some liturgical scholars have complained that the wider Protestant tradition has collapsed any semblance of confession into the Supper,[60] losing Luther's intended tie to baptism, Luther himself also connected penance with the Eucharist. To that point, during Christmas in 1521, when Luther was sequestered in Wartburg Castle, Andreas Karlstadt lifted the requirements of auricular confession before the Supper, along with dispensing with vestments, distributing both kinds (bread and cup), and officiating the Supper in the vernacular. Many of Karlstadt's reforms appear to be consistent with the trajectory of Luther's previous work, yet as Walter Sundberg observes, "Luther was not always ready to embrace the fullest implications of his own teaching."[61] Thus, by 1524 Luther overturned Karlstadt's omission of confession before the Supper and required each Christian in Wittenberg, under civil decree, to have his faith and conduct examined by a priest before receiving the Eucharist.[62] Therefore Luther connected penance to baptism, but then

57. Bagchi, "Sacramentality of Penance," 119.

58. H.-M. Barth, *Theology of Martin Luther*, 247.

59. Bayer, *Luther's Theology*, 270.

60. White claims, "For most Protestants, penance became subsumed in the penitential eucharist, . . . did not disappear, . . . and simply attached itself to the eucharist" (*Sacraments*, 123).

61. Walter Sundberg, *Worship as Repentance: Lutheran Liturgical Traditions and Catholic Consensus* (Grand Rapids: Eerdmans, 2012), 70.

62. Subsequently, from 1525 to 1591, some fifty Lutheran church ordinances mandated individual confession before a person is admitted to the Supper. Typically, the penitent is to be examined and make confession before the priest at least four times a year. Such a mandate, however, must be viewed in the best light, for Luther. As he notes in the Large Catechism, "True Christians who cherish and honor the sacrament will of their own accord urge and impel themselves to come." *BC* 451. See Thomas Tentler, "Confession," in Hillerbrand, *Oxford Encyclopedia of the Reformation*, 1:403; Sundberg, *Worship as Repentance*, 85.

again to the Supper. He required an examination by the priest before each Eucharist while also arguing that penance is done best when done voluntarily.

One may then easily deduce that Luther strongly connected penance with the other sacraments in his ongoing development of the rites. Yet in much of his writing it remains equivocal whether confession serves as scaffolding around the twin pillars of baptism and Supper or stands as a third sacramental pedestal. In his Small Catechism, for instance, the Reformer placed "Confession and Absolution" between "The Sacrament of Holy Baptism" and "The Sacrament of the Altar." In the wider evangelical tradition, the Augsburg Confession sandwiches articles 11 and 12, on confession and repentance, between article 10, on baptism and the Holy Supper of our Lord, and article 13, on "the use of the sacraments." Again, in Melanchthon's "Instruction for Visitation of Pastors in Saxony," to which Luther himself wrote the foreword, penance is again listed as a sacrament.[63] Thus, sometimes Luther seemed to approve of the sacramentality of penance; in other places where penance is not regarded technically as a sacrament unto itself, it appears to function as one, or at least is so strongly connected in practice with the other two Protestant sacraments that it requires its own subdivisions under the sacramental sections of the early evangelical confessions.

Just as bafflingly, after repeatedly arguing in previous writings that Christians need not go to the church (that is, to the priest) with their sins for confession, in 1529 Luther wrote "A Short Order of Confession before the Priest for the Common Man." Then in 1531, Luther, perhaps paradoxically, wrote "How One Should Teach Common Folk to Shrive Themselves." But in both writings, the Wittenberg professor emphasized that penance is "an intimate act within the fellowship of believers in which Christians, burdened by their sins and repentant, make oral confession to a fellow Christian, usually a minister, and receive assurance: 'As thou believest, so be it done unto thee' [Matt. 8:13]. And I, by the command of Jesus Christ our Lord, forgive thee all thy sin."[64] Daily repentance, then, can be made to another fellow struggler in the faith, but the Christian should seek out his priest regularly, too. The Reformer did not remove the priestly role in hearing confession but merely the priestly power potentially to abuse the rite.

Hence Luther's exact placement of penance as a sacrament is not altogether clear, even if it is tied tightly to baptism and the Supper. David Bagchi noticed that Luther's "ambivalence on the question of sacramentality led to a much wider ambivalence concerning penitential practice within the Lutheran [and

---

63. Bagchi develops this point in "Sacramentality of Penance," 122.
64. Here from Sundberg, *Worship as Repentance*, 83; see also LW 53:121.

broader Protestant] tradition as a whole."[65] In Luther's theology of confession, it is clear that penance is indispensable to understanding his entire project of salvation by grace alone through faith alone, his ecclesiology of a priesthood of all believers, his anthropology of the bound will and the redeemed becoming *simul iustus et peccator* (simultaneously justified and a sinner), his second use of the law (that "men thereby may be led to the knowledge of sin"), his understanding of the believer's attitude in worship and life, his conception of the power of the spoken word, and his reliance exclusively on the work of Christ for salvation. All of these central themes in the Reformer would be at least diminished and misunderstood without their proper reference to penance.

Any change in sacramental status for Luther regarding this practice should in no way, then, be interpreted (as many indolently often have) as indicating that he reduced its import as an ecclesial ceremony. While baptism is the basis upon which one may draw faith and assurance of being a Christian, forgiven by God for one's condition of sinfulness, penance springs forth from baptism as the ongoing apparatus by which Christians continue to grow in sanctification despite being burdened by their fleshly, sinful nature for the remainder of this life. Utilizing Paul's words from Romans 6:4, Luther in his teaching on baptism declared, "It signifies that the old creature in us with all sins and evil desires is to be drowned and die through daily contrition and repentance."[66] If the Christian remains a sinner while becoming a saint in Luther's anthropology,[67] then the very early conviction that "the life of the believer [ought to] be one of daily repentance" remains in Luther's mature theology, which continues to assert that daily repentance is an important act of faith and a means by which the promised grace of God may be lived. This practice was one that Luther himself then exercised with fellow colleagues through daily confession throughout his life.

By the concept of "private confession," Luther did not mean to indicate an exclusively personal practice. Christians are to confess to one another. Yet believers are liberated from being compelled to bring their confessions repeatedly to the church—that is, to the priest—out of a now-rejected theology of sacerdotalism.

65. Bagchi, "Sacramentality of Penance," 119–20.
66. Luther, "The Sacrament of Holy Baptism," in the Small Catechism; via Lull, 326; cf. BC 360.
67. In fact, Bagchi points out that in his lectures on Romans, Luther used not only the Latin *simul iustus et peccator* but also, significantly, *semper peccator, semper penitens, semper iustus* (always a sinner, always repentant, always justified), stressing even more the need for daily repentance.

Thus, while he did indeed declassify penance as a sacrament in the fall of 1520 (in *Babylonian Captivity*), Luther in no way sidelined its importance both in the theology and the ethics of the Christian faith. As Hans-Martin Barth has observed, for Luther, "who all his life strove to explain and proclaim the message of justification, confession was at the center of his thought and spiritual practice."[68] Penance is therefore not optional but is an essential exercise for the ongoing journey of the Christian.

Though fundamental to the life of the believer, penance is clearly at the same time not to be seen as a good work (that is, as something produced by a person to achieve better standing before God). The work of God is already accomplished by Christ alone, Luther reasoned. It is Christ who has already prayed, "Father, forgive them, for they know not what they do" (Luke 23:34). As Walter Sundberg explains Luther's thought, "We do not participate in the atonement; it is the work of Christ alone done on our behalf. But we must prepare to receive it in and through confession of sins."[69] The traditional Roman practice of doing penance led to the Scylla of overconfidence in the work of the rite, or to the Charybdis of doubt concerning its effectiveness for the believer. Albrecht Peters characterizes Luther's redefinition of penance: "Faith in God's unqualified declaration of innocence is all that can keep our act of confession from taking on the character of a work; faith allows the confession to be saturated with [the] selfless, divine love of Christ. . . . The Reformation flamed up precisely because of Luther's efforts to incorporate Confession into the foundational [sacramental] framework of promise and faith."[70]

Like the sacraments of baptism and the Supper, then, penance, once the third Protestant sacrament, remained for Luther a gift of God and a welcomed means for receiving God's grace. Moreover, penance persisted for Luther as both indispensable practice and human disposition appropriate to the Christian and as an essential key to understanding the other principal themes of his theology.

Later Protestant Reflections on Penance

Following his German predecessor, Philip Melanchthon repudiated compulsory confession, requirements for proper remorse, and notions of human

68. H.-M. Barth, *Theology of Martin Luther*, 246.
69. Sundberg, *Worship as Repentance*, 171.
70. Albrecht Peters, *Commentary on Luther's Catechisms: Baptism and Lord's Supper* (St. Louis: Concordia, 2012), 19, 17–18.

cooperation with God to achieve forgiveness. Also like Luther, Melanchthon emphasized repentance as a daily endeavor for the Christian, and he underscored the restoration of the sinner to righteousness through mortification and regeneration exclusively as a work of God in and through the person.[71] "This means that repentance and satisfaction are not something that the penitent himself performs, something that could win him the forgiveness of sins: we are made righteous only by faith in God's action, which reconciles the sinner."[72] Like justification itself, a penitent's restoration occurs by faith alone. Melanchthon encouraged confession to one's pastor or even one's neighbor, emphasizing that personal absolution came as good news and words of comfort to the penitent. Over the latter half of the sixteenth century, the Lutheran tradition mandated its adherents to pastoral examination as a qualification for admission to the Lord's Supper.

Other Reformers contemporary to Luther did not hold the church official in such high regard for the function of confession. In his Sixty-Seven Theses, Ulrich Zwingli posited:

> God alone remits sins through Jesus Christ, his Son, our only Lord. He who gives this authority to an individual takes away the honor due to God to give to one who is not God. This is real idolatry. Hence the confession which is made to the priest or other person shall not be regarded as remission of sin, but only a seeking for advice. Acts of penance imposed by human counsel . . . do not cancel sin but are imposed to deter others. Christ has borne all our toil and sorrows. Hence whoever attributes to works of penance that which belongs to Christ alone, errs and dishonors God.[73]

Thus Zwingli, founder of the Swiss Reformed tradition who famously rebuffed Luther's sacramentalism, viewed confession as nothing more than brotherly counsel and consolation.

His successor in the Reformed tradition, John Calvin, was more circumspect but correspondingly uncertain about the place and function of private confession for the Christian. On the one hand, Calvin saw private confession to the priest as a "butchery of conscience," wherein the Christian might be left to personal turmoil in order to adequately produce an acceptable level of remorse before God and God's clerical representative.[74] On the other hand,

71. Philip Melanchthon, *Loci communes* 8:63–64; here via Jürgen Werbick, "Penance," in *Dictionary of the Reformation*, ed. Klaus Ganzer and Bruno Steimer (New York: Crossroad, 2004), 239.
72. Werbick, "Penance," 239.
73. Theses 50–54 of Ulrich Zwingli, Sixty-Seven Theses; here via *Huldrych Zwingli*, ed. G. R. Potter (New York: St. Martin's Press, 1977), 24–25.
74. Tentler, "Confession," 403.

Calvin positively wrote that genuine "repentance not only constantly follows faith, but is also born of faith." While God saves each believer with justification through faith alone, the believer's actual alteration comes through the "free imputation of [divine] righteousness."[75] Therefore, "this restoration does not take place in one moment or one day or one year; but through continual and sometimes even slow advances God wipes out in his elect the corruptions of the flesh . . . that they may practice repentance throughout their lives and know that this warfare will end only at death."[76] While extreme cases of sin may still require public acts of penance through fasting, Calvin stressed the practice of internal discipline as conventional. And because the fleshly nature maintains sinfulness even after redemption, each Christian must practice the "mortification of the flesh" and the discipline of self-denial throughout life.

Calvin also retained the practice of private confession, especially to fellow Christians, seeing that Scripture, "not expressly determining on whose bosom we should unburden ourselves, leaves us free choice to confess to that one of the flock of the church who seems most suitable." At the same time, pastors should especially be chosen as those "better fitted" due to their calling in Christian instruction and consolation. They are available for the "cure of souls" to benefit every Christian. Pastors, then, serve this function normatively, but Calvin also observed that "where God prescribes nothing definite, conscience [ought not to] be . . . bound with a definite yoke."[77] Calvin then counseled Christians to seek private confession freely, especially for those who particularly desire or need it.

While Calvin referred to them as "those who marvelously exult in being considered spiritual,"[78] the Anabaptists practiced repentance as integral to church discipline in a manner distinct from both Catholics and magisterial Protestants, yet also sharing something in common with the other two Western traditions. Rejecting the magisterial ecclesiology of an invisible church, the Anabaptist tradition attempted to build a believers' church around the ordinances of baptism and the Supper, (re)instituting adult believer's baptism as the proper entry into the church, wherein each believer being baptized pledged to follow Christ and the discipline of the congregation. Before each Supper could be observed, individuals would need to examine themselves, and any offense by one member against another would need to be resolved in order for true communion to take place with the common loaf and cup. However, in the case of unrepentant sins, when members had first attempted

75. Calvin, *Inst*. 3.3.1; LCC 20:593.
76. Calvin, *Inst*. 3.3.8; LCC 20:601.
77. Calvin, *Inst*. 3.4.12; LCC 20:636–37.
78. Calvin, *Inst*. 3.3.2; LCC 20:595.

individual admonition and congregational reconciliation with a sinner, the unrepentant sinner would be banned, in varying degrees, from communion, the church services, and even Christian fellowship altogether. While each Anabaptist congregation exacted its own specific discipline, as one first-generation Anabaptist theologian put it, "It [was] an exclusion and separation of such a nature that from then on no Christian [could] have fellowship with such a man [or woman], not in words, meat or drink, in grinding or baking, or in any other way," until the individual was willing to be reconciled to the brothers and sisters once again. "It is done for the good of the sinner, that he may look into his own heart, take stock of himself, and abandon sin." After sin is finally abandoned, the church "receives him again joyfully, . . . opens the doors of heaven to him, and lets him reenter the fellowship of the Lord's Supper," the sign that represented ecclesial belonging.[79]

Thus, like Luther in his early Protestant writings, the Anabaptists were open to private confession, in this case between those who had observed or were affected by an individual's iniquities and the individual transgressor. As in the early church's practice, the Anabaptists also restored public confession as a last resort, when private intervention was not successful. Like Catholicism, the Anabaptists called for a dis-fellowshiping of the unrepentant, even if ideally seen as only a temporary punishment, because a number of early Anabaptists also viewed the church as salvific. But in contrast to the magisterial Protestants, they saw the commission to bind and to loose as one that the entire congregation was responsible for exercising, not simply as an obligation carried out by the clergy on behalf of the group. Thus the great leader and organizer of Dutch Anabaptism, Menno Simons, admonished the second-generation Anabaptists: "I command you with holy Paul, by the Lord Jesus Christ, . . . diligently to observe each other unto salvation, in all becoming ways teaching, instructing, admonishing, reproving, warning, and consoling each other as occasion requires, . . . until we increase in God and become united in faith and in the knowledge of the Son of God."[80]

During the years of the English Reformation, Thomas Cranmer's original 1549 Prayer Book made private confession before a priest optional. Instead, "the generall confession to the churche" during worship before the Eucharist appears to have supplanted the regular practice of private penance. Private confession, on the other hand, functioned to appease the conscience by "avoyding

79. Balthasar Hubmaier, "A Christian Instruction," in "The Writings of Balthasar Hubmaier," collected and photographed by W. O. Lewis, trans. George Duiguid Davidson (microfilm of typescript in Conrad Grebel College Library, Waterloo, ON, 1939), 293.

80. Menno Simons, A Kind Admonition on Church Discipline, in The Complete Writings of Menno Simons, ed. J. C. Wenger (Scottdale, PA: Herald Press, 1956), 411.

[avoiding] of all scruple and doubtfulness."[81] Thus, as Bauerschmidt observes, private confession was reduced to a "pastoral tool among others."[82] In the 1552 revision of the Prayer Book, the custom of private confession as a church discipline had dissipated, replaced only with confession to clergy essentially as a means for counseling the troubled. The emphasis on regular repentance lingered only within corporate confessions in the Prayer Book's liturgies, with Lenten services providing a seasonal accentuation to the discipline.

Repentance for Contemporary Protestants

It is true that Martin Luther ultimately eliminated penance as a sacrament of the church. Unfortunately, many Protestants have unwittingly distorted Luther's intention by discarding confession as a common Christian practice altogether. Luther intended neither the abolition nor even the diminution of repentance in the daily life of the Christian. Luther's theology of repentance for Protestants valiantly attempted to endorse the importance of daily confession while simultaneously upholding the Protestant principle that each Christian's restoration was the achievement of God. The Christ event was the only satisfaction needed for a Christian's genuinely confessed sins. Yet, as Thomas Tentler points out, "On the other hand, when Luther proclaimed 'Christian liberty,' denied that ordination conferred on priests an inherent power to absolve, affirmed that all believers had the right to pronounce forgiveness, discouraged detailed inquiry into sins (especially secret sins), and rejected the possibility of a complete confession, he prepared the way for the decline and eventually demise of confession, even though religious and secular authorities in Lutheran Germany tried to maintain it."[83]

Consequently, Protestant Christians today have, for the most part, allowed the discipline of confession to atrophy in their practice of the faith. A recovery of the Lenten tradition of corporate confession from Ash Wednesday through the six Sundays of Lent in preparation for Easter has given more liturgically oriented Protestant traditions a seasonal outlet for confession. But most Protestants understand, or at least practice, ongoing confession only as a "private" matter of personal prayer through a Christian's spiritual pilgrimage. The fact that "sin" itself has undergone a great deal of redefinition and reduction in meaning cannot be unrelated to confession's insidious disappearance for many

81. E. C. S. Gibson, ed., *The First and Second Prayer-Books of King Edward the Sixth*, Everyman's Library 448 (London: J. M. Dent, 1910), 217.

82. Bauerschmidt, "Godly Discipline," 688.

83. Tentler, "Confession," 403.

Protestants. When believers began theologically to temper the perils of the spiritual poison of iniquity, its regular antidote through continual penitence correspondingly dissipated.

At best, Protestants tie confession to the Lord's Supper, an excellent theological connection to be made, to be sure, but one that is inadequate in isolation from other avenues for repentance. Lutheran, Reformed, Anglican, and free-church traditions all demonstrate the eucharistic tie to repentance, with many Lutherans still advocating for notifying one's pastor before receiving communion. Reformed church liturgies call for weekly repentance in worship and also even more intentional confession before communion, when observed. The free-church tradition, whose origin, ironically, at least partly originated in Anabaptist ecclesiology, has mostly abandoned both private and public forms of confession. And every Christian tradition, Protestant, Catholic, and Orthodox, can testify to the universal truth that but a fraction of the Easter Sunday crowd can be found two or three days earlier at Maundy Thursday and Good Friday services, not to mention six weeks earlier, at the outset of the penitential season of Lent, at observances for Ash Wednesday. Western Christians love to hear the good news of God's forgiveness but not focus on the burden of human sin, the reason for Christ's sacrifice, and the depravity of each human's postfallen nature.

Undoubtedly Protestant Christians have lost a sense of the value of confession for several reasons. First, due to their misunderstanding of their own tradition, they have begun to develop what Dietrich Bonhoeffer famously called a "cheap grace." In 1937 Bonhoeffer decried the condition of Christianity along these lines, observing that the church had developed a

> grace which amounts to the justification of sin without the justification of the repentant sinner who departs from sin and from whom sin departs. Cheap grace is not the kind of forgiveness of sin which frees us from the toils of sin. . . . Cheap grace is the preaching of forgiveness without requiring repentance, baptism without church discipline, Communion without confession, absolution without personal confession.[84]

If Bonhoeffer's observations about the church were true in the early twentieth century, they must be all the more true now in the twenty-first.

A second reason for the loss of the practice and theology of confession is, as stated previously, that many Protestants misunderstand Luther and his successors' original intentions in ultimately rejecting penance as a sacrament.

84. Dietrich Bonhoeffer, *The Cost of Discipleship*, trans. R. H. Fuller with some revision by Irmgard Booth (German, 1937; New York: Touchstone, 1995), 44–45.

While penance no longer was categorized as "sacrament" under Luther's strict definition of a "promise accompanied by a sign," Luther and many other Reformers and subsequent Protestant leaders still highly valued the practice of confession as essential to one's continual sanctification, integral to growing and being drawn increasingly into union with Christ. And what baptism accomplished through initial faith for the forgiveness of sins, continual repentance rehearses and renews through its daily discipline. Luther even counseled those troubled at the promise of daily forgiveness that if the devil were to torment them with their past sins and thus with a lack of assurance for forgiveness, they should respond, "I am a son of God. I have been baptized. I believe in Jesus Christ, who was crucified for me. Let me alone, Devil."[85] Then doubts would pass away as believers would remember that forgiveness was first accomplished for them through their baptism. Daily repentance, daily assurance, and daily sanctification are rooted in one's first confession and the baptismal waters. Thus it is in this context that Luther finally concluded: "The sacrament of penance, which I [initially had] added to [baptism and the Lord's Supper], lacks the divinely instituted visible sign, and is, as I have said, nothing but a way and return to baptism."[86]

Over time, and through the various formative traditions within Protestantism, most Protestants moved first from Luther's injunction of private confession to the pastor or to one another, eventually adopting the Reformed practice of congregational corporate confession during worship. But as congregational confession only went so far (or was diminished by subsequent liturgies), and in a post-Enlightenment world where empirical science is deemed absolute truth but religion is considered only a personal and subjective belief, the increased privatization of the faith gradually moved Christians to a practice of self-confession, merely praying privately to God, with no other human intermediary, a practice that both distorts Luther's idea of the priesthood of all believers and mangles his intentions for confession. But the blame for the privatization of confession cannot be laid squarely at the feet of postmodernity.

Protestant Christians could have created, and once did create, intentional countercultures alongside their self-consumed neighbors. Christian churches are to be distinct fellowships of ethical accountability if such notions of community are not to be refracted in the public square. Genuinely caring for one another, praying for each other, and listening to each person's burdens and

85. Martin Luther, cited in *Luther: Letters of Spiritual Counsel*, ed. Theodore G. Tappert, LCC 18 (Philadelphia: Westminster, 1955), 134.
86. Luther, *Babylonian Captivity*, LW 36:124.

confessions was Luther's hope for the ongoing priesthood of all believers among modern Christians. Sadly, today in its present impoverished stage, where contemporary worship and Christian life are inexorably pressured to be upbeat, watered down, and artificially happy, the practice of confession is often completely lost in many quarters, so removed is this discipline from its initial Protestant moorings. The privatization of faith and the corresponding loss of genuine community undoubtedly play significant roles in this regression. An unfortunate outcome of Protestantism five centuries following the Reformation has been the ambivalence about or, worse, the discontinuance of confession by many Christians. At best, believers have made repentance a merely "personal" matter. In fact, an argument can be made that some (though clearly not all) of the work of the psychologist is to serve as the "secular priest" of sorts to a generation without "safe" priests to whom they might properly confess. Thus, like many things in Western culture, the sciences have even here replaced religion to meet basic human needs; in this case psychological counseling often replaces private confession as a means to soothe the soul and ease the conscience. Yet most Protestant believers find the long-held tradition of private confession and fraternal absolution to be completely foreign.

The Reformer who is often blamed for the diminution of the discipline of repentance may, unexpectedly, also provide guidance for restoring its practice among Protestants. The practice of private confession (i.e., of seeking out a brother and sister to receive, and also to grant absolution for, an individual's confession) was the ideal, "for when we have laid bare our conscience to our brother and privately made known to him the evil that lurked within, we receive from our brother's lips the word of comfort spoken by God himself." This, Luther believed, was "a cure without equal for distressed consciences."[87] The Reformer's rejection of the Catholic practice was his interpretation that penance was practiced as a work, not as a glorious means of grace.[88] Luther's admonition to repent daily could be recovered by establishing accountability partners in the life of each Christian, whether it be an ordained pastor or simply a trusted friend in Christ, who is theologically just as much a member of the royal priesthood of Christ. After believers lament and confess their sins, God works through their neighbor "when he absolves [the penitent] through the word placed in the mouth" of the neighbor. "Thus," Luther concluded,

87. Ibid., LW 36:86.
88. In the Large Catechism, e.g., Luther wrote, "There has been no law quite so oppressive as that which forced everyone to make confession on pain of the gravest mortal sin." BC 476. Rightly understood, confession is beneficial, comforting, and strengthening to each believer's conscience, claims Luther in *Babylonian Captivity*, LW 36:86.

"we teach what a wonderful, precious, and comforting thing confession is, and we urge that such a precious blessing should not be despised, especially when we consider our great need. If you are a Christian, you need neither my compulsion nor the pope's command at any point, but you will compel yourself and beg me for the privilege of sharing in it."[89]

As long as Christians continue the sacrament of baptism, they should maintain a high view of the discipline of confession, for this practice is inextricably tied to the first sacrament. Rejecting Jerome's understanding of repentance as the "second plank" after shipwreck (i.e., after postbaptismal sin), Luther encouraged Christians to relieve their consciences with the retort, "But I am baptized! And if I am baptized, I have the promise that I shall be saved and have eternal life, both in soul and body." Thus, instead of searching for a plank on the seas of despair, Luther admonished Christian sinners to continue to make use of their baptisms. "The ship does not flounder since, as we said, it is God's ordinance and not a work of ours. But it does happen that we slip and fall out of the ship. If anybody does fall out, he should immediately head for the ship and cling to it until he can climb aboard again and sail on in it as he had done before."[90] Such is the work of daily repentance for the Christian.

Luther took sin seriously as a daily challenge to one's faith, but he understood its remedy within the context of grace and not works. By each Christian seeking out the help of other "priests," Luther understood private confession as integral to spiritual growth. Complemented by both Calvin's understanding of corporate confession in worship and the Anabaptist attempt to restore a stronger Protestant ecclesiology through congregational watch-care of the church for and to each Christian member, the Protestant understanding of penance might again be reestablished to its ideal balance of human responsibility constituted on God's grace alone. Repentance can be again appreciated not as an outward requirement but as an inward, heartfelt aspiration. The Protestant tradition itself has demonstrated both corporate and individual forms for the practice of repentance. Provided Christians continue to acknowledge the existence of sin, its antidote is accessible by the power of the Spirit in the church's worship, fellowship, and private counsel with one another.

89. Luther, Large Catechism, in *BC* 460. In his Small Catechism, Luther even outlined examples of one's confession to another Christian, how one may confess, and how the other may give words of comfort and absolution; see *BC* 350–51.

90. Luther, Large Catechism, *BC* 466.

2

Confirmation

A Ceremony for the Laying On of Hands

Baptism and water have come. You have been penetrated, as it were, so that you may come to the form of bread. But it is not yet bread without fire. What therefore does fire represent? It is chrism. For the oil of our fire is the sacrament of the Holy Spirit.

Augustine

The question is whether by the decision of humans oil receives a new and secret power of the Spirit as soon as it will have pleased them that it be called chrism. For there is no one who makes mention of oil—not from the ancients, nor even from that middle age which abounded with many faults. Therefore although they may clatter, they will accomplish nothing by denying that they are insolent towards the Spirit of God as long as they transfer his power to fetid oil.

John Calvin

Confirmation as the bishops want it should not be bothered with. Nevertheless we do not fault any pastor who might scrutinize the faith from children. If it be good and sincere, he may impose hands and confirm.

Martin Luther

CONFIRMATION IS A POSTBAPTISMAL RITE long practiced by many Western Christian traditions that, as exercised today, may come immediately following the baptism of an adult or as a conscious acknowledgment of one's previous baptism and declaration of faith by one of age who was baptized as an infant or child. The acknowledgment of baptism and personal faith often follows a prescribed period of catechesis. The ceremony itself often involves laying hands on the confirmands and/or anointing them with oil (chrism), in many traditions done by a bishop, as a blessing or consecration of the act. However, a review of the early history of confirmation demonstrates that the ritual was not initially a freestanding ceremony in its own right but gradually developed originally as inextricably linked to a larger service of initiation of new believers into the Christian community, which included water baptism and first Eucharist.

Confirmation within the Rite of Initiation in Early Christianity

In the first several centuries of early Christianity, there was no rite called "confirmation." Confirmation was not practiced by early Christians independently, as its own ordinance, but was developed in the second to third centuries as a ritual attached to the conclusion of baptism. At the turn of the third century, Tertullian recorded in his work *On Baptism*: "Then having gone up from the bath we are anointed with a blessed anointing of ancient discipline, by which people were accustomed to be anointed for priesthood, by oil from a horn from which Aaron was anointed by Moses. For this reason we were called 'christs' ('anointed ones') from 'chrism,' which is the ointment which lends its name to the Lord."[1] This physical act, Tertullian explained, served also to benefit the baptizants spiritually as an anointing of the Holy Spirit, just as the physical water of immersion baptism "has a spiritual effect" to free the neophyte from sin. The baptismal ceremony was concluded with a laying on of hands, "calling and inviting the Holy Spirit." The action of chrism, Tertullian explained, was drawn from the witness of Acts, where Christ was referred to as having been anointed by God (Acts 10:38).

A generation later, around 215–35, Hippolytus, in his *Apostolic Tradition*, added to the description of the nascent practice what many now view as simply a baptismal dismissal rite:[2]

The neophytes are anointed by the presbyter from the oil consecrated by the bishop. He says, "I anoint you with holy oil in the name of Jesus Christ." And

1. See Paul Turner, ed., *Sources of Confirmation: From the Fathers through the Reformers* (Collegeville, MN: Liturgical Press, 1993), 11–12; cf. Tertullian, *Baptism* 7.1; *ANF* 3:672.
2. Aidan Kavanagh, *Confirmation: Origins and Reform* (New York: Pueblo, 1988), 69–72.

thus, drying themselves, the individuals are vested, and afterwards are brought in the church.

But the bishop, imposing his hand on them, prays by saying: "Lord God, who made them worthy to merit the forgiveness of sins by the bath of rebirth of the Holy Spirit, send your grace onto them, that they may serve you according to your will. For to you is the glory, to the Father and to the Son with the Holy Spirit in the holy Church, both now and for ever. Amen."

Afterwards, pouring the consecrated oil from his hand and imposing it on the neophyte's head, let him say, "I anoint you with holy oil in the Lord, the Father Almighty, and Christ Jesus, and the Holy Spirit." And consigning the neophyte on the forehead, let him offer the kiss and say, "The Lord be with you." And let those who have been signed say "And also with you." Let him do the same to each individual.[3]

These two patristic witnesses give the earliest descriptions of the integral parts of a developed single rite of initiation framed around baptism and the newly inducted Christian's first Eucharist. From these early sources, it appears that, following the water baptism by the presbyter, a variety of rituals were practiced in local congregations: a prayer by the bishop, laying on of hands, anointing, and signing. As Kenan Osborne recognizes, "There is no unified and generalized development of these additional ceremonies, and in fact local churches tended to be quite varied in the use or non-use of these ceremonies."[4] But what is clear is that the entire service was linked with the giving of the Holy Spirit, which is the probable reason a bishop's participation was apparently requisite, as a successor to the apostles. These services developed gradually, with water baptism being the only described initiation practice prior to the advent of the third century. Incrementally, the initiation service added a "multiplicity of coordinated events," which represented a web of interrelated meanings for the baptizants.[5] Regardless, following the baptism and some kind of episcopal blessing, the candidates were fully received into the faith community, signified through their first Eucharist as the final movement of the initiation rite.

The early church found biblical guidance for the bishop's blessing following baptism in such Scripture passages as Acts 8:15 and 19:6, which portrayed the apostles as laying hands on the baptized and witnessing evidence of the Holy Spirit's presence permeating the new believers, apparently replicating the descent of the Holy Spirit following the baptism of Christ in the Gospel

3. Hippolytus, *Apostolic Tradition*; here via Turner, *Sources of Confirmation*, 12–13.
4. Kenan B. Osborne, *The Christian Sacraments of Initiation: Baptism, Confirmation, Eucharist* (New York: Paulist Press, 1987), 120.
5. Aidan Kavanagh, *The Shape of Baptism: The Rite of Christian Initiation*, 2nd printing (Collegeville, MN: Liturgical Press, 1991), 53.

accounts. This "sealing by a bishop," as Eusebius called the episcopal portion of the rite, normatively and appropriately happened immediately following baptism.[6] But by the fourth century, the Western church became aware of a growing problem in situations where the episcopal ideal was no longer practical: the bishop could not always be present immediately following a baptism. Although the church had practiced a protracted catechesis process for the neophytes before baptism and typically prepared for the Easter season to baptize the catechized collectively in the presence of the bishop, scenarios began to arise in which individuals were baptized in cases of emergency. In one well-known circumstance, a Novatian was baptized by aspersion on his deathbed only to recover, yet not having received the benefits of the episcopal seal.[7] For the church then to continue its practice in an orderly fashion, such candidates were admonished to receive the imposition of hands and anointing at the earliest opportunity.[8]

To this point, by the latter half of the fourth century, Jerome warned of the potential outcome for those who received only baptism by the local presbyter but not the laying on of hands by the bishop: "If only at the invocation of a bishop does the Holy Spirit descend, they are to be mourned who have been baptized by presbyters and deacons in villages and hamlets and in the more distant places, and have fallen asleep before they could be visited by bishops."[9] Nevertheless, for reasons of distance, emergencies, and other logistics, it gradually became more commonplace for an interval of time to transpire between the baptism of neophytes and their anointing.

This particularly became the case between the fourth and sixth centuries as the church grew and bishoprics expanded. Through the first three centuries of existence, Christianity had remained mostly in urban centers, until the cessation of Christian persecution. Now in these latter centuries, Christianity had spread from its urban hubs to more remote and rural communities. Country bishops (*chōrepiscopoi*) and local priests (presbyters) were granted the authority to baptize and perform other rites. But the Western church was concerned with liturgically connecting its isolated Christians and congregations with the wider church and hence preserved the requirement of the bishop's presence at some juncture to anoint all baptized Christians.[10] Consequently the interval

---

6. Eusebius, *Ecclesiastical History* 6.43; NPNF² 1:289; here via Turner, *Sources of Confirmation*, 13.

7. Eusebius, *Ecclesiastical History* 6.43.

8. J. D. C. Fisher, *Christian Initiation: Confirmation Then and Now* (Chicago: Hillenbrand, 2005), 127.

9. Jerome, as paraphrased in ibid.

10. Fisher, *Confirmation*, 140. In 416, Pope Innocent decreed that the "consignation of infants . . . should not be done by any but the bishop." See Gerard Austin, *Anointing with the*

between baptism by the priest and anointing by the bishop steadily grew such that baptism and what would eventually be known as "confirmation" began to separate in Western Europe.[11]

As the rites of initiation continued to develop, it is worth recognizing that not all the church fathers found biblical precedent for the varied movements of the rites. In the late fourth century, for instance, Basil the Great observed:

> We also bless the water of baptism, the oil of anointing, and even the baptized themselves. By virtue of what writings? Is it not by virtue of the protected, secret, and hidden tradition? Indeed! Even the oil of anointing, what written word has taught about that? The triple immersion, from where does it come? And everything that surrounds baptism: the renunciation of Satan and his angels—from what Scripture does that come?
>
> Is it not from that teaching held private and secret, which our fathers kept in silence, protected from anxiety and curiosity, knowing well that in keeping quiet one safeguards the sacred character of the mysteries? For how would it be reasonable to divulge by writing the instruction, that which is not permitted to the uninitiated to contemplate?[12]

Although Basil clearly wrote these words as an explanation for the necessity of protecting the hidden mysteries of the faith from outsiders, his words ultimately seem to be a concession to parallel Luther's and other subsequent Reformers' objections to the elevation of the entire confirmation service as a sacrament on par with baptism and Eucharist. The theological substance of confirmation, the Reformers concluded, is not supported in Scripture.

In 380, Emperor Theodosius established Nicene Christianity as the state church of the Roman Empire, and by 500 most of the population of Rome itself was Christian. Such a Christian hegemony affected both cultural and liturgical practices of the church. Most Roman children were now raised in Christian homes, and infant baptism became increasingly common. Adult conversions and catechesis correspondingly almost disappeared entirely. Consequently, only Christian parents' newly born children at risk of death received baptism without the episcopal anointing and blessing, but the bishop's postbaptismal hands-laying and chrism were still performed at a later date for those children who survived. This subsequent service finally received the

---

Spirit: The Rite of Confirmation (New York: Pueblo, 1985), 12; cf. Turner, *Sources of Confirmation*, 56, no. 102.

11. Osborne, *Sacraments of Initiation*, 122–23.

12. Basil, *The Holy Spirit*, chap. 27; see NPNF[2] 42; here via Turner, *Sources of Confirmation*, 13–14.

label "confirmation" in southern Gaul in the fifth century and evolved into a freestanding sacrament only by the Middle Ages.[13]

Confirmation Solidified as a Separate Rite in the Medieval Period

For over a millennium confirmation developed slowly. Just as all documents regarding Christian initiation mention only water baptism until third-century additions and innovations, so confirmation as a distinct rite was not the normative practice in the West[14] until the eleventh century. Augustine's doctrine of original sin, which articulated baptism as its antidote, had taken root over this period, such that parents were encouraged to have their local priest baptize their newborn children immediately, even if the children appeared healthy, rather than risk awaiting the episcopal visit on Easter or Pentecost, whereas children in previous centuries had customarily been presented to the bishop. Baptizing a newborn within eight days became the established practice throughout Europe.[15] Consequently, the episcopal visit and its associated service of confirmation became further separated from baptism as baptism became an ordinance observed not only at holy seasons but throughout the year.

Further diminishing the importance of episcopal chrismation (confirmation), the church in many regions of the West allowed younger children to partake of the Eucharist even if they were only baptized.[16] Confirmation then was no longer considered attached to baptism and the rites of initiation. The rite became further delayed not only because of the more sporadic visits of the bishop to each community but also because of parental neglect, as fewer Christians apparently appreciated the purpose and effect of confirmation and its episcopal blessing. Eventually the church completely reversed its original design in many regions by insisting that infants were not fit for confirmation since it had become a rite of passage for those who had reached an age of reason. When parents became negligent in seeing their children subsequently confirmed, the church in various regions of Europe made efforts to set early age requirements for confirmation to take place, in some cases even by threatening penalties against both parents and parochial clergy if it were delayed beyond this time.[17] However, such efforts apparently had only a marginal effect on dilatory parents.

13. Fisher, *Confirmation*, 128–29, 135.
14. Chrismation (confirmation) was never traditionally practiced independently of baptism in the East.
15. Fisher, *Confirmation*, 108–9.
16. Osborne, *Sacraments of Initiation*, 123.
17. The Constitution of Odo of Paris (1193), e.g., instructed parents not to await the visit of the bishop but proactively to take their children to him when he is in the vicinity of their

Just as, or perhaps because, parents may have disregarded the rite, church authorities heightened the stature and value of confirmation through its rhetoric. The Venerable Bede (d. 735) observed that of all the places where he could have withdrawn so that he might be discovered by his betrayer, Jesus chose the Mount of Olives. Such a place was intentional, the medieval English monk maintained, so "that he might designate all those baptized in his death to be confirmed with the most noble chrism of the Holy Spirit."[18] By the twelfth century, Lombard included confirmation not only as a separate rite but also as one of the seven sacraments of the church. The substance of the sacrament, explained Alexander of Hales (d. 1245), was not its form of words as imparted from the Lord or the apostles but its anointing with chrism on the forehead.[19] For good measure, Bonaventure (d. 1274) explained:

> Christ did not institute confirmation, because those believing after his ascension had to be confirmed. Hence the apostles dispensed neither the matter nor the form but the *res sacramenti* without the form, by the Holy Spirit confirming unmediated, and without the element or the matter, because in giving the Holy Spirit visible signs appeared. And therefore there was no need of the element. But afterwards the successors had to give the Spirit to the instituted rites on the strength of words and invisibility. Therefore it was necessary that a sensible element be instituted.[20]

To the medieval church, then, for the Holy Spirit to be communicated, the oil of confirmation became just as essential as the bishop in his role as mediator. Aquinas affirmed that the "grace of the Holy Spirit is designated in the oil" and that the oil is therefore "suitable for the matter of this sacrament." The oil, Aquinas continued, was mixed with balsam to bring it a fragrance so as to fulfill 2 Corinthians 2: "We are the good aroma of Christ" (cf. 2:15). The sacrament was then to give renewed strength as commensurate with those

---

townships. But the Constitution of Richard Poore (ca. 1217) denies entry to the church for parents who have not seen their children confirmed by age five. See Fisher, *Confirmation*, 121–23.

18. Bede, "Explanation of the Gospel of Luke," Luke 22:39, in CCSL 1 (Turnhout: Brepols, 1954): 120:385; here via Turner, *Sources of Confirmation*, 78. Scholars have observed that Bede, who also called the Mount of Olives the Mount of Chrism, saw Jesus's place of prayer before his arrest as by divine design and full of powerful meaning. When mixed with balm and spices, olive oil made chrism, the consecrated oil for confirmation. See Bede, *Commentary on the Acts of the Apostles*, trans. Lawrence T. Martin (Kalamazoo, MI: Cistercian Publications, 1989), 23.

19. Alexander of Hales, "Comments on Peter Lombard's *Sentences* in Four Books," in Bibliotheca Franciscana scholastica medii aevi 15, ed. PP. Collegii S. Bonaventurae (Quaracchi, Florence: Typographia Colegii S. Bonaventurae, 1957), 421; here via Turner, *Sources of Confirmation*, 68.

20. Bonaventure, "Commentary on the *Sentences*," 7.7.2; here via Turner, *Sources of Confirmation*, 69.

baptized now being of "a mature age."[21] However, it was not until the Council of Florence (1439) that confirmation was officially earmarked as a sacrament and summarized as having to use "chrism blessed by a bishop" and being "made from oil which consciously signifies excellence, and balsam, which signifies the aroma of good character." The spoken form of the chrismation[22] was "I sign you with the sign of the cross, and I confirm you with the chrism of salvation. In the name of the Father and of the Son and of the Holy Spirit."[23]

Luther's Repudiation of Confirmation as a Sacrament: "A Deceitful Mumbo-Jumbo"

Martin Luther wrote very little on the topic of confirmation relative to the space he gave to the Western church's other six sacraments. In his famous diatribe against five of the seven sacraments, *The Babylonian Captivity of the Church*, Luther devoted a mere three paragraphs to confirmation. His brevity in no way suggests uncertainty regarding the rite: Luther asserted in no uncertain terms that confirmation was not a sacrament. But this ceremony simply did not seem to enliven or incite the Wittenberg Reformer as some of the other church practices had. Luther did not believe that the way Rome practiced confirmation was satisfactory or even tolerable. But as with a number of other ordinances, Luther did not necessarily suggest the elimination of the practice but simply a proper understanding and simpler observance of the rite, though he did little to encourage its continuation.

As with baptism, penance, Eucharist, and ordination, Luther undoubtedly would have participated in the Western church's practice of this sacrament, likely being confirmed as a youth in Mansfeld between 1491 and 1497.[24] At the advent of the Reformation, Luther did not seem to be unsettled by this established practice.[25] By December of 1519, in a private letter, he shared

21. Thomas Aquinas, *Summa theologica* 3:72.2; here via Turner, *Sources of Confirmation*, 69.

22. The form was not originally worded by the fifteenth-century council but had been in use at least since the fourteenth century. Jean Gerson (d. 1429) cited the same form in his *Theological and Canonical Summary in Six Books*. See Turner, *Sources of Confirmation*, 70.

23. Council of Florence 1.2; via *Concilia omnia, tam generalia, quam particularia, ab apostolorum temporibus in hunc usque diem a sanctissimis patribus celebrata, & quorum acta listeris mandata, ex vestustissimis diversarum regionum bibliothecis haberi potuere*, ed. Petrus Crabbe (Cologne: Petrus Quentel, 1538), 128–29; here via Turner, *Sources of Confirmation*, 70.

24. Denis Janz makes this suggestion in his "Confirmation," in *Westminster Handbook to Martin Luther*, 28.

25. For instance, while lecturing to his noonday class on Heb. 6 sometime between the springs of 1517 and 1518, Luther simply concurred with Lombard and "all theologians" that the sacraments of baptism and confirmation cannot be repeated; LW 29:180.

with George Spalatin, the Elector of Saxony's secretary, that he would not be including confirmation in his three-part series of sermons on the sacraments since it, along with ordination, marriage, and extreme unction, did not appear to him to be a sacrament "since there is no sacrament except where a divine promise is expressly given and evokes faith."[26]

Luther finally gave his public justification for stripping the term "sacrament" from confirmation in his 1520 *Babylonian Captivity*. The special service was a simple but beautiful laying on of hands, without all the pomp and circumstance. The Reformer mocked the church's biblical interpretation to justify the service as a "sacrament." If what makes it a sacrament is that the apostles saw evidence of the Holy Spirit being imparted to the participants (Acts 8:14–17), why not make even preaching a similar sacrament? The Reformer then stated wistfully and then sarcastically: "Would that there were in the church such a laying on of hands as there was in apostolic times, . . . but there is nothing left of it now but what we ourselves have invented to adorn the office of bishops, that they may not be entirely without work in the church."[27] If the bishops were truly the successors to the apostles, their priority would not be in ceremonies but in the plain preaching of the gospel, Luther argued. But after delegating the essential tasks of ministry to their underlings, it is not surprising that they would replace their apostolic duties with something completely contrived, "for whatever human wisdom has decreed must be held in honor among men!"[28]

The problem with the current practice of confirmation for Luther was thus multifaceted. First, he saw no biblical justification for delegating the basic ministerial practices of the church to parochial clergy while reserving this tangential ceremony exclusively for the church's bishops. "For a bishop who does not preach the gospel or practice the cure of souls—what is he but an idol in the world [cf. 1 Cor. 8:4], who has nothing but the name and appearance of a bishop?"[29] What instead makes a person a genuine priest and a minister of the Holy Spirit is not the office but the quality of the individual. Second, Luther maintained that there is no scriptural evidence that confirmation is a divine ordinance. In reference to Luther's previously delineated definition of "sacrament," confirmation lacks a divine promise. Although Christ and his apostles laid hands on numerous people, and individuals were healed, such instances were descriptive and never specifically divinely prescriptive for subsequent generations.

26. WA Br 1:19–24; via Lohse, *Luther's Theology*, 128n3.
27. LW 36:91.
28. Ibid.
29. Ibid.

For the next several years, Luther's primary attack on confirmation focused on its perceived weak biblical support. For instance, in the summer of 1522, Luther had been informed by his friend Nicholas Hausmann that the suffragan bishop of Meissen had announced his intention to come to Hausmann's town of Zwickau in order to confirm the children there. On August 3, 1522, Luther wrote a letter in response to Hausmann's news, encouraging him to confront the bishop upon his arrival in Zwickau and advising Hausmann to show the bishop the evidence from Scripture that confirmation was unbiblical; if the "episcopal idol," in turn, couldn't justify his practice biblically, Luther admonished Hausmann to warn the children of his church against trusting in and relying on the ritual as a sacrament.[30]

Perhaps to give further commentary on the subject, along with the letter to Hausmann, the Wittenberg Reformer enclosed a tract on Leviticus 18 that, while seemingly unrelated in topic, concluded with particularly colorful words by Luther regarding the Reformer's renunciation of the episcopal rite: "Especially to be rejected is confirmation, that deceitful mumbo-jumbo of the episcopal idols. It has no foundation in Scripture. The bishops are only deceiving people with their lies when they say that grace, a character, a mark are conferred in confirmation. It is rather the character of the beast, Revelation 13."[31] Luther was undoubtedly rejecting Aquinas's and the Council of Florence's assertion that baptism, confirmation, and holy orders all imprint "an indelible sign" on the soul of their recipients to grant them a distinctive, permanent character.[32] Luther now eschewed the notion that these rites should make such an ontological change: "A Christian should not, at the peril of his soul, base his faith on human fantasy, which will surely betray and deceive him, but only on the Word of God, who does not lie."[33]

Then in May of 1523, Luther wrote a short treatise, in response to a request by the citizens of Leisnig, who had recently joined the Reformation, explaining the biblical rationale for its congregational authority and polity, especially in the privilege of calling its own clergy. In the midst of elucidating the supreme importance of preaching among the various duties of a cleric, Luther added this vivid flourish: "Thus it becomes evident that our present-day

---

30. LW 45:5; WA Br 2:584–85.

31. Luther, "The Persons Related by Consanguinity and Affinity Who Are Forbidden to Marry according to the Scriptures, Leviticus 18," LW 45:8–9.

32. The "indelible mark" (*character indelebilis*) was authorized by Eugene IV in his 1439 bull *Exultate Deo*, where the pope explains that baptism, confirmation, and ordination "indelibly impress upon the soul a character, i.e., a certain spiritual mark which distinguishes them from the rest"; cited in Carl Mirbt, *Quellen zur Geschichte des Papsttums und des römischen Katholizismus*, 2nd ed. (Tübingen: Mohr, 1901), no. 150; here via LW 44:129n22.

33. LW 45:8–9.

bishops are spiritual idols and not bishops. For they leave the high office of
the word, which should be their own, in the hands of the very lowest [orders].
. . . In the meantime, however, they administer confirmation, consecrate bells,
altars, and churches which are neither Christian nor episcopal duties and
which they themselves invented. They are perverted and blind masks and true
child-bishops [*Kinderbischöfe*]."[34]

Finally, in 1531, in his *Commentary on the Alleged Imperial Edict*, the
Wittenberg professor decried the claim that confirmation was clearly founded
in the Gospels. He retorted:

> It is, after all, nothing else but their "holy inspiration" and the new "holy
> gospels" with which they have now refuted our confession. They have found
> these gospels at Augsburg either in the chimney flue or in the privy, that is to
> say, they have invented them and fabricated them out of their false, mendacious
> hearts. For our gospels, which are known in all the world, say nothing about
> their confirmation and anointing.[35]

The Scriptures, then, should be central, according to Luther, both in rightly
interpreting the sacraments and in deciphering the homiletical responsibilities of ordained clerics.

Luther's Positive Place for Confirmation as an Ecclesial Ceremony

Luther's reappraisal of confirmation was characteristically provocative but not
entirely negative. The dismissal of the Catholic classification aside, Luther's
assessment of confirmation in *The Babylonian Captivity*, though the brief-
est of his treatments of the seven sacraments, may bring the best insight into
the Reformer's intentions with the five former sacraments. In decrying what
seemed to the Reformer a willy-nilly use of sacramental terminology, Luther
conceded: "I am not saying this because I condemn the seven sacraments as
usages, but because I deny that it can be proved from Scripture that these
usages are sacraments."[36] This passage is crucial to understanding Luther's

34. Luther, "That a Christian Assembly Has the Right to Judge," LW 39:314. Eric Gritsch
astutely observed that the term "child-bishop" was commonly used by schoolboys in a traditional
game held on December 6, St. Nicholas Day, wherein the children would select one student to
play "bishop" and rule over them for the day. The game had been explicitly prohibited by Pope
Gregory XII in a 1407 bull, yet the tradition apparently persisted. See LW 39:252n8.

35. Luther, "Dr. Martin Luther's Commentary on the Alleged Imperial Edict Promulgated
in the Year 1531, after the Imperial Diet of the Year 1530," LW 34:87.

36. Luther, "The Pagan Servitude of the Church"; here via Dillenberger, 324; cf. LW 36:91,
which renders this sentence: "I do not say this because I condemn the seven sacraments, but
because I deny that they can be proved from the Scriptures."

broader intentions regarding the ceremonial practices of the church. Specifically on confirmation Luther explained, "For these reasons, it is enough to regard confirmation as a rite, or a ceremony, of the church, like the other ceremonies of the consecration of water, and similar things. If in all other cases physical objects may be sanctified by preaching and prayer, surely there is greater reason for thinking that a man may be sanctified by them."[37] But since sermons, prayers, and the like do not fit the criteria of possessing both signs and accompanying divine promises, they may be useful to the church and still minister to Christians, but they are simply not sacraments on which all Christians' faith must rely and which may serve to rescue transgressors from sin and facilitate their salvation.

What Luther was attempting to articulate was not the repudiation of the rite itself but of the supernatural substance, which seemed to imply something beyond and different from what the service was originally intended to convey. Thus Luther wanted to emphasize that the ceremony need not be carried out exclusively by a bishop, does not convey an extra measure of divine grace or an indelible mark on the confirmed, and has no biblical grounding. Yet Luther saw the original purpose of confirmation as a kind of blessing or seal from a pastor on those who had completed the catechetical process, a blessing of being authorized in and by the church. Along these lines, the ritual does no harm and even has spiritual value, provided that neither the presiding minister nor the confirmed nor the congregation as a whole returns to its medieval superstitions: "I would permit confirmation," he conceded, "as long as it is understood that God knows nothing of it, and has said nothing about it, and that what the bishops claim for it is untrue."[38] With these caveats in place, the Reformer accepted the simple laying on of hands as a celebration of and graduation from catechetical instruction.[39] In a 1523 sermon, Luther acquiesced: "We do not find fault if every pastor examines the faith of the children to see whether it is good and sincere, lays hands on them, and confirms them."[40] Though he never himself provided a rite for confirmation, Luther guardedly approved of its inclusion in the 1540 Brandenburg Church Order. But the rite could still be viewed as developmentally important, a source of spiritual encouragement to the confirmed, and a way of surrounding newly committed Christians with prayer, spiritual support, and the blessings of their pastor and congregation.

37. Luther, "Pagan Servitude of the Church," via Dillenberger, 325; cf. LW 36:92.
38. Luther, "The Estate of Marriage," LW 45:24–25.
39. WA 11:66.29–32.
40. Here via Fisher, *Confirmation*, 173.

Confirmation among Other Protestant Reformers

Luther allowed for regional variety in many of the church's worship practices, with the Reformer himself even supplying two different services for corporate worship, the Formula Missae and the Deutsche Messe. But most evangelical churches in Germany did not utilize a rite for confirmation in Luther's day, many interpreting it to be a "Roman" ceremony with no biblical substance. At the same time, Lutheran churches began to address the developmental and pedagogical needs of teaching more about their Protestant understanding of baptism and the Lord's Supper to the laity. For his part, Melanchthon concurred with Luther's flaccid understanding of the rite, and in his Instructions for the Visitors of Parish Pastors, a guiding document to accompany consultants who were to study and enforce aspects of German parish life in the late 1520s, Melanchthon advised on how baptism should be understood among the evangelical churches, stressing particularly that faith completes baptism. Concerning confirmation, he simply added: "One need not quarrel over the use of chrism. The true chrism with which all Christians are anointed by God himself is the Holy Spirit."[41]

In Zurich, Ulrich Zwingli began instituting a catechetical curriculum on the principles of Christian faith for adolescents of the Swiss Reformation that culminated in a public renewal of the baptismal commitment. Unlike a Catholic or even Lutheran sacrament, this rite did not encompass the conveyance of divine grace but served as a human response to grace by which the catechized confirmed their faith and affirmed the meaning of their baptisms.[42]

A group partly made up of some of Zwingli's former students, led by Conrad Grebel (d. 1526) and Felix Manz (d. 1527), developed a complete rearrangement of the then-established initiation patterns to match what they believed was the original order of the early church. For these and other Anabaptists in various regions of Western Europe,[43] the rite of passage on which a person first confessed a conscious faith in Christ was not the "confirmation" of one's infant baptism but a believer's baptism, coinciding with one's

41. The 1538–39 version of the Instructions added that "chrism is an unnecessary, free matter." See Melanchthon, Instructions for the Visitors of Parish Pastors in Electoral Saxony, LW 40:288.

42. Theodore R. Jungkuntz, Confirmation and Charismata (Eugene, OR: Wipf & Stock, 1997), 52.

43. Most Anabaptist scholars today understand the movement not to originate exclusively with the Grebel circle but instead to have had a polygenesis in various Central and Western European regions. See, e.g., James M. Stayer, Werner O. Packull, and Klaus Deppermann, "From Monogenesis to Polygenesis: The Historical Discussion of Anabaptist Origins," Mennonite Quarterly Review 49, no. 2 (April 1975): 85–86.

pledge of commitment to church discipline, which collectively constituted the full induction of the believer into the church community in one service, just as the original believers would have confessed faith preceding their baptisms and incorporation into the church in the first century. In many ways, the Anabaptists were more restorationists than Reformers, desiring not simply to rectify perceived medieval abuses of church doctrine and practice but also to reorganize the church by what they believed were the original designs drawn from the New Testament. Interestingly, observing the ceremonial vacuum created when a child was born within their "believers' church," where paedo-baptism had been deemed inappropriate, Balthasar Hubmaier (d. 1528), an important Anabaptist theologian and liturgist of the movement's first generation, developed an infant dedication service in order to bless children and replicate the child dedications of the temple ("Children were being brought," etc., Matt. 19:13).[44] In essence, then, the Anabaptists flipped the sequence for the initiation rites of passage: community blessing of the neophytes and later water baptism. The Anabaptists were mercilessly persecuted and martyred by Swiss Reformed, Catholic, and various political authorities for this radical reorientation of Christian initiation.

Perhaps the most unappreciated Reformer of the sixteenth century, Martin Bucer of Strasbourg, may be more responsible than any other figure for the retention and redefinition of the practice of confirmation in Protestantism. Often called a "champion of Christian unity" and the "father of Protestant confirmation," Bucer wrote a catechism by which he recommended Protestant churches examine young initiates as an "evangelical confirmation," an alternative to medieval episcopal chrism services. After completing a public examination of catechumens before the congregation, the pastor formally imposed hands on the catechized. Bucer also worked through ecumenical enterprises both within magisterial Protestantism and with Anabaptists in an attempt to settle theological differences regarding initiation rites, which had been so divisive among these groups. With Melanchthon, Bucer produced a "Consultation" for the Archbishop Hermann of Cologne, which included a rite called "Confirmation of Children Baptized and Solemn Profession of Their Faith in Christ, and of Their Obedience to Be Showed to Christ and to His Congregation," as a short-lived attempt to bring Lutheran reforms to that city. Following the examination and imposition of hands, the presiding minister would pray: "Confirm this thy servant with thy Holy Spirit, that he may continue in the obedience of thy gospel."[45]

44. See Brewer, *Pledge of Love*, 35, 98–99.
45. Cited in Fisher, *Confirmation*, 202, and White, *Sacraments*, 48.

In 1538, Landgrave Philip of Hesse directed Bucer to intermediate on behalf of Lutherans with a group of Anabaptists who had been arrested for their initiation practices there. In his dialogue with the group, Bucer conceded that infant baptism by itself was not a full incorporation into the church and that a personal vow or pledge of obedience to God and one's church was necessary for each individual for proper admission to the Lord's Supper and full communion in the life of the church. Bucer then craftily maintained infant baptism while incorporating the substance of the nascent Anabaptist initiation rites into confirmation, insisting that the catechized also demonstrate the fruits of genuine faith through their lives as a prerequisite for full admission to the church. Because this Protestant rite answered much of the Anabaptist protest there, Bucer was apparently able to persuade some two hundred Anabaptists to (re)join the state church. His 1539 order became foundational to Protestant confirmation practices for those adolescents who had previously been baptized as infants. Candidates answered a series of questions beyond rote memorization of the Apostles' Creed, vowed to remain obedient to the discipline of the church, received the laying on of hands as a blessing of the Holy Spirit, and were prayed over on behalf of the entire congregation as a completion of their confirmation. Protestant confirmation became an intermediate rite of passage, then, between baptism and the Lord's Supper and was linked with both sacraments as a "sacramental ceremony."[46]

Bucer was also instrumental in revising Cranmer's original 1549 Book of Common Prayer, since the sacramentality of confirmation had been under great dispute in England. Cranmer's initial prayer book required the bishop to preside and required a catechism, an episcopal signing of the forehead, and a sacramental prayer formula: "Confirm and strengthen them with the inward unction of thy Holy Ghost." Bucer's 1552 revision maintained the episcopal rite but removed the controversial prayer and the signing, replacing them with a prayer for the seven gifts of the Spirit to be made manifest within and a simple imposition of hands on the catechized. In his 1550 treatise to the young King Edward VI of England, Bucer paralleled confirmation, as a believer's pledge to the eternal commonwealth, to a citizen's oath of allegiance to that earthly kingdom, adding:

46. See Rhoda Schuler, "Confirmation," in *The Encyclopedia of Protestantism*, ed. Hans J. Hillerbrand (New York: Routledge, 2004), 1:503; and Denis R. Janz, "Confirmation," in Hillerbrand, *Oxford Encyclopedia of the Reformation*, 1:405. Schuler (503), on the one hand, states: "This early form of the rite . . . bore little resemblance to the Roman Catholic sacrament, which was not preceded by instruction in the faith, included no profession of faith, and was not the gateway to the Lord's Supper"; Janz (405), on the other hand, observes, "Whether intentional or not, the wording of Bucer's rite echoes that of the Council of Florence and suggests that, in the last analysis, he regarded confirmation as sacramental."

Since, then, whatever matters with regard to arousing men to a true obedience of Christ is to be taken advantage of with utmost zeal by all who seek Christ's Kingdom, who would doubt that this applies particularly to the churches of Christ? They should require of individual Christians their personal profession of faith and Christian obedience: of adults, before they are baptized; and of those who are baptized as infants, when they have been catechized and instructed in the gospel of Christ; and if any do not permit themselves to be catechized and taught and refuse to follow all the precepts of Christ and to make a legitimate profession of faith and of the obedience to be rendered to Christ and his Church, they ought to be rejected from the company of the saints and the communion of the sacraments, because those who are of this kind openly repudiate the grace of Baptism and altogether separate themselves from the Kingdom of Christ.[47]

Such a requirement, Bucer argued, was justified by the ordering of the Great Commission, according to which those who were baptized must be taught the substance of the faith.

If there was any other Reformer as irreverent about the medieval practice of confirmation as Luther, it was John Calvin. Negatively, Calvin saw confirmation as one of the five "bastard Sacraments" of Rome with no scriptural foundation. Although Calvin conceded that the Catholic ritual and formula for chrism are "beautifully and charmingly done, . . . the Word of God, which promises the presence of the Holy Spirit," is glaringly absent.[48] Instead, it is "a deceptive promise of the devil." The sign of confirmation is also illusory and baseless: "We see the oil—the gross and greasy liquid—nothing else. . . . Let them, I say, bring forth [the] word, if they would have us see in the oil anything else than oil." But if the sign and the command to confirm are both absent, the Romanists are left with nothing else than "sacrilegious boldness."[49]

Positively, Calvin conceded beyond Luther both that the apostles laid hands on the baptized and that the Holy Spirit was conveyed on the new believers. But such an event was temporary, since the apostles initially only baptized in Jesus's name and the Holy Spirit's presence was only subsequently experienced in Acts. This was an interim period.[50] Ultimately baptism itself conveyed the sealing of the Spirit. Consequently, confirmation in the early church became

47. Martin Bucer, "What the Kingdom of Christ Is, and What Is Necessary for Its Restoration," in *De Regno Christi*; here via *Melanchthon and Bucer*, ed. Wilhelm Pauck, LCC 19 (Philadelphia: Westminster, 1969), 229–30.

48. By "Word of God" here Calvin was drawing upon Augustine's understanding of sacrament as containing a "word" or divine promise along with the element. In each case, the divine promise assured the recipient(s) of the presence and work of the Holy Spirit in some way. See, e.g., Augustine, *John's Gospel* 80.3, PL 35.1840; NPNF[1] 7:344.

49. Calvin, *Inst.* 4.19.5; LCC 21:1453.

50. Calvin, *Inst.* 4.19.6; LCC 21:1454.

an examination of the substance of Christian faith for the children of adult believers who had themselves been instructed in the mysteries of the faith and confessed their faith before the bishop. These children, having previously been baptized, were now presented by their parents so that the children might confess the same faith before the bishop sometime "at the end of their child-hood or at the beginning of adolescence."[51] The early church added the rite of the imposition of hands not as a sacrament but merely, yet importantly, to give "more reverence and dignity" to a ceremony already "weighty and holy." This significant ceremony, Calvin proposed, should be restored in its simplicity and purity not as a sacrament but "as a form of blessing."[52]

Contemporary Protestant Appropriations of Confirmation

In many ways, Luther's and the subsequent Protestant reforms of confirma-tion from a sacrament to a simple rite of affirmation of faith and clerical blessing were a helpful transition to preserve something of the established practice, to undergird its catechetical and transitional substance, but to keep it from unwarranted and extrabiblical superstitions. Magisterial Protestants also maintained confirmation with its original link to baptism while impor-tantly also connecting it to the Lord's Supper. Such an ordering is a helpful placement, clarifying baptism as only the initial rite on the spiritual journey and adding further meaning to the Lord's Supper as a sign of incorpora-tion into the church body through the conscious affirmation of its faith and practice. Arguably, then, by demoting confirmation from its sacramentality, the Reformers paradoxically strengthened the sacramental significance of baptism and Eucharist. Such principles could provide helpful guidance for today's mainstream Protestant heirs to the magisterial Reformers.

At the same time, the free church, which at least typologically descends to some degree from the Anabaptist tradition, serves as a continual radical check to the magisterial Protestant assumptions regarding the entire practice of confirmation. This tradition makes a powerful case for inverting the two related initiation rites, arguing for the blessing to come at the birth of a child to Christian families through infant-dedication services, whereby the covenantal nature of obligations of parents and church are still affirmed, and reserving baptism for adolescence and adulthood contingent upon a candidate's per-sonal articulation of the faith as the true entrance into the church. The free church then assumes that individuals come to salvation not through cognitive

51. White (*Sacraments*, 49) suggests Calvin likely saw a child of ten as the ideal age.
52. Calvin, *Inst.* 4.19.4; LCC 21:1452.

appropriation of the Christian history, denominational tradition, and recitation of creedal formulas but through the heartfelt reception of God's grace. These ideas remain central to the free-church tradition.

Having affirmed these various Protestant churches in their approaches to adolescent initiation, both mainline and free-church congregations also must recognize the problems associated with the theological and liturgical traditions inherited from their Reformation ancestors. The tacit theology behind many Protestant confirmation classes is that the substance of the faith is exclusively cognitive (i.e., can simply be taught). However, numerous confirmed Christians, accepted into full membership of their churches, often later come to genuine faith or, conversely, never experience a personal appropriation of the faith beyond their formal catechesis. Churches that utilize confirmation must face the reality that persons cannot fully "confirm" their baptism simply through catechesis and rote memorization of creeds. A change of the heart and the reception of divine grace are necessary. Although Cranmer utilized the Great Commission as the biblical justification for catechism (i.e., "baptize, teaching them," etc.) to follow baptism, the context of Matthew 28 was undoubtedly the *ordo salutis* for adult believers who hear the preaching of the Word, are baptized upon confession of faith, and are taught more of the substance of Christianity following their baptisms. Mainline paedobaptist churches that utilize confirmation must also make room for spiritual appropriations of the faith that cannot be reduced to catechesis and heritage lessons before a genuine spiritual confirmation rightly takes place.

Conversely, free-church credobaptist congregations must restore infant dedications to their original covenantal intent of obligating church and family to raise the children up in the faith and tradition of their congregations, and their pastors must make intentional efforts to bless the children of Christians in these ceremonies. All too often, such ceremonies today are reduced to introductions of the parents and child and the presentation of a gift to the family. Second, the free-church tradition must combine its long-held emphasis on evangelism of its youth with a greater intentionality of offering them catechesis of the theological depths of the faith combined with a period of teaching the heritage of their tradition. Without these latter elements, free-church Christians are left to spiritual experiences without the grounding of community, text, and tradition. This Protestant tradition must utilize catechesis classes for those who do come to faith spiritually. It is an unfortunate circumstance that many free-church congregations often baptize individuals based solely upon the baptizant's subjective experience of salvation, often without offering catechesis on the Christian life and even without detailed explanation of the spiritual and water baptisms through which the candidate is incorporated into the local and universal church. Catechism courses should be required by every free-church congregation after an individual professes faith and before baptism, as was the case in early Christianity, as a way of not only maintaining the congregation's conversionist convictions but now also combining them with basic teaching about baptism, the Lord's Supper, the church, and the ongoing practices and discipline of their congregation and respective denomination. Such a move would likely balance the hyperindividualistic and exclusively experiential understandings of conversion and church membership that often go unchecked in the contemporary free church.

In essence, it seems that the churches requiring believer's baptism and those that utilize confirmation of previous baptism both need something of the other tradition that has all too often been neglected in their own traditions. No doubt numerous churches are making great strides to compensate for these gaps, but they are unfortunately still the exception rather than the rule. Regardless of the timing of baptism and blessing, genuine confession of faith complemented by a rigorous training in the Scriptures and in the customs of their respective churches should be obvious to both broad traditions of Protestantism.

There is much to appreciate in both Luther's and other Reformers' theological meliorations of confirmation. Luther was instrumental in laying the groundwork for understanding that, to be developmentally and, especially, spiritually valuable, a liturgical ceremony need not be considered a sacrament. If the church acknowledges that the ceremony is merely an ecclesial service, without the burdens of divine ordination or scriptural precedent, confirmation can be useful and even laudable. The pastor's imposition of hands can also be a highly valuable gesture for symbolizing the affirmation and blessings of the local congregation. Likewise, Calvin's emphasis that confirmation comes as the completion of the church's scrutiny and spiritual review of adolescents to transition them to full membership is particularly helpful today. Conversely, the Anabaptists' restorationist instinct to replicate the early church's practice of baptizing only mature converts who can claim faith for themselves and submit themselves to the church's teaching would rectify many of the associated theological issues facing the increased dropout rate of young adults. If daringly applied in churches today, the Anabaptist approach could give greater opportunity for genuinely individual commitments to the faith rather than commitments made during adolescence under pressure from parents or peers.

Likewise, Balthasar Hubmaier's construction of a Christian parallel to the temple's long-held practice of dedicating newborns to the Lord helps to place the ceremony of child inductions in a fitting perspective for many

Christian traditions burdened by new Protestant superstitions of christening, according to which parents and family sometimes even depart from services immediately following the child's baptism. Infant initiation is a commitment on the part of parents and gathered congregation, obligating themselves to spiritually nurture their children in the church: it is a beginning, not an end.

Regardless, the reclamation of Martin Bucer's theological contribution to the rite of confirmation may be most applicable of all the Reformers' contributions to the contemporary Protestant context, in mainline and free churches alike. Bucer understood well the significant distinctives of both radical and magisterial Reformers, harnessing many of the principles of the two traditions to build a more spiritually comprehensive catechism, while placing baptism and pastoral blessings in more appropriate contexts. What is most important is that, as the final act of initiation, regardless of which Protestant tradition, candidates would consciously accept the faith, accede to the church's teachings, and submit themselves to the regulation of its incumbent discipline and responsibilities in order to be fully united in Christ's body.

3

Marriage

A Public Ordinance

It is truly just and right, proper and helpful for our salvation. You have joined the marriage pact with the sweet yoke of concord and the indissoluble bond of peace, so the chaste fruitfulness of holy spouses might be preserved for the adoption of children. For your providence, O Lord, and your grace arrange both of these: generation adds to the splendor of the world, regeneration leads to the increase of the church.

The Hadrianum

Although the other sacraments took their rise after sin and on account of sin, we read that the sacrament of marriage was instituted by the Lord before sin, yet not as a remedy, but as a duty.

Peter Lombard

There has been such a thing as marriage itself ever since the beginning of the world, and it also exists amongst unbelievers to the present day. Therefore no grounds exist on which the Romanists can validly call it a sacrament of the new law, and a function solely of the church.

Martin Luther

IN MANY WAYS MARRIAGE is the most complex of all the rituals that became the Western church's seven sacraments, most significantly because the institution of marriage predates both Christian and Jewish origins, finding its source in the foundations of human society. Acknowledging its provenance, yet discussing its "holy standard" before God, has always created a precarious tightrope walk for theologians. It follows then that at least a brief discussion of the cultural origins of marriage is necessary before outlining the institution's development through the early and medieval centuries and, ultimately, Protestant Reformers' reflections on it and new instructions for it.

For centuries, marriage has been a part of the customary norms of society, albeit in varying forms of monogamy and polygamy, though historically and normatively understood as a permanent mutual relationship between two parties, one male and one female, who unite for purposes of companionship and love and establish a home as a proper context for procreation of and nurturing children in a family. Alongside Jewish customs, much of the framework for the institution of marriage in the West has been inherited from Greek and Roman precedents. Classical laws and thought of the West upheld marriage as "both a private good for members of the household and a public good for the broader community or polis."[1] The Greek valuation of monogamous marriage as leading to an orderly society was adopted by Roman philosophers and jurists, who subsequently grounded this relationship as established in natural law. Marriage was both a private relationship that, according to Aristotle, was established in the natural feeling of love for one's mate, providing the proper context for cohabitation and procreation, and also a relationship designed "to provide whatever is necessary to a fully lived life. . . . Accordingly there is a general agreement that the conjugal affection combines the useful with the pleasant."[2]

But classical thought also demonstrated that such private relationships served a public good of securing the continuation of humanity in general and the local community in particular, establishing an orderly mechanism for perpetuating the family, its property, and its household.[3] Yet, as the Roman Stoic moralist Musonius Rufus observed, marriage is not merely for the purpose of procreation, lest the sexual union be no more advanced and refined than that of any other sexual relationship or that of the animal class; instead, "in marriage there must be above all perfect companionship and mutual love of husband and wife, both in health and sickness and under all conditions, since it was with desire for this as well as for having children that both entered upon

1. John Witte Jr., *From Sacrament to Contract: Marriage, Religion, and Law in the Western Tradition*, 2nd ed. (Louisville: Westminster John Knox, 2012), 17.

2. Aristotle, *The Nicomachean Ethics*, ed. Hugh Tredennick, trans. J. A. K. Thompson (repr., New York: Penguin, 1976), 8.12; here via Witte, *From Sacrament to Contract*, 19.

3. See Judith Evans Grubbs, *Law and Family in Late Antiquity: The Emperor Constantine's Marriage Legislation* (Oxford: Clarendon, 1995), 64; and Witte, *From Sacrament to Contract*, 24.

marriage."[4] Classical teachings on marriage were subsequently appropriated in Christianity, in both the East and the West, by the church fathers through the first five centuries and again later by the West in canon law and theological treatises by the high medieval period.

The Hellenistic influences that shaped Western European thought regarding the institution were only surpassed by the Jewish elevation of marriage as a covenant (Mal. 2:14), as part and parcel of their understanding of the new agreement God established with Israel at Mount Sinai, in which God promised divine favor and blessings in return for the people's acquiescence to Mosaic law, which included regulations governing marriage, sexual relations, and family obligations. Through "covenant," each side committed to surrender something of each one's own freedom in deference to the other. Later prophetic literature represented God's relationship to Israel as parallel to, resembling, and to be refracted in the marital relationship of husband and wife. As God's divine being is willingly conformed in order to be bound to one nation, so a man surrenders himself to be bound to his wife.[5] The covenant became a union not merely confirmed by the community after the union's consummation but one that, while entered into by both individuals, was determined by the community *ab initio* through a ceremony requiring public commitment and concomitant witnesses. This custom eventuated into a two-step process of betrothal and then full consummation; the latter was immediately preceded by what eventually became a ten-day ceremonial celebration of the impending union.[6] The public celebration of this private event was established through the Jewish understanding that marriage was divinely designed for humans as the basic structure of and for the natural order. God created the first humans male and female, not only as companions but also as partners in marriage, with the command to multiply. Although through much of Hebrew patriarchal society a man would marry a woman after initiating a contractual agreement with the woman's father, it was the wife who, on the occasion of infertility, would give her slave to her husband in order to carry out this divine command and continue the family line.[7] "It is within the marital household that many of the goods of creation are enjoyed. Moreover, it is through lineage

---

4. Musonius Rufus, in *Musonius Rufus: The Roman Socrates*, trans. and ed. Cora E. Lutz (New Haven: Yale University Press, 1947), 89; here via Witte, *From Sacrament to Contract*, 21.

5. Witte, *From Sacrament to Contract*, 38–39.

6. David Novak, "Jewish Marriage: Nature, Covenant, and Contract," in *Covenant Marriage in Comparative Perspective*, ed. John Witte Jr. and Eliza Ellison (Grand Rapids: Eerdmans, 2005), 27–46.

7. See, e.g., Gen. 16. Yet in some Old Testament contexts polygamy also became a sign of wealth and power (e.g., Solomon's 700 wives and 300 concubines). See Kelly, *Sacraments Revisited*, 152–53.

that familial identities, and more broadly the identity of Israel as a people, are maintained over time."[8] Following the diaspora, the acceptance of polygamy (and the ease of divorce) dissipated and was viewed as morally repugnant. Increasingly the union between husband and wife was seen to parallel God's love for his chosen people. Consequently, monogamy became the inherited presupposition for Jewish marriage at the advent of Christianity.

That the original Christian tradition did not place the same emphasis as its Hellenist and Jewish predecessors did on the security of marriage and the establishment of family for the flourishing of society and tradition may come as an unanticipated observation. The New Testament is, instead, ambiguous regarding the importance of marriage and family. On the one hand, Jesus affirmed the necessity of maintaining marital commitments by condemning divorce, grounding such human obligations in God's design for creation: "Have you not read that the one who made them at the beginning 'made them male and female,' and said, 'For this reason a man shall leave his father and mother and be joined to his wife, and the two shall become one flesh'? So they are no longer two, but one flesh. Therefore what God has joined together, let no one separate" (Matt. 19:4–6). On the other hand, Jesus warned that even the rival obligations of family relations need to be checked in light of one's relationship to the Messiah: "Whoever loves father or mother more than me is not worthy of me; and whoever loves son or daughter more than me is not worthy of me" (Matt. 10:37). The New Testament records Jesus as seemingly giving the Christian community a higher standing in the Christian's life than that of biological relations—"My mother and my brothers are those who hear the word of God and do it" (Luke 8:21)—leaving many believers to understand the relations of the church as the new family of God. Likewise, the apostle Paul appears to present a mixed message regarding marriage. According to Paul, marriage is a necessary estate to curb the weakness of the flesh: "But because of cases of sexual immorality, each man should have his own wife and each woman her own husband" (1 Cor. 7:2). Paul provided instructions on the management of the household, with application to Christ and the church (Eph. 5:21–33), yet he maintained that singleness and chastity provide opportunity for greater devotion to Christ. Whether as a critique of the Hellenist civic duty of marriage and procreation in its Roman cultural setting[9] or as an apostle anticipating persecution and/or the imminent end of the age, Paul generally advised Christians to maintain the status quo: "Are

8. Brent Waters, "Marriage," in *The Oxford Handbook of Sacramental Theology*, ed. Hans Boersma and Matthew Levering (Oxford: Oxford University Press, 2015), 517.

9. For this claim, see Waters, "Marriage," 517–18.

you bound to a wife? Do not seek to be free. Are you free from a wife? Do not seek a wife" (1 Cor. 7:27). But as the Christian tradition not only flourished through early persecution but ultimately became the codified religion and worldview for Western Europe, the church fathers of the first five centuries provided additional instruction and clarification for the ordering of marriage and family life.

Marriage in the Patristic Era

In the postbiblical patristic era, it seems that the church made room both for the life of celibacy and for marriage, with various church fathers making one or the other normative and most proper for the Christian. By 105, Ignatius wrote his *Letter to Polycarp*, directing that both options be exercised in an orderly manner and under the supervision of the bishop:

> Tell my sisters to love the Lord and to be content with their husbands physically and spiritually. In the same way command my brothers in the name of Jesus Christ to love their wives, as the Lord loves the church. If anyone is able to remain chaste to the honor of the flesh of the Lord, let him so remain without boasting. If he boasts, he is lost; and if it is made known to anyone other than the bishop, he is ruined. And it is proper for men and women who marry to be united with the consent of the bishop, that the marriage may be in accordance with the Lord and not due to lustful passions. Let all things be done for the honor of God.[10]

By the end of the second century, Clement admonished Christians to find a "suitable" time and spouse, "for everyone is not to marry, nor always. . . . Neither ought everyone to take wife, nor is it every woman one is to take"; rather, marriage is appropriate under the proper circumstances and for the purpose of propagating children.[11] Meanwhile, Jerome (d. 420) utilized 2 Corinthians 5:17 ("Old things have passed away; behold, all things have become new" [cf. KJV]) to argue for celibacy or continence as the new freedom in Christ: "For when we were in the flesh, the sinful passions, which were through the law, wrought in our members to bring forth fruit unto death. But now we have been discharged from the law, having died to that wherein we were holden; so that we serve in newness of the Spirit, and

---

10. Ignatius, *Letter to Polycarp*, chap. 5; here via *The Apostolic Fathers*, ed. Michael W. Holmes, trans. J. B. Lightfoot and J. R. Harmer, 2nd ed. (Grand Rapids: Baker, 1989), 116–17.
11. See Clement, *The Stromata, or Miscellanies*, chap. 23; ANF 2:377.

not in oldness of the letter."[12] Those who desire marriage and its ongoing sexual relationship remain in the animal state, according to Jerome, and are not guided by the Spirit of God.

While other church fathers rejected his condemnation of the conjugal union of marriage among Christians, Jerome's position was only moderated by others to give marriage a second-class position to that of celibacy. Augustine (d. 430) described this idea of marriage as a lesser good when compared to the greater good of celibacy. In fact, for Augustine, all sexual acts postfall were mired in sin, such that the institution of marriage might only make this act "less sinful," as it carried out God's prefall injunction to multiply. While marriage and celibacy are both laudable vocations, the call to singleness is of a higher spiritual plane, and the sexual intercourse that was created good for the first humans has been disfigured after the fall, redeemed by God only through the gift of offspring. Thus, while marriage is good, it maintains a compromised interdependence with the fallen world. Regardless, marriage provides for lifelong friendship, mutuality in faithful service, and "a foundation for the task of ordering creation in anticipation of Christ's kingdom."[13] Thus marriage fulfills much of God's intention for the temporal world, while celibacy serves God's transcendent world.[14]

Marriage in the Medieval Period

Augustine's interpretation of these complementary vocations guided Christian sexual ethics into and through much of the Middle Ages, with most medieval theologians using the bishop of Hippo's understanding as their frame of reference: they interacted with it, modified it, or appropriated it as their own. The early medieval period was a time of confusion for the Western empire, confusion that translated into a diversity of understanding and practice of marriage. Celibacy was ultimately mandated for clerics and codified by the Lateran Council in 1123, partly as a means to restrict priests from diverting funds from properties deeded to the church and giving those funds to their heirs,[15] and partly as a continuation of more transcendent themes presented by some of the fathers.

As formerly non-Christian people groups were assimilated into Christendom through Western expansion and the slow dissolution of the Roman

12. Jerome, *Against Jovinianus* 1.37; NPNF² 6:374.
13. Waters, "Marriage," 519. See esp. Augustine, *Of the Good of Marriage*; NPNF¹ 3:399–413; and Michael Parsons, *Reformation Marriage: The Husband and Wife Relationship in the Theology of Luther and Calvin* (Eugene, OR: Wipf & Stock, 2011), 49–76.
14. Waters, "Marriage," 519.
15. Martin E. Marty, *Martin Luther: A Life* (New York: Viking Penguin, 2004), 101.

Empire, both the state and the church were also forced to address various practices of divorce and remarriage formerly accepted in these varied cultures. Although the church demonstrated a strange and inconsistent tolerance (and even allowance) for divorce through the eighth century, by the ninth century many theologians again appealed to Augustine's idea that marriage paralleled and depicted Christ's union with the church, and thus they restored the Christian ideal that marriage was indissoluble.[16] But what remained inconsistent, as its practice fluctuated from one corner of Europe to another, was the place of the church and its priest or bishop in the wedding service itself. Even as medieval theologians were reading Ephesians 5:32, "This is a great *mystery*" (*mystērion*, Greek), as instead "a great *sacrament*" (*sacramentum*, Vulg.), Aquinas did not require a priest to officiate the service in order to sanctify the rite, for the married couple, in this case, *were* the ministers of the sacrament, through which a specific grace was still conferred to the couple, an idea later confirmed by Duns Scotus (d. 1308). Some Scholastics suggested a place for the priest at least following the wedding service, since his blessing might ameliorate the sinful qualities, per Augustine's theology, of the marriage bed.

Church scholars then even debated whether it was the nuptials by the couple or the sexual consummation itself that finally established the marriage. Pope Alexander III (d. 1181) ultimately ruled that marriages were determined by the mutual consent of the couple, and the Fourth Lateran Council in 1215 merely recommended that couples seek parental permission, provide witnesses at the ceremony, make public their marital status, and request premarital counseling from a priest. But in various places throughout Europe, wedding services were often held in homes, at the door of the church, and at the church's altar.[17] And even in his famous *Four Books of Sentences*, which was determinative for establishing marriage as one of the seven sacraments of the Western church, Peter Lombard admitted to its unique character among the other six rituals: "Although the other sacraments took their rise after sin and on account of sin, we read that the sacrament of marriage was instituted by the Lord before sin, yet not as a remedy, but as a duty."[18] This statement later led liturgy scholar James F. White to conclude that marriage "barely makes it onto the list of seven sacraments," as it admittedly did not fit Lombard's own sacramental rubric.[19]

16. Kelly, *Sacraments Revisited*, 159.

17. Witte, *From Sacrament to Contract*, 91.

18. Lombard, *Sentences* 4, in *Peter Lombard and the Sacramental System*, 243; here via Johnson, *Sacraments and Worship*, 296.

19. White, *Documents*, 225.

Luther's Understanding and Reform of Marriage

Many of the concerns that were the foci of Luther's writings on marriage in treatises, sermons, and letters were culturally shaped by his time and are of little concern to the reader five centuries removed. Questions pertaining to the impediments to marriage (e.g., whether a faithful Christian might marry her cousin or the brother of her deceased husband) are no longer widely debated in most Christian circles of the West. Suffice it to say that Luther repudiated most of the restrictions that both the state and the church had placed on men and women who intended to marry, characterizing these rules as extraneous, unfounded in Scripture, and "impious, man-made laws."[20] The bulk of Luther's writings on this matter were directed toward such cultural legalisms[21] and his corollary arguments for greater freedom for selecting a mate. Nevertheless, one may observe that many of Luther's remaining words on marriage and proposed theological reforms thereof are largely important to and applicable for not only his day but also contemporary discussions of the institution. Furthermore, Luther's understanding of marriage, inexorably shaped by his Augustinian training, nevertheless saw a deliberate reform as consistent with his overarching sacramental project. In many ways, Luther's view of marriage is filled with paradoxes. He spoke highly of the institution of marriage, yet he chose not to participate in it himself until he was in his early forties. He simultaneously elevated the importance of marriage in society and demoted it as something less than a sacrament in the church. Luther was a product of his society in seeing women as inferior to men, yet he elevated women (including his wife, Katie [Katharina von Bora]) in ways more familiar to modern egalitarian marriages. Finally, he took marriage out of the jurisdiction of the church by characterizing it as a public institution, yet he outlined some distinctively Christian underlying principles for its purpose and meaning.

It is not surprising that the early Luther, an Augustinian monk, was highly influenced by his order's namesake. Even in 1519, many of Luther's views on marriage, celibacy, and sexuality were still grounded in Augustine's teachings, especially the notion that marriage serves as a kind of antidote to sexual immorality. His foray into the general topic came in January of that year in the form of a homily on the wedding at Cana in John 2, "A Sermon on the Estate of Marriage." Here the Reformer pointed to Genesis as recording the

---

20. Luther, *Babylonian Captivity*; here via Dillenberger, 330; cf. LW 36:96.

21. Yet entertaining they remain. Luther opined, e.g., "Good God! It is dreadful to contemplate the audacity of the Roman despots, who both dissolve and compel marriages as they please." LW 36:96.

origins of marriage, observing that God is there portrayed as creating a wife for Adam. Luther then advised Christians intent on marriage likewise to pray, asking God to provide a proper spouse, for "a wife is given by God alone [cf. Prov. 19:14]."[22] In this way, marriage was a uniquely human estate, ordained to transcend the natural mating of the animal world.

Drawing again upon the Augustinian school, Luther concurred that marriage maintained three purposes. First, still in 1519 the Reformer affirmed marriage as a sacrament, in this case, as a sacred sign of the union of Christ's human and divine natures, signifying this spiritual reality. Second, marriage served as a "covenant of fidelity," to be a sacred bond between husband and wife, so that each completely surrenders himself or herself to the other, a bond that cannot be severed except by the death of the spouse. While the flesh must be kept in check, the marriage bed "permits even more occasion than is necessary for the begetting of children."[23] Marriage of husband and wife then serves as the proper outlet for sexual relations, an outlet that, after the fall, is to counteract the lusts of the flesh. Third, God designed marriage as the context for begetting and raising children. It is incumbent upon Christians to recognize the obligations of not spoiling children as unbelieving parents do, but to rear them "to serve God, to praise and honor him, and want nothing else of them."[24] Luther added that this is the highest work that a couple can perform in life: "They can do no better work and do nothing more valuable either for God, for Christendom, for all the world, for themselves, and for their children than to bring up their children well."[25] Such work surpasses building churches, endowing masses, going on pilgrimages, or any other good work and is "their shortest road to heaven."[26]

This trifold benefit and purpose to marriage, Luther argued, was predicated upon the discrimination between the three loves a human might experience: false love, natural love, and married love. False love is self-serving, one that distorts sexual relations into fulfilling one's own pleasures; it is a love that corresponds with a human's aspirations for wealth, power, position, and possessions. Natural love is that instinctive love between parents, siblings, family relations, and good friends. But married love is the purest of all since it is selfless, seeking the fulfillment only of the other. Here Luther repined: "If Adam had not fallen, the love of bride and groom would have been the loveliest thing. Now this love is not pure either, for admittedly a married

22. Luther, "A Sermon on the Estate of Marriage," LW 44:8.
23. LW 44:11.
24. LW 44:12.
25. Ibid.
26. Ibid.

partner desires to have the other, yet each seeks to satisfy his desire with the other, and it is this desire which corrupts this kind of love."[27] Thus marriage now, regretfully, serves as a "hospital for incurables which prevents inmates from falling into graver sin."[28] Regardless, Christian couples can experience a measure of this the purest and greatest of loves, both enjoyed within faithful mutuality and through their higher calling of discipling their children rather than spoiling them.

While Luther's subsequent writings on marriage retained the Augustinian trifold purpose to marriage, the nomenclature was slightly altered to include "children, loyalty, and love."[29] Love now served as the key replacement to the medieval understanding that marriage was a sacrament. In fact, just one year after his "Sermon on the Estate of Marriage," Luther detailed the evolution of his thought in *The Babylonian Captivity of the Church*, explaining just why marriage should not be considered a sacrament: "Figures or allegories are not sacraments."[30] The simple fact that marriage serves as an illustration or analogy for Christ's dual nature or for Christ and the church does not mean it is the equivalent of what it resembles. Returning to his twofold definition of a sacrament as requiring a promise with an accompanying sign, Luther acknowledged that God nowhere instituted marriage in Scripture and thus promised no specific grace to those who participate in it, concluding that "a sign alone cannot be a sacrament." And since marriage finds its origin not in redemption but in creation and has always included believers and nonbelievers alike, it cannot be properly categorized as a sacrament of the new covenant for the Christian church: "The marriages of the ancients were no less sacred than ours, nor are those of unbelievers less true marriages than those of believers, and yet they are not regarded as sacraments."[31]

At this point, however, Luther was keenly aware that he himself previously utilized Ephesians 5 ("The two shall become one. This is a great sacrament" [cf. 5:31–32 Vulg.]) as a prooftext to defend the sacramentality of marriage. Now in 1520 Luther perceived this as both a misreading of the passage and a mistranslation of (the Greek) *mystērion* as (the Latin) *sacramentum* and not straightforwardly as "mystery." Luther reasoned that elsewhere in Scripture when *mystērion* appears, it "denotes not the sign of a sacred thing, but the

---

27. LW 44:9.
28. Ibid.
29. WA 34:52.5–6 ("Eine Hochzeitpredigt über den Spruch Hebr. 13,4"); here via Scott Hendrix, "Luther on Marriage," in *Harvesting Martin Luther's Reflections on Theology, Ethics, and the Church*, ed. Timothy J. Wengert (Grand Rapids: Eerdmans, 2004), 172.
30. Luther, *Babylonian Captivity*, LW 36:92.
31. Ibid.

sacred, secret, hidden thing itself," just as Christ himself is called a great
mystery in 1 Timothy 3:16 and is not, because of the proper translation of
this latter passage, viewed as the eighth sacrament! But elsewhere Rome has
arbitrarily "transformed the Scriptures according to their own dreams, making
anything out of any passage whatsoever," turning every other use of *sacramentum* into a sign and attaching new customs and ceremonies to it. "Thus
they continually chatter nonsense about the terms: good work, evil work,
sin, grace, righteousness, virtue, and almost all the fundamental words and
things. For they employ them all after their own arbitrary judgment, learned
from the writings of men, to the detriment of both the truth of God and of
our salvation."[32] But the real "sacrament"—Luther underscored in this section of his treatise, just as at the beginning of this seminal work—is that the
real mystery is Jesus Christ himself. This mystery is hidden to the wise and
the rulers of the world and is revealed to the foolish who believe in Christ.
"Therefore," Luther concluded, "a sacrament is a mystery, or secret thing,
which is set forth in words, but received by the faith of the heart."[33] Paul,
then, used the notion of the two becoming one flesh as an illustration of the
the great sacrament "to mean Christ and the church" (Eph. 5:31–32).[34] The
sarcastic Luther then classically opined: "See how well Paul and these men
agree! Paul said he is proclaiming a great sacrament in Christ and the church,
but they proclaim it in terms of [a] man and a woman! If such liberty in the
interpretation of the sacred Scriptures is permitted, it is small wonder that one
finds here anything he pleases, even a hundred sacraments."[35] Although Luther
had arrived at a new position regarding the status of marriage within the
church's sacramental system, his understanding of marriage within the order
of creation and within the lives of Christians was just beginning to develop.

However, Luther's life circumstances took a dramatic turn following his
hearing before the Diet of Worms in April of 1521. Prince Frederick of Saxony
had Luther taken into protective custody at Wartburg Castle from May of
that year until March of 1522, for his own protection from Imperial arrest.
In isolation from the company of friends, Luther found himself in what may
have been the deepest struggles with his vows of celibacy. To further complicate matters, in his absence from Wittenberg, three priests in Magdeburg
and Meissen were married, precipitating a debate on the matter throughout
the region on whether clerical vows were binding. Those twin events, one
of personal struggle and one of external controversy, served as catalysts in

32. LW 36:94.
33. Ibid.
34. Ibid.
35. LW 36:94–95.

Luther's mind, leading him to conclude that the required vows of celibacy for clergymen were extrabiblical, false mandates, and inventions of the church.[36]

Although he continued to see celibacy as a gift of God, not a human work, and understood the life of singleness as a greater gift than that of marriage, one that provided a liberating and concentrated devotion to the ministry of the church itself, Luther nevertheless saw no biblical mandate from the New Testament for all priests to observe this lifestyle and recognized from his own experience and that of others that drudgery in this matter belied the reality of such a blanket divine gift to the entire priestly class. Yet marriage was still not the ideal for a cleric, in Luther's mind, but was a necessity for some: "How much happier a state of affairs it is to tolerate a marriage irksome twice over than to be tortured by the constant pangs of conscience!"[37] Luther was yet to see the benefits of marriage and family as the normative environment "for experiencing and enacting the gospel."[38] And yet, provided it was not "contrary to love," such decisions should be a matter of free choice for each cleric: "Therefore, we may keep the vow, but we are not bound to keep it, since nothing is binding on us except to love one another. . . . It is easy to see why dispensations can and ought to be made with respect to the vow of chastity and, in fact, in all vows. . . . No one is harmed if you marry."[39]

Luther began markedly to modify his stance on marriage in general and sexual relations in particular in his 1522 treatise *The Estate of Marriage*. The Wittenberg professor began the treatise by rehearsing the creation narrative in Genesis, citing 1:27, where "God created man; . . . male and female he created them" (RSV), and stressing that God declared this creation to be "very good" (1:31). Luther then made the obvious observation, just as in Genesis, that God continues to create all people as either male or female, "a he or a she."[40] Since "each one of us must have the kind of body God has created us," we cannot declare ourselves to be a different gender but should honor the body that God created as good. Genesis then continues, Luther pointed out, with the divine injunction to "be fruitful and multiply" (Gen. 1:28).[41] One can readily observe Luther's gradual parting from both Augustinian and medieval notions of marriage as the second-rate sacrament out of necessity

36. For Luther's own considerations during this time, see LW 48:277–79 and esp. LW 44:251–400; Hendrix, "Luther on Marriage," 176; Jane E. Strohl, "Luther on Marriage, Sexuality, and the Family," in *The Oxford Handbook of Martin Luther's Theology*, ed. Robert Kolb, Irene Dingel, and L'ubormir Bàtka (Oxford: Oxford University Press, 2014), 372–73.
37. LW 44:395.
38. Strohl, "Luther on Marriage, Sexuality, and the Family," 373.
39. LW 44:393.
40. Luther, *The Estate of Marriage*, LW 45:17.
41. LW 45:17–18.

for laypeople and his developing openness to marriage as a blessing intended from creation for all willing people. Long gone is the notion that marriage is a "hospital for incurables." Instead, since human bodies are indeed "good," he reasoned, and since people cannot follow God's "ordinance" without coming together, "it is not my prerogative to be without a woman."[42]

Sexual relations, then, are not sin but are "a natural and necessary thing" in the context of marriage, for which God designed them. Resisting marriage is instead what leads to sinfulness for all but eunuchs! To promise to live otherwise is to deny the purpose of the gender for which God made each person, "even if you should make ten oaths, vows, covenants and adamantine or ironclad pledges"; one cannot promise not to be a man or a woman.[43] Thus church and civil impediments should be overcome because "the created order of marriage spills over into the realm of law and gospel."[44] And since God designed sexual relations and procreation to be as natural as walking, eating, drinking, and emptying the bowels and bladder, it is an ordinance such that ignoring it would prove unnatural and even rebellious to God's desire. Marriage between a man and a woman is designed as part and parcel of natural law and divine ordinance.

Parenthetically, Luther was not unaware of the practice of homosexuality in his day. Elsewhere in his writings, Luther characterized such as "uncleanness and effeminacy," citing Romans 1, 1 Corinthians 6, and Ephesians 5, and concluding that those who practice same-sex relations have exchanged God's truth for a lie and the worship of God for that of an idol.[45] Perhaps his greatest denunciation of homosexual behavior came in his *Lectures on Genesis*, where, commenting on the episode at Sodom in Genesis 19:4–5, Luther identified homosexual behavior as an almost unspeakable sin condemned by God:

> I for my part do not enjoy dealing with this passage, because so far the ears of the Germans are innocent of and uncontaminated by this monstrous depravity; for even though this disgrace, like other sins, has crept in through an ungodly soldier and a lewd merchant, still the rest of the people are unaware of what is being done in secret. The Carthusian monks deserve to be hated because they were the first to bring this terrible pollution into Germany from the monasteries of Italy. Of course, they were trained and educated in such a praiseworthy manner at Rome.[46]

42. LW 45:18.
43. LW 45:19.
44. Strohl, "Luther on Marriage, Sexuality, and the Family," 374.
45. Luther, *Lectures on Romans*, LW 25:164–65.
46. Luther, *Lectures on Genesis*, LW 3:251–52.

Naturally, Luther was able to attach what he viewed as iniquity both to non-German and monastic origins, combining sexual ethics with his German nationalistic and anticlerical sentiments. Yet the overarching message regarding what Luther viewed as the proper exercise of sexuality remains as he admonished his people to "fear God and to arm [them]selves against the flesh and the devil, in order that [they] may not fall into similar disgraceful sins which God cannot allow to go unpunished."[47] The men of Sodom had wives and children and thus should have lived according to "discipline and modesty." Such was the case with Lot, who "maintained discipline and chastity to the utmost of his ability, while the others indulged freely and without shame in adultery, fornication, effeminacy, and even incest to such an extent that these were not even regarded as sins but as some pastime."[48]

At this point Luther clarified that sexual relations between a single man and an unattached woman were not a "cleansing of the nature, which seeks an outlet," as some canons in Italy and Germany had apparently suggested.[49] He maintained that it was not only inappropriate sexual behavior but also was, in its essence, still sin. In place of sinful relations, marriage was always to be the context for the passions of the flesh to be satisfied, according to God's design. Clearly at this juncture Luther now understood such urges not to be evil in nature but as having a divine origin and needing to be carried out for a divine purpose. "The heinous conduct of the people of Sodom," on the other hand, "is extraordinary, inasmuch as they departed from the natural passions and longing of the male for the female, which was implanted into nature by God, and desired what is altogether contrary to nature. Whence comes this perversity? Undoubtedly from Satan, who, after people have once turned away from the fear of God, so powerfully suppresses nature that he blots out the natural desire and stirs up a desire that is contrary to nature."[50] In Luther's reading, so spiritually calloused were the men of Sodom that they called on the angels of the Lord to be brought outside, for their sins were now openly practiced, and they were unashamed of them.[51]

The lifelong commitment of husband and wife was God's design both for individuals and for the society as a whole. While Luther considered only a few reasons for the tragedy of divorce (namely, adultery, natural or bodily

---

47. LW 3:252.
48. LW 3:254.
49. Ibid.
50. LW 3:255.
51. For further discussion of Luther and homosexuality, see William H. Lazareth, "ELCA Lutherans and Luther on Heterosexual Marriage," *Lutheran Quarterly* 8, no. 3 (Autumn 1994): 235–68; John T. Pless, "The Use and Misuse of Luther in Contemporary Debates on Homosexuality: A Look at Two Theologians," in *Lutheran Forum* (Pentecost/Summer 2005): 50–57.

deficiency, or refusing one's conjugal duty), he otherwise encouraged Christians in particular to remain married and "endure the other's ill behavior, that would doubtless be a wonderfully blessed cross and a right way to heaven."[52] Thus Luther did not leave marriage as simply a public ordinance with an overarching natural law to guide all humans. What is often overlooked by many contemporary researchers of this topic is that Luther outlined singularly Christian principles for marriage as well, highlighting that there is something specific to the ways Christians abide in marital fidelity that speaks to God's ultimate purpose behind the institution.

While Christians should not allow the fleshly, sinful nature to overtake the sanctified spiritual nature, Luther read the apostle Paul as giving instructions for marriage as the normative Christian ethic for overcoming bodily passions. Doing otherwise, attempting a life of singleness despite one's struggles, would place one in spiritual peril. Luther then encouraged men to overcome the pagan worldview that saw women as an annoyance and a necessary evil. The Reformer humorously considered an inverted situation: "I imagine that if women were to write books they would say exactly the same thing about men."[53] Instead, Christians should understand that both man and woman are products of God's good creation. He critiqued parents who dissuaded their children from marriage by enticing them to take on monastic vows, reducing marriage to a life of tribulation and sorrows: "Thus do they bring their own children home to the devil, as we daily observe; they provide them with ease for the body and hell for the soul."[54] But Christians understand that men and women were made for one another from God's own hand: "Do not criticize his work, or call that evil which he himself has called good. He knows better than you yourself what is good and to your benefit" (Gen. 2:18). Those who listen to such parents or the wicked advice of pagan books follow in the way of the devil, who himself detests the estate of marriage. For Solomon advised: "He who finds a wife finds a good thing, and obtains favor from the LORD" (Prov. 18:22).[55]

For Luther, then, there is a difference between simply "being married" and truly recognizing its estate—that is, its divine origin and purpose. One can be married and find all the misery to which the pagan customs referred. But understanding that in the struggles of marriage and parenting a spouse finds God's blessing—that is quite another approach altogether. This particularly Christian consciousness allows husbands "to see that their life and conduct

52. LW 45:34.
53. LW 45:36.
54. LW 45:37.
55. LW 45:38.

with their wives is the work of God and pleasing in his sight." Luther then mused: "Could they but find that, then no wife would be so hateful, so ill-tempered, so ill-mannered, so poor, so sick that they would fail to find in her their heart's delight and would always be reproaching God for his work, creation, and will."[56] Such a spiritual approach would bring "peace in grief, joy in the midst of bitterness, [and] happiness in the midst of tribulations, [just] as the martyrs have in suffering."[57] And parenting is seen not as drudgery, with a loss of independence, but with an understanding of holy responsibility such that the parent can acknowledge to God:

> I confess to thee that I am not worthy to rock the little babe or wash its diapers, or to be entrusted with the care of the child and its mother. How is it that I, without any merit, have come to this distinction of being certain that I am serving thy creature and thy most precious will? O how gladly will I do so, though the duties should be even more insignificant and despised. Neither frost nor heat, neither drudgery nor labor, will distress or dissuade me, for I am certain that it is thus pleasing in thy sight.[58]

Christian parents, then, when recognizing their divine calling and duty to care for spouse and child, will be humbled and honored, both recognizing marriage and family as part and parcel of God's calling on their lives and expressing thanks for such menial but holy labors.

Thus, while marriage does not fall into Luther's overarching sacramental framework, the estate is nevertheless infused with mystery as part of God's design and is a divinely ordained institution to be lived out by faith in God's ways and will. This understanding of Christian marriage is lost when individuals and culture interpret marriage's worth by one's feelings and self-centered desires rather than being open to God's works and direction through it: "Nothing is so bad, not even death itself, but what it becomes sweet and tolerable if only I know and am certain that it is pleasing to God."[59] When human reason finds marital relations to be self-entrapment and parenting to be an unnecessarily arduous life of to-do lists, Christian faith "opens its eyes, looks upon all these insignificant, distasteful, and despised duties in the Spirit, and is aware that they are all adorned with divine approval as with the costliest gold and jewels."[60] When marriage and its oft-accompanied responsibility of parenting meet with God's perfect pleasure, the husband and the

56. Ibid.
57. LW 45:39.
58. LW 45:39–40.
59. LW 45:39.
60. Ibid.

wife recognize that they are not even worthy of their incumbent tasks. For instance, Luther even told husbands that washing the baby's diapers is acting in the Spirit of God, for which God and the angels smile. But the Christian spouse and parent must act and live in faith in order to see God's purposes: "No one can have real happiness in marriage who does not recognize in firm faith that this estate together with all its works, however insignificant, is pleasing to God and precious in his sight."[61]

While much of Luther's early writing on marriage pertained to the duties of each spouse and of parenting, his theology of marriage was also mostly solidified by 1522, interestingly still some three years before his own marriage. The modern reader may wonder about Luther's own wrestling with his vows in the early 1520s and his ultimate elevation of the vows of marriage over those of celibacy. Admittedly, Luther conceded that the celibate is not as burdened with the cares and anxieties of the world, has the support of God's Word in the examples of Paul and Christ, and may place his entire focus on the ministerial task; yet the estate of marriage, he maintained, is God's normative and blessed design for humanity. In 1522 Luther suggested that only "one in a thousand" was capable of celibacy.[62] By the following year, he conjectured it as only one in a hundred thousand.[63] Still in 1522, Luther retained an Augustinian view of intercourse as "never without sin"; thus marriage was a remedy against such iniquity wherein God excuses sex within the estate by divine grace. But Luther almost paradoxically understood marriage as also an "estate of faith,"[64] wholly blessed by God, and by 1525 he discerned that sexual desire is "God's word and work."[65]

Although Luther's works gave encouragement and approval for a number of German monks, priests, and nuns to be married, Luther was slow to join the estate himself until 1525, when on June 13, at age forty-two, he married the runaway nun Katharina von Bora (1499–1552). In a letter written to Nicholas von Amsdorf in the days between the ceremony of exchanging vows and the customary marriage banquet, Luther stated that he now intended to grant his father's wish for grandchildren. Further, Luther wrote, "I also wanted to confirm what I have taught [regarding marriage] by practicing it; for I find so many timid people in spite of such great light from

---

61. LW 45:42.
62. WA 10/2:279.19–21; here via Janz, "Marriage," in *Westminster Handbook to Martin Luther*, 90.
63. WA 12:115.20–21; here via Janz, "Marriage," 90.
64. See LW 44:9n1; William H. Lazareth, *Luther on the Christian Home: An Application of the Social Ethics of the Reformation* (Philadelphia: Muhlenberg, 1960), 233–34.
65. WA 18:275.19–28; here cited in Janz, "Marriage," 90.

the gospel."[66] For Luther, the Christian understanding of and responsibility in marriage were the rediscovery of this great gospel light. The remainder of his remarks on marriage reflect his teaching regarding the struggles and blessings of marriage and family, as he and Katharina enjoyed six children, two of whom preceded them in death. As Luther's time was consumed with writing and preaching, Katharina hosted a continuous rotation of house guests and students in their home, the former monastic cloister, while she also bred pigs, brewed beer, grew vegetables, and managed the household finances. Martin Marty wrote of the Luther marriage: "The verdict on the married couple and the family was that overall they were happy and rewarded. The word Luther liked to use for his attitude toward Katharina was that he esteemed her, and he had good reason to."[67] It is then not surprising to learn that Luther broke with the custom of his day in bequeathing in his will his remaining possessions not to his surviving children, as was expected, but the transfer of all goods to his widow.

By 1529, Luther recorded the highest praise of the estate of marriage in the Large Catechism, mentioning "how highly God honors and praises this walk of life." Luther explained:

> [God] has established it before all others as the first of all institutions, and he created man and woman differently (as is evident) not for indecency but to be true to each other, to be fruitful, to beget children, and to nurture and bring them up to the glory of God. God has therefore blessed this walk of life most richly, above all others, and, in addition, has supplied and endowed it with everything in the world in order that this walk of life might be richly provided for. Married life is no matter of jest or idle curiosity, but it is a glorious institution and an object of God's serious concern. For it is of utmost importance to him that persons be brought up to serve the world, to promote knowledge of God, godly living, and all virtues, and to fight against wickedness and the devil.[68]

In the catechism Luther argued that marriage is no secondary walk of life but is sanctioned and endorsed by God's Word. "Because of this Word it is not a walk of life to be placed on the same level with all the others, but it is

---

66. Luther, "Letter to Nicholas von Amsdorf, June 21, 1525," in WA Br 3:541.4–8. Luther went on to explain that the marriage was without passion but that he deeply cherished Katharina. According to Scott Hendrix ("Luther on Marriage," 343), by these words Luther was showing all the more that his apparent primary motivation for marrying was to be an example to others. Also see Scott Hendrix, *Martin Luther: Visionary Reformer* (New Haven: Yale University Press, 2015), 166.

67. Marty, *Martin Luther*, 111.

68. Luther, Large Catechism, *BC* 414.

before and above them all, whether those of emperor, princes, bishops, or any other. . . . It is not a restricted walk of life, but the most universal and noblest, pervading all Christendom and even extending throughout all the world."[69]

It is on his "universal" or "public" point that many misunderstand Luther's teaching on the institution. When he perceived marriage to belong to the worldly estate, which should be adjudicated by the state and not by the church, Luther did not have in mind the secularization of marriage (or any other matter) as understood by the modern Western democratic notion of the separation of church and state. Although much of the language utilized by Luther and other Reformers can be exploited as if to support such a claim, the understanding of Luther's two kingdoms is then completely overlooked in doing so. Luther's secular kingdom is still overseen by a God who is active in appointing its leaders, who should in turn be faithful to the framework of natural law and be doing Christian justice as God's representatives in the political realm. And although Luther no longer classified marriage as a sacrament of the church, as Hendrix reports, "nevertheless, Luther continues to insist that marriage is a divinely-willed estate and that Christians are to live in marriage in a special way."[70] Pastors would still bless marrying couples through church ceremonies. Marriage bans would continue to be published in church.

But Luther proposed reassigning marriage to be regulated by the state as a reaction (arguably an overreaction) to the church's apparent recent heavy-handedness in regulating marital impediments and turning away candidates for marriage because of what Luther viewed as arbitrary rules regarding age, previous marital history, previous vows to the church, kinship to their betrothed, and so forth. In his typical hotheaded style, the Reformer simply recommended removing marriage from the sovereignty of ecclesial clerics and placing it in the hands of those whom he hoped would be Christian princes (just as he would do, even more puzzlingly, with ordination) in the context of a Christian state, wholly different from the modern secular (now a-religious) states of the present century. Luther found grounding in such a move because the state is to govern the physical world of God's creation, the church is to manage the spiritual realm of God's redemption, and God, the Reformer maintained, has established marriage as part of his handiwork from the outset of creation, for "it is not good that the man should be alone" (Gen. 2:18).

Thus, for Luther, as Denis Janz explains, "the denial of marriage's sacramentality is by no means a devaluation of marriage but the opposite."[71] To that

---

69. Ibid.
70. Hendrix, "Luther on Marriage," 345.
71. Janz, "Marriage," 90.

point, in a 1531 wedding sermon, Luther underscored the divine framework and blessing of marriage:

> God's Word is actually inscribed on one's spouse. When a man looks at his wife as if she were the only woman on earth, and when a woman looks at her husband as if he were the only man on earth; yes, if no king or queen, not even the sun itself sparkles any more brightly and lights up your eyes more than your own husband or wife, then right there you are face to face with God speaking. God promises to you your wife or husband, actually gives your spouse to you, saying "This man shall be yours; the woman shall be yours. I am pleased beyond measure! Creatures earthly and heavenly are jumping for joy." For there is no jewelry more precious than God's Word; through it you come to regard your spouse as a gift of God and, as long as you do that, you will have no regrets.[72]

Marriage is thus intended for all human beings generally but is realized more fully by Christians particularly because the estate, no longer a sacrament conveyed and controlled by the church, is dialectically elevated to be more valuable in God's eyes than chastity as one of the "holy orders and true religious institutions established by God."[73]

Subsequent Protestant Reforms of Marriage

Just as in Germany, so also in Switzerland the reformation of marriage began to unfold in the early 1520s. Ulrich Zwingli petitioned the bishop of Constance in July of 1522 to accept clerical marriage. Zwingli explained what he perceived to be a reality obvious to all: "How inadequately and poorly the priests from times past to the present have commonly upheld the rule of celibacy. It was easy enough to give orders, but it was not possible to ensure that orders could be carried out." Even if the bishop could not endorse the marriage of clergy, Zwingli boldly asked him to turn a blind eye and "not to oppose it."[74] This was not merely an academic but also a deeply personal issue for the Zurich Reformer, because months earlier he had secretly been betrothed to Anna Reinhard, a widow in the community. Their cohabitation was apparently common knowledge locally, and their public nuptials finally took place in April 1524, just three months before their first child was born.[75]

---

72. In WA 34:52.12–21; here via Hendrix, "Luther on Marriage," 347.

73. Luther, "Confession concerning Christ's Supper," WA 26:504.30–31; LW 37:364; see also Hendrix, "Luther on Marriage," 346.

74. Zwingli, "Petition to the bishop of Constance, 2 July 1522" here via Potter, *Huldrych Zwingli*, 18.

75. G. R. Potter, *Zwingli* (Cambridge: Cambridge University Press, 1976), 80.

Like Luther, Zwingli argued, particularly in his Sixty-Seven Theses in January of 1523, that not all those who are called into the service of the church are likewise granted the gift of celibacy; "hence marriage is permitted to all human beings." Turning the Roman clerical customs on their head, Zwingli contended that, upon realizing that they do not possess this gift, clerics actually commit sin if they do not protect themselves through marriage.[76] The present circumstance, under Roman policies, has left the church mired in hypocrisy and scandal: "Priests are not allowed to take lawful wives but may keep mistresses if they pay a fine."[77] By May of 1525, a civil court was created to replace church courts in order to supervise marriages in the Zurich city-state. Civil authorities were increasingly used by Zwingli for the purpose of enforcing the proper practice of religion and its responsibilities, "to set forth the word of God." Among Zwingli's regulations were that marriage must take place publicly in a church and that the pastor officiating the wedding keep records of the event.[78]

Beyond the endorsement of clerical unions, the theology and practice of marriage was addressed most thoroughly among early Swiss Reformers by John Calvin. Calvin carefully underscored the ordinariness of marriage as akin to "farming, building, cobbling and barbering [as] a good and holy ordinance."[79] However, the Geneva Reformer demonstrated how the Vulgate had mistranslated the Greek *mystērion* as *sacramentum* in Latin ("This is a great sacrament," Eph. 5:32). In its place, Calvin interpreted the "mystery" or "secret," as it might be more readily rendered, to refer to the relationship of Christ and the church that the union of husband and wife are called by Paul to replicate. Christ, then, is the husband's "prototype" for how to embrace his wife: "For as he poured out his compassion upon the church, which he had espoused to himself, thus he wishes every man to feel toward his own wife."[80] As Christians recognize their union to Christ by joining his body, they become one with him in his bones and flesh. This is the mystery to which marriage serves as a kind of sign or parable (akin to how a vine and branches or shepherd and his sheep might remind believers of their relationship to the Messiah). "But," as Calvin provocatively noted, "anyone who would classify such similitudes with the sacraments ought to be sent to a mental hospital."[81]

76. See theses 28–30 in Zwingli, Sixty-Seven Theses; here via Potter, *Huldrych Zwingli*, 23.
77. Thesis 49; via Potter, *Huldrych Zwingli*, 24.
78. Zwingli, "Regulations [re Matrimony]"; here via Potter, *Huldrych Zwingli*, 68–69.
79. Calvin, *Inst.* 4.19.34; LCC 21:1481.
80. Calvin, *Inst.* 4.19.35; LCC 21:1482.
81. Calvin, *Inst.* 4.19.34; LCC 21:1481–82.

Calvin flagged a level of inconsistency in the Roman notion of marriage being elevated as a holy sacrament on the one hand and of its diminution as sullied by sinful intercourse on the other, such that priests could not participate in that sort of "uncleanness and pollution and carnal filth." One cannot have it both ways, Calvin maintained: "How absurd it is [for the church] to bar priests from the sacrament. . . . They affirm that in the sacrament the grace of the Holy Spirit is conferred; they teach copulation to be a sacrament; and they deny that the Holy Spirit is ever present in copulation."[82] Finally, like Luther and Zwingli before him, Calvin criticized the innumerable impediments the church had placed on marriages, including holy days and seasons, kinship to the seventh degree, and the overall bureaucracy of the church, which arbitrarily delayed and denied unions. There is good reason, the Reformer observed, why no one referred to marriage as a "sacrament" until the medieval papacy of Gregory VII (r. 1073–85), through the writings of Peter Damiani.[83]

For his part, Calvin articulated the positive and Christian responsibility of marriage for both husband and wife in his 1542 service book, The Form of Prayers, wherein, drawing from his previous 1540 Strasbourg marriage rite and William Farel's 1533 service, the Geneva Reformer emphasized the divine institution of marriage as coming before the fall in paradise. Husband and wife would obligate themselves to one another through their vows, each pledging to bear responsibility for the spouse and live in holiness with the spouse. The presiding pastor would then pray over and bless the couple.[84]

While much of the language of Calvin's Institutes appears to parallel Luther's understanding of marriage, Calvin's later sermons, lectures, and commentaries found new language to describe marriage as "covenant."[85] Even though, as John Witte Jr. points out, "The idea of a divine covenant or agreement between God and humanity had long been taught in the Western church," Calvin began to observe how often the Bible uses the same term to describe marriage (e.g., "The LORD was a witness to the covenant between you and the wife of your youth," Mal. 2:14). Thus, Calvin concluded, the term "covenant" applies not only to pledges binding God to humanity but also to promises binding humans to one another. The Lord then draws the husband and wife together in covenant, to live in faithful service to God and each other. God is

82. Calvin, Inst. 4.19.35; LCC 21:1483.
83. Calvin, Inst. 4.19.37, 34; LCC 21:1484, 1481.
84. White, Sacraments, 129.
85. The "covenant" language is not new to Calvin. The Anabaptists had already begun to appropriate the same term for marriage. See George Huntston Williams, The Radical Reformation, 3rd ed. (Kirkville, MO: Sixteenth Century Journal Publishers, 1992), 420–21.

then the one who has established marriage, Calvin concluded.[86] In a sermon on Ephesians 5, Calvin wrote:

> When a marriage takes place between a man and a woman, God presides and requires a mutual pledge from both. Hence Solomon in Proverbs 2:17 calls marriage the covenant of God, for it is superior to all human contracts. So also Malachi [2:14] declares that God is, as it were, the stipulator [of marriage], who by his authority joins the man to the woman, and sanctions the alliance. . . . Marriage is not a thing ordained by men. We know that God is the author of it, and that it is solemnized by his name. The Scripture says that it is a holy covenant, and therefore calls it divine.[87]

Because of God's presence in the family, community, government, and church, the parents of the couple, peers, the minister, and the magistrate all played important roles in the Geneva wedding ceremony in representing God's action in uniting the couple. Following Calvin's lead, by the mid-sixteenth century Western society as a whole also generally required the mutual consent of the couple, parental approval, witnesses, civil registration, and ecclesial blessing.[88]

Finally, one might argue that Thomas Cranmer's most (in)famous act as archbishop of Canterbury pertained to the dissolution of a marriage: the granting of the annulment between Henry VIII and Catherine of Aragon. What is more to the point of this book, however, is the positive Protestant reforms to marriage that its leaders advanced. On this issue, Cranmer's greatest such contribution to Protestantism came in his service for matrimony in the English Prayer Books of 1549 and 1552. Drawing much of the traditional English marriage vows from the fourteenth-century Manual of York Use,[89] Cranmer's Book of Common Prayer calls upon couples to be married in the body of the church, with gathered family and friends, to sing hymns, hear the gospel and sermon, and exchange vows. In the now-well-known "Dearly beloved" introduction, the presiding minister would acknowledge marriage as "signifying unto us the mystical union that is betwixt Christ and his church," demonstrating Cranmer's christocentric interpretation of Ephesians 5, which was parallel to that of Luther and Calvin. Couples were to enter into marriage "reverently, discreetly, advisedly, soberly, and in the fear of God, duly considering the causes for which matrimony was ordained," which Cranmer

86. Witte, *From Sacrament to Contract*, 184–85.
87. Calvin, "Sermon on Eph. 5:22–26, 31–33"; here via Witte, *From Sacrament to Contract*, 186.
88. Witte, *From Sacrament to Contract*, 187.
89. See "Marriage Vows in the Vernacular," in Johnson, *Sacraments and Worship*, 297.

delineated as procreation of children, a remedy against sin, and for the mutual society, help, and comfort of one another.[90]

Interestingly, the Reformed Strasbourg theologian Martin Bucer, who assisted Cranmer by proposing changes to the original prayer book in its subsequent edition, also presented to the new king, Edward VI, a book in 1550, *De regno Christi* (On the kingdom of Christ), wherein Bucer devoted more than a quarter of what would be his final work to the proposed Protestant theology of marriage, in the hopes that Protestantism would take root under the young king's reign: "Christ our King and his Church ask of Your Majesty that he also assume proper responsibility for the ordering of marriage." Bucer asked the king to adjudicate marriage's proper candidates and advisers and to govern the ceremony so that it might be one which was heartfelt, orderly (by virtue of the BCP), and reverent.[91] It is properly the king's responsibility, Bucer maintained, to ensure that "pious princes and governors" oversee this holy institution, for without such governance, morality would be neglected, "plainly all righteousness will also fail, all fear of God will be struck down, and true religion will become entirely obsolete, . . . [esp. regarding] the purification and the conserving of purity of holy matrimony, the seedbed of the human race and font of good citizens."[92]

A Contemporary Protestant Christian Understanding of Marriage

At first blush, by demoting marriage from its "sacramental" status and removing it from the oversight of the church in society, Luther and other Protestant Reformers "secularized" marriage, making the institution so earthly and public that it had few transcendent and ecclesial qualities remaining. Such a shallow reading of the Reformers' intentions makes them into easy targets to blame for the contemporary social issues of rising divorce rates and confusion regarding same-sex marriage. After all, one may argue, if the state and not the church determines the definition and purpose of marriage, these developments would be natural outgrowths of an ever-evolving and otherwise-ambiguous institution.

But what is commonly misunderstood about Luther's view of marriage is not that it is merely "public and, thus, not Christian." Such reductionism leaves many modern readers to believe that the Reformer held a pessimistic view of marriage for Christians. But quite to the contrary and in keeping with

90. See *The First English Prayer Book* (Winchester, UK: John Hunt, 2008), 59–60.
91. Martin Bucer, *De regno Christi*, in LCC 19:315–33.
92. Ibid., LCC 19:333.

his notions of the universal priesthood and the divine purpose of both church and state, much of Luther's overarching project was to tear down the wall of false dualisms the medieval church seemed to build up between the sacred and secular. More broadly still within Augustinian fashion, all things belong to God. While Christians and non-Christians alike participate in marriage, it is still a divinely ordained relationship, and when Christians, though still sinners like their unbelieving counterparts, find marriage and child rearing a pleasure and not a necessary burden, a gift and not merely a responsibility, mutuality instead of sexism, then they draw closer to God's intent in prefall creation and postfall redemption. Scott Hendrix rightly observes: "Although Luther endorses marriage between Christians and non-Christians and even calls marriage a worldly thing, he is not trying to secularize marriage in the sense of separating it from God or religion. It is no longer a sacrament, to be sure, but marriage is intended by God for most people and, as we have seen, it is the genuinely religious form of life."[93] Maintaining this distinction, while understanding that all marriage is to conform to natural law, brings clarity for the limited roles that both church and state exercise in its stewardship.

Some of Luther's marriage reforms are particularly important to apply to the contemporary church setting, such as his positive statements regarding the Christian purposes of marriage and vocation in marriage. Understanding that God takes pleasure in the husband and wife's selfless and menial acts of bearing with a partner for a lifetime and the caring for and raising of children, with all of its tedious and draining tasks, can be a transformative way to reframe the institution and encourage its participants. Luther's pastoral words regarding finding satisfaction in one's spouse and finding Christian identity in the calling of husband, wife, parent, and friend liberate instead of bind both husband and wife in their respective roles and mutual responsibilities.

John Calvin, who mirrored the Anabaptists in utilizing the terminology of "covenant," also brings a helpful constitution to marriage. A covenantal understanding of marriage, at least for believers, underscores the intended permanency of the relationship, rather than seeing the merger as a temporary or convenient secular contract. If the saying is true that "contracts are meant to be broken," covenants are intended to be kept, with severe spiritual consequences for their dissolution. And while Christendom no longer exists and perhaps is not even desirable to twenty-first-century citizens, Calvin's understanding of placing marriage within the context of the union of families (whose parents still often present the bride and bless such bonds), churches (whose pastors still preside over such ceremonies), and magistrates (who still

93. Hendrix, "Luther on Marriage," 340.

grant licenses and legal recognition of the marriage)—this understanding gives a helpful balance for appreciating the multilayered responsibility each couple bears to one another, their community, their church, and the larger society. In our modern context fewer couples seem as interested in the commitment of marriage, and others participate without heeding Cranmer's advice of doing so "reverently, discreetly, advisedly, soberly, and in the fear of God, duly considering the causes for which matrimony was ordained." Hence a reclamation of Luther's positive notion of marriage as calling and Calvin's covenantal framework as commitment would at least bring a helpful foundation for the recovery of distinctively Christian marriages among Protestant believers. Such marriages could exhibit God's ideals in the marriage relationship and thereby witness to other Christians and even to a secularized post-Christian world, which is unconsciously longing for order, meaning, and substance.

By removing the "sacramental" label from the estate, Luther intended to promote marriage beyond Christians to all people as the divine intention for living in God's created world. Because God granted to the vast majority of people the desire for company and intimacy, God blessed the means of marriage to fulfill the divinely intended purposes for a measure of fulfillment in life, the blessings of children, and the betterment of society. If these things are so, then Calvin was right that God is the founder of marriage, and Christians can experience what Luther said of this divine union, that "there is no more lovely, friendly, and charming relationship, communion, or company than a good marriage."[94]

94. Luther, Table Talk, WA Tr 2, no. 292.

4

Ordination

"A Man-Made Fiction"

There are seven grades or orders of spiritual office, as is clearly taught us in the words of the holy Fathers, . . . seven on account of the sevenfold grace of the holy Spirit, and those who do not participate in this grace, enter the ecclesial grades unworthily.

Peter Lombard

Now we, who have been baptized, are all uniformly priests in virtue of that very fact. The only addition received by the priests is the office of preaching, and even this with our consent.

Martin Luther

ORDINATION, OR "HOLY ORDERS," that ceremonial act of consecrating or setting apart clergy for the specific task of church ministry, has long been observed and honored since the earliest days of Christianity. The etymology of the word "ordination" probably derives from its use in ancient Rome of appointing civil servants; the term was adopted by the church in the eleventh century to apply to its holy orders.[1] Regardless of the lexicon, the church looked to this practice as having biblical precedent and serving as a means by

1. Wolfgang Klausnitzer, "Ordination," in Hillerbrand, *Oxford Encyclopedia of the Reformation*, 3:177.

which it might officially affirm, both spiritually and ceremonially, an ordinand's calling to ministry as a livelihood of service. Additionally, the rite of setting an individual apart, often through the use of laying on of hands, has usually been a means of demonstrating the church's recognition of the candidate's gifts, character, and, often, proper training for a ministerial vocation.

Over the centuries, however, the Western church began to solidify in its understanding that ordination was one of three services through which the recipient may receive an indelible mark and, in the case of this service, one that was interpreted as elevating the individual's position with God, among the church leadership and above those the church hierarchy was to serve. The Reformers challenged such a notion by insisting that ordained ministry was simply an official installation of a person to fulfill an ecclesial or liturgical function for the church (e.g., preaching, administering the ordinances, pastoral care, leadership, etc.); the Reformers generally eschewed the notion that the rite conveyed an ontological reality (i.e., a special and particular way of being that was unparalleled in the life of a layperson).

Biblical Background and Assumptions

Christians have turned as far back as the Old Testament to find biblical precedent for the rite of ordination. Isaac blessed Jacob instead of Esau through the laying on of hands in Genesis 27, thus setting the younger son apart with authority and inheritance. Jacob, in turn, blessed the sons of Joseph by laying his hands on the boys (Gen. 48:8–22). Subsequently, blessings were passed down from one generation to another, but these blessings had binding implications upon the recipient. When Samuel anointed Saul and later David (1 Sam. 9–10 and 16, respectively), it was to grant them God's leadership of the chosen people.[2] The priesthood of Judaism was hereditary.

Likewise, Christians look to the Jewish precedent of ordination for rabbis and add to that background the New Testament passages that describe a kind of formal induction into an office (Titus 1:5; Heb. 5:1; 8:3). The church also began to develop the practice of laying on of hands as indicative of a biblical and solemn event for all those involved (Acts 6:6; 13:3; 1 Tim. 4:14; 5:22; 2 Tim. 1:6). Additionally, the New Testament seems to name offices or at least specifically designated roles in the church, with these positions sometimes being accompanied by an apostolic imposition of hands. Acts 6 is undoubtedly the most prominently cited passage along these lines, one

2. Alton H. McEachern, *Set Apart for Service* (Nashville: Broadman, 1980), 12–13.

that is often viewed as a precedent for diaconal ordination. Here the apostles were struggling both to carry out the main tasks of their ministry and to handle conflicts and logistical details within the church at the same time. Consequently, they instructed the church:

> "It is not right that we should neglect the word of God in order to wait on tables. Therefore, friends, select from among yourselves seven men of good standing, full of the Spirit and of wisdom, whom we may appoint to this task, while we, for our part, will devote ourselves to prayer and serving the word."
> . . . They had these men stand before the apostles, who prayed and laid their hands on them. (6:2–6)

Along with the diaconal ministry, the Scriptures named individuals who were set apart for other designated offices. In Acts 20, Paul sent a message to Ephesus to have the elders (*presbyterous*, v. 17) meet him and informed (or reminded) them that the Spirit made them "overseers" (*episkopous*, v. 28) under the Great Shepherd (cf. Heb. 13:20; 1 Pet. 5:4). First Timothy describes the qualifications for serving as bishop and as deacon, while frustratingly describing little of the responsibilities of the office or how such individuals are to be commissioned by the church, save for Paul's admonishment of Timothy to "not neglect the gift that is in you, which was given to you through prophecy with the laying on of hands by the council of elders" (1 Tim. 4:14). Timothy was to "not ordain anyone hastily" (5:22) but was to "rekindle the gift of God" by means of the imposition of Paul's own hands (2 Tim. 1:6). As the church developed in the next several centuries, three ecclesial offices developed as bishop, presbyter, and deacon, with various liturgical ceremonies often involving the imposition of hands as a continuation of the apostolic practice.

Early Christian and Patristic Practice of Ordination

Two of the earliest postbiblical sources of Christianity were 1 Clement (ca. 96) and the *Didache* (late first to early second century). In the former, the church of Rome described Christian polity to the church of Corinth, outlining their own commitment to do the work of Christ "in an orderly fashion." The services of worship were prescribed by God, the letter stipulates, to be done "not in a careless and disorderly way, but at the times and seasons he fixed." Such ordering includes a divine prescription for how and by whom the services are led, so that the worship of God would meet divine approval. Just as the high priests, the priests, the Levites, and the laypeople had their assigned tasks, so also Jesus was sent by God, and the apostles were sent by Christ to appoint the first bishops and deacons among the early believers after testing their faith.[3] God then directed an orderly fashion for appointing and assigning the tasks of ministry so that Christian worship would be rightly exercised and congregational discord would be avoided.

One might observe in 1 Clement not only the injunction to do things in an orderly fashion but also the fact that the apostles were those who appointed the initial officers of the churches. However, by the time of the *Didache* the title of "apostle," it seems, was still utilized for an itinerant teacher, though the local clerical officers of each congregation appear to have been appointed by each church:

> Now concerning the apostles and prophets, deal with them as follows in accordance with the rule of the gospel. Let every apostle who comes to you be welcomed as if he were the Lord. . . . But if he stays three days, he is a false prophet. . . . If he asks for money, he is a false prophet. . . .

> Therefore appoint for yourselves bishops and deacons worthy of the Lord, men who are humble and not avaricious and true and approved, for they too carry out for you the ministry of the prophets and the teachers. You must not, therefore, despise them, for they are your honored men, along with the prophets and teachers.[4]

While appointed in each community, the bishops and deacons of each church carry a spiritual authority locally as from the Lord and are deserving of the same respect as that of the visiting prophet or apostle.

By the early second century, particularly commencing with the writings of Ignatius of Antioch, the local parish or parishes in each community seem to have moved from a plurality of bishops to obeying the leadership of a single episcopate, while the presbyters and deacons remain in the plural. In 116, Ignatius stipulated even something of the assigned ministerial tasks of each office: "Let the bishop preside in God's place, and the presbyters take the place of the apostolic council, and let the deacons (my special favorites) be entrusted with the ministry of Jesus Christ."[5] Ignatius admonished the churches to follow the leadership of their bishop, respecting the presbytery as they would the apostles, and the deacons as they would the law of God.

---

3. See 1 Clement 40–42, trans. Cyril C. Richardson, in LCC 1:62–63; here via Johnson, *Sacraments and Worship*, 315–16.

4. *Didache* 11 and 15; here via Holmes, *Apostolic Fathers*, 155–57; cf. Richardson, in LCC 1:176, 178.

5. Ignatius of Antioch, *To the Magnesians* 6, in Richardson, LCC 1:95; here via Johnson, *Sacraments and Worship*, 317–18.

But the bishop was to preside over the congregation, and the Eucharist's validity was contingent upon the bishop's approval, as he or one whom he had appointed must officiate. Likewise, baptism and love feasts were also to be observed under the bishop's supervision.[6] Thus, while clerical authority and the local hierarchy were clarified early in the church, the liturgical means for such appointment was apparently left obscure and was perhaps inconsequential to and not uniformly designated for early Christianity due to other, more pressing concerns.

Though scholars have suggested that the early Christians drew from the customs of the Old Testament and the rabbis—and perhaps even the Essene community's practice of ranking their offices, as uncovered in Qumran and elsewhere—to shape the hierarchy of the first Christian communities, it is most likely that the actual ordination service with the imposition of hands was primarily fashioned by the missional impulses of early Christianity within the Roman Empire.[7] In this setting, baptism was the means of commissioning laity to be missionaries in their walks of life, while the laying on of hands began to emerge as the practice for commissioning the bishop, presbyters, and deacons for their respective ministerial tasks of leadership within the church. Regardless, each Christian was called to carry on the ministry "in his own rank."[8] By the third century, ordination itself became the framework for upholding the hierarchy, order, and various delegated responsibilities of the church.

Also in the third century, *The Apostolic Tradition* of Hippolytus demonstrates that the rite of ordination had moved from the simple imposition of hands to a more formal, elongated ritual. The bishop, elected by the people, became the requisite individual to lay hands on other bishops; and deacons, the latter group that Hippolytus described, were assigned to give assistance to the bishop. Meanwhile, presbyters were empowered to lay lands only on other presbyters. In addition to the laying on of hands, Hippolytus recorded that a third-century ordination service included prayers of consecration by a bishop, the kiss of peace offered by all, a responsive thanksgiving, Eucharist, and at least the sporadic use of the thanksgiving for oil, cheese, and olives.[9]

By the mid-third century, one may observe a corresponding elevation of ordination with the heightened description of the Lord's Supper as a sacrifice.

6. Ignatius of Antioch, *To the Smyrnaeans* 8, trans. Cyril C. Richardson, in LCC 1:115; here cited in Johnson, *Sacraments and Worship*, 318.
7. Glenn Hinson, among others, makes this argument. See E. Glenn Hinson, "Ordination in Christian History," *Review and Expositor* 78, no. 4 (Fall 1981): 486.
8. See 1 Clement 41, citing Isa. 60:17e–f LXX (http://ccat.sas.upenn.edu/nets/edition/).
9. Hinson, "Ordination in Christian History," 487–88.

Not only would the priest who presided over this sacrificial ritual obviously be carrying on in place of Old Testament high priests; Cyprian of Carthage also stated that, as he mixed water with wine, the priest represented Christ himself through these actions.[10]

Though hailing from the Eastern church in the mid-fourth century, in 390–91 John Chrysostom testified to something of the elevation of ordination within Christianity when he, the "golden-throated" preacher, reported that felt himself unworthy of the rite. Some six years before being appointed archbishop of Constantinople, Chrysostom described ordination as something beyond human and as a little lower than the angels, something "discharged on earth, but [ranking] among heavenly ordinances." Since it is an ordinance begun by Christ, its recipients must take on an especial spiritual purity "as if standing in the heavens themselves in the midst of those powers." Even as one stands upon the earth, a priest, once ordained, has "an authority which God has not given to angels or archangels." Chrysostom saw the authority to baptize as a higher honor than earthly kingship and more honorable than parenthood, and he saw the authority to "forgive sins" as the ultimate spiritual power and "a position of greater responsibility and more fearful judgment."[11]

Medieval Development of Ordination

As Christianity grew from an underground, persecuted religious movement to the official religion of the empire, the ministerial office appropriated unprecedented powers and responsibilities, both ecclesially and culturally. As its developed hierarchy mirrored that of the secular nobility, with "princes of the church" (e.g., cardinals and bishops) ruling their own ecclesial principalities, ordination became the primary means for social promotion for underprivileged classes and for the potential maintenance of a high lifestyle for the younger brothers of dynastic aristocratic families within an otherwise socially fixed feudal system. The Middle Ages, then, saw an increased cleavage between clergy and laity in social stature and authority as the clerical hierarchy reserved "the church" as its own collective title and, as Chaucer observed, was esteemed as the "First Estate" in medieval European society.[12] Even many of the civil benefits granted to secular officeholders, especially exemptions from

10. Cyprian, *Epistles* 62.14; *ANF* 5:362; here via Hinson, "Ordination in Christian History," 488.
11. Chrysostom, *Priesthood* 3.4–3.6; 2.2; 6.1–2; *NPNF*¹ 9:46–47; here via Hinson, "Ordination in Christian History," 489.
12. See the General Prologue to Chaucer's *Canterbury Tales* for an example of what would later be called "Estates Satire" (http://www.librarius.com/cantales/genpro.htm).

military service and paying taxes, were also conferred upon clergy.[13] Hence, ordination became a societal demarcation to spiritually empower clergy over the peasantry and, to a degree, even over the nobility.

The essential clerical distinction that ordination now fostered was reflected in the evolving ordination ritual itself, which had moved from its apparent incipient simplicity to an increased complexity "by grafting onto the primitive core secondary elements symbolic of the conveyance of power."[14] Such clerical distinctions were signified by the anointing of hands, the handing over of the instruments of the specific order (e.g., chalice, book, and keys), and the gradual enhancement of vestments. Naturally, an expanded theology of ordination paralleled these ever-developing liturgical enhancements, with one alternately leading the other through this period.

Commencing with Augustine at the beginning of the fifth century, it became traditional to use the terminology of "character" being "stamped" or "marked" through the rites of baptism, confirmation, and holy orders. Before the medieval period, many patristic writers utilized the biblical terminology of "seal"[15] to describe the objective work of God in these special church practices through which the recipient would be granted divine salvation, enter the kingdom of God, and be illuminated by the Holy Ghost. From the late first- to second-century Shepherd of Hermas, which associated "seal" with baptism, its use ultimately expanded to the other two ordinances. But Augustine precipitated an ecclesial shift to adopt a different analogy and terminology by 400, apparently drawing on a former military image in reference to a particular brand a soldier received that was unique to the troops of his commanding general. Just as the soldier now "belonged" to his general through obedient service, so too does the Christian soldier belong to and fight for God. Baptism and ordination, for Augustine, mysteriously embossed the recipient as God's own, a stamp that was indelible in character.

The context for Augustine's analogy was in *Against the Letter of Parmenian*, where he challenged the Donatist sect and argued that the rebaptism or reordination of schismatic Christians was inappropriate and spurious because, regardless of their previous wandering, the individual had still received a *character indelebilis*, a divine imprint that cannot be removed. Although an apostate may lose the grace conveyed in the rite, the mark itself was irrevocable, a permanent and divinely objective reality.[16]

13. Kelly, *Sacraments Revisited*, 137.
14. White, *Sacraments*, 131.
15. E.g., 2 Cor. 1:21–22; Eph. 1:13; 4:30; and Rev. 9:4.
16. See Augustine, *Contra epistolam Parmeniani*, in PL 43:33–108; Emmanuel J. Cutrone, "Sacraments," in *Augustine through the Ages: An Encyclopedia*, ed. Allan D. Fitzgerald (Grand Rapids: Eerdmans, 1999), 741–47.

Following Augustine's trajectory of thought, medieval theologians expanded on the nature and divinely bestowed power of such a permanent mark on the soul of the clergy. This notion, when combined with the medieval idea of sacerdotalism, the notion that all propitiatory sacrifices of a Christian required the intervention of a priest, placed the ordained as the intermediary between the individual and God, thus between the individual and the means of divine grace. By virtue of this indelible character, the minister became the conduit through which God ordered the conveyance of mercy in baptism, Table, and confession. The power of the keys to bind and to loose sins, the privilege to preside over the sacrifice of the Eucharist, and the authority to grant absolution for the forgiveness of sins—these are examples of the decisive spiritual dominion that the medieval First Estate held over the other classes. Admittedly, however, this ultimate clerical hegemony led to various forms of priestly abuse, which were denounced by late medieval critics and sixteenth-century Reformers.

By the twelfth century, the school of Saint Victor promoted ordination from a rite to a sacrament that conveyed authority to the ordinand to celebrate the Eucharist. A generation later (ca. 1152), Peter Lombard followed by not only promulgating its sacramentality but also dividing ordination into seven graces pertaining to the seven ecclesiastical grades of the church.[17] The Council of Florence codified ordination as a sacrament in 1439, stating in the Decree for the Armenians that the ordinand receives "the power for the offering of sacrifice in the Church for the living and the dead," and requiring the bishop as the rite's ordinary minister. "The effect," the decree declared, "is the increase of grace, that whoever is ordained may be a fit minister."[18]

Luther and the Universal Priesthood

Over the centuries a number of challenges to the Western church's understanding of ordination as a sacrament emerged. Scholars have brought to light various counterarguments for a more egalitarian priesthood, dating as early as the Waldensian movement in the twelfth century and continuing through the Lollard and Hussite movements in the fourteenth and fifteenth centuries, as evidence of pre-Reformation attempts at a shared notion of

17. Peter Lombard, *Sentences* 4, in *Peter Lombard and the Sacramental System*, 224.
18. See Council of Florence, Decree for the Armenians, in DS 336; here via Johnson, *Sacraments and Worship*, 327.

a universal priesthood for all Christians.[19] However, much of the modern Protestant understanding of ordination originates most directly from Martin Luther.

One cannot fully grasp Luther's rejection of the prevailing Catholic notion of holy orders as a sacrament, with its associated indelible mark and sacerdotal gifts, until one first comprehends Luther's notion of the priesthood of all believers, because, for Luther, ordination was contingent upon the church as the universal priesthood being the source for the authority of and responsibility for clerical appointments. Hence, in this case, Luther's negative stripping away of the sacramental can only be grasped by following his constructive reform of the ministerial office.

Three of Luther's most noted Reformation treatises were published in 1520, in proximity to the crucible season between Pope Leo's June 15 *Exsurge Domine*, warning Luther to recant, and Leo's impending *Decet Romanum*, issued on January 3, 1521, which officially excommunicated Luther and his followers. Each of Luther's treatises *To the Christian Nobility*, *The Pagan Servitude of the Church*, and *The Freedom of a Christian*, in part, demonstrated a theology of ordination that the Reformer had been developing for some time, a theology that further embroiled him in controversy. Luther wrote that "if this sacrament and this fiction [of the spiritual elevation of the clergy through indelible marks] ever fell to the ground, the papacy with its 'characters' will scarcely survive. Then our joyous liberty will be restored to us; we shall realize that we are all equal by every right."[20]

The first of these treatises, *To the Christian Nobility*, was written in August as a lengthy open letter to appeal to political authorities to intercede in reforming the church in Germany. At the outset of this petition, Luther argued why civil authorities held a share of sovereignty over ecclesial matters: "The pope or bishop anoints, shaves heads, ordains, consecrates, and prescribes garb different from that of the laity, but he can never make a man into a Christian or into a spiritual man by so doing. . . . [But] as far as that goes, we are all consecrated priests through baptism [1 Pet. 2:9; Rev. 5:9–10]."[21] Luther completely rejected the notion that the medieval divisions of the clerical hierarchy wholly constituted the spiritual estate while princes, lords, artisans, and farmers made up the temporal estate. Instead, he wrote, "all Christians

---

19. Richard L. Greaves is one scholar who has outlined these attempts as predating the sixteenth century; see his study "The Ordination Controversy and the Spirit of Reform in Puritan England," *Journal of Ecclesiastical History* 21, no. 3 (July 1970): 225.

20. Luther, *Babylonian Captivity*, LW 36:117.

21. Luther, *To the Christian Nobility of the German Nation concerning the Reform of the Christian Estate*, LW 44:127.

are truly of the spiritual estate, and there is no difference among them except that of office [1 Cor. 12:12–13] . . . for baptism, gospel, and faith alone make us spiritual and a Christian people."[22] In other words, it is God who ordains and consecrates, not the pope or the bishop. "If we had no higher consecration than that which pope or bishop gives, no one could say mass or preach a sermon or give absolution."[23]

Although he recognized how hard this concept was for a stratified society that had uncritically accepted the sacred-profane dualistic worldview of the medieval church, Luther nevertheless argued theologically that, in the sight of God, "there is no true, basic difference between laymen and priests, princes and bishops, between religious and secular. . . . They are all of the spiritual estate, all are truly priests, bishops, and popes."[24] With Christ as the head, all Christians compose the body, with no divisions between sacred and secular. Luther supported this claim christologically: just as Christ did not possess two separate bodies—one earthly, mundane, and temporal and the other transcendent, exalted, and spiritual—but maintained one unified body, so there is no partition within the people of God.[25] They share, instead, in their spiritual authority and service.

This now-famous egalitarian notion is repeated in Luther's other two important 1520 treatises. In *The Babylonian Captivity of the Church*, published in October, he again underscored that "all of us that have been baptized are equally priests."[26] Baptism became the rite of ordination for all Christians to practice the faith and live Christian lives of mutual ministry. In eschewing the hierarchical priesthood now established in the Western church, Luther instead figuratively and theologically rent asunder the temple curtain for all by arguing for the priesthood of every Christian. Thus, in the then-new Protestant thought, all Christians bear most of the responsibilities for and the privileges of ordained ministry.[27] In both his latter 1520 treatises, Luther cited 1 Peter 2:9 as a biblical basis for the egalitarian priesthood, translating the passage as declaring: "You are a chosen race, a royal priesthood, and a priestly royalty."[28]

22. Ibid.
23. LW 44:127–28.
24. LW 44:129.
25. LW 44:130.
26. LW 36:112.
27. Luther wrote: "If [the Catholic Church] were forced to grant that all of us that have been baptized are equally priests, as indeed we are, and that only the ministry was committed to them, yet with our common consent, they would then know that they have no right to rule over us except insofar as we freely concede it." LW 36:112.
28. Luther paraphrased what is normally rendered "holy nation" as "priestly royalty" or "priestly kingdom." LW 36:113; Dillenberger, 345.

In his *Freedom of a Christian*, published in early November 1520, Luther bestowed on Christians the dual title of priests and kings, emphasizing in the latter the Christian's new position above all things, which are now made subject to the believer. But even more important than kingship is the holy priesthood,

> for as priests we are worthy to appear before God to pray for others and to teach one another divine things. . . . Thus Christ has made it possible for us, provided we believe in him, to be not only his brethren, co-heirs, and fellow-kings, but also his fellow priests. Therefore we may boldly come into the presence of God in the spirit of faith and cry "Abba, Father!" pray for one another, and do all things which we see done and foreshadowed in the outer and visible works of priests.[29]

This revolutionary shift in ecclesial power became what Alister McGrath later called "Christianity's dangerous idea,"[30] an idea that liberated laity to participate in the functions of ministry, to pray for and forgive one another, and to read and interpret Scripture without clerical hegemony—an idea that democratized the early modern church in Saxony. Additionally, the layperson is seen as having the same access to God as any clergyman has and as being free to come before God's presence. Robert G. Torbet remarked that this idea served less to "defrock the clergy [than to ordain] the laity."[31]

Luther, Lay Vocation, and the Public Ministry

However, left to its own, Luther's egalitarian priesthood would likely prove problematic for the day-to-day functioning of a church and the ordering of its worship without also recognizing the Reformer's counterbalancing description of the purpose and necessity of ordination and the pastoral office. It is here especially that Luther's theology of ordination should not be viewed as merely negative, tearing down Roman monasticism, but also as constructive for the Protestant tradition. Luther saw the universal priesthood as an important framework for the spiritual status that in theory is theologically shared by all but that is not practiced so as to disqualify or make redundant the role of the clergy.

29. Luther, *Freedom of a Christian*, LW 31:355.
30. Alister McGrath, *Christianity's Dangerous Idea: The Protestant Revolution—a History from the Sixteenth Century to the Twenty-First* (New York: HarperOne, 2007), title and throughout, esp. 50–56.
31. Robert G. Torbet, *The Baptist Ministry: Then and Now* (Philadelphia: Judson, 1953), 9. Likewise, Karlfried Froehlich wrote: "Luther did not eliminate priests or do away with the priesthood. Instead he eliminated the laity!" See Froehlich, "Luther on Vocation," in *Harvesting Luther's Reflections on Theology, Ethics, and the Church*, ed. Timothy J. Wengert (Grand Rapids: Eerdmans, 2004), 127.

While all Christians share the same authority in regard to the Word and sacrament, for the sake of good order only a person who has received the consent of the congregation or been called by the majority thereof should actually administer them. Ironically, then, it is in the actual regular tasks of proclamation (i.e., preaching) and dispensing the sacraments that Luther finally separates clergy from laity. The ordination of every Christian through the waters of baptism gives each believer a vocation, not to leave work but to find in occupations and family relations a new calling through Christ. Luther expressed this idea powerfully:

> If you are a manual laborer, you find that the Bible has been put into your workshop, into your hand, into your heart. It teaches and preaches how you should treat your neighbor. Just look at your tools—at your needle or thimble, your beer barrel, your goods, your scales or yardsticks or measure—and you will read this statement inscribed on them. Everywhere you look, it stares at you. Nothing that you handle every day is so tiny that it does not continually tell you this, if you will only listen. Indeed, there is no shortage of preaching. You have as many preachers as you have transactions, goods, tools, and other equipment in your house and home. All this is continually crying to you: "Friend, use me in your relations with your neighbor just as you would want your neighbor to use his property in his relations with you."[32]

Thus, for Luther, to become a called Christian did not necessarily mean a new vocation; every occupation and station in life encompassed a divine purpose and Christian calling. "Every occupation has its own honor before God, as well as its own requirement and duties. . . . God is a great lord and has many kinds of servants."[33]

But Luther still had a special place for the work of clergy in the egalitarian church. Since the laity were to find God's calling in carrying out their everyday work as a "butcher, baker, and candlestick maker," or as mother, father, sister, and brother in family relations, now in a Christian manner, so also the clergy were called to perform the public tasks of preaching, baptism, and the Supper as their own respective callings; these activities of preaching and dispensing the sacraments were the exclusive demarcated privileges and normative responsibilities of an ordained priest. For the purpose of good order, only the properly ordained priest was, under normal circumstances, to minister the Word in public worship.[34] The layperson must always be on

32. LW 21:237.
33. Luther, "Sermon on Keeping Children in School," LW 46:226.
34. In his treatise *Concerning the Ministry*, Luther maintained, "The community rights demand that one, or as many as the community chooses, shall be chosen or approved who,

the ready to minister the Word in private, in daily life, vocation, family, and activities. Regardless, Luther was protective of the work of the clergy as a particularly public role, which should be kept from charlatans and from those who misinterpret the "priesthood of all" as conveying a kind of universal theological authority. Scolding any who might attempt to shape or reprove the direction of the pastor's homilies, for instance, Luther wrote: "You fool, you simpleton, look to your own vocation; don't you take to preaching, but let your pastor do that."[35] While in emergencies any Christian must and should preach and perhaps even baptize and give absolution,[36] the selected minister(s) are particularly chosen by each congregation to teach what the church needs to hear. These individuals are selected to be "ministers, deacons, stewards, [or] presbyters," but they are not spiritual leaders of the church by their own authority, nor do they assume alone what belongs to the entire church. Yet in one's own vocation and family relations, each "preaches" and ministers to the other.

Luther's Notion of Congregational Authority and Order

Although he was vehemently opposed to monasticism and any ontological claims of clerical privilege, Luther was in no way in favor of eliminating a functioning clergy in favor of the universal priesthood. Instead, the officiating minister functioned in the place and on behalf of the gathered congregation, "all of whom have like power."[37] For the sake of good order and because of the communally recognized gifting and subsequent selection of an individual, the bishop "takes a person and charges him to exercise this power on behalf of the others."[38] In his treatise To the Christian Nobility, Luther presented an analogy that the aristocracy could easily grasp: "It is like ten brothers, all king's sons and equal heirs, choosing one of themselves to rule the inheritance in the interests of all. In one sense they are all kings and of equal power, and yet one of them is charged with the responsibility of ruling."[39] Therefore, there is no substantive difference between clergy and

---

in the name of all with these rights, shall perform these functions publicly. . . . Publicly one may not exercise a right without consent of the whole body or of the church." LW 40:34; WA 12:189.21–27.

35. Luther, "Exposition of John 1 and 2," WA 46:735; here via Wingren, Luther on Vocation (Philadelphia: Muhlenberg, 1957), 114.

36. LW 44:128.

37. Ibid.

38. Ibid.

39. Ibid.

laity "except for the sake of office and work." Just as temporal authorities are authorized to police, judge, or rule on behalf of the community, which empowers the magistrate to act in the public's stead, so too do the bishop and pastors serve as the church's ministers in the place and on behalf of the community of "priests."

But the clergyman does not own and cannot domineer with his authority. Such authority is instead granted by God through the discernment and approbation of the entire church. Luther warns, "No one may make use of this power except by the consent of the community or by the call of a superior. (For what is the common property of all, no individual may arrogate to himself, unless he is called.)"[40] Consequently, the meaning of ordination is the "common consent," congregational affirmation, and episcopal certification of an individual to the ministry of the Word. Those ordained were to be seen as "ministers chosen among us . . . as servants of Christ and stewards of the mysteries of God [cf. 1 Cor. 4:1]."[41]

By 1523, Luther argued in *Concerning the Ministry* that the biblical purpose of ordination was to provide the people of God with ministers of the Word. Ordination was intended to be the mechanism by which the mysteries of God are made known through the public ministry of the Word. It follows, then, for Luther that ideally a person is not ordained "by the authority of the bishop alone without any consent or election by the people over whom they are to be placed."[42] The bishop should confirm no candidate without the proper say of the congregation in which the minister is intended to serve. But having been properly chosen by the church, the minister performs the functions of preaching and dispensing the sacraments on behalf of the others to bring order and avoid confusion regarding the public ministry. Without this calling by God and church,[43] all papal "shaving, anointing, putting on of vestments, and other rites arising out of human superstition, do not convince us otherwise, even were they given by angels from heaven."[44]

Those who serve in this public ministry, then, should not be called "priests," since all Christians are members of the holy priesthood, but those who preach and give the sacrament to the people should be called "servants" or "ministers." Their only qualification, Luther held, was that they were able to teach the

---

40. LW 36:116.

41. LW 36:112–13.

42. LW 44:11.

43. Although he most often referred to a calling in reference to the congregation, Luther assumed that this call came initially from God and that the office of pastor was divinely established. See LW 26:17; 37:364; Janz, "Ministerial/Pastoral Office," in *Westminster Handbook to Martin Luther*, 95.

44. LW 40:35.

Word entrusted to them (2 Tim. 2:2).[45] The Word then becomes the basis for the remaining biblical functions of ministry, including baptizing, consecrating, binding, loosing, praying, and judging doctrine. Luther called the office of preaching the gospel both apostolic and the greatest office of the church, the fountain from which the other functions of ministry flow.[46] Consequently, the congregation must be discerning about its teachers, for "a priest is not identical with a presbyter or minister—for one is born to be priest, one becomes a minister."[47] And the congregation was responsible to continue to discern that the Word is faithfully proclaimed and, if need be, to reprove and even dismiss their ministers for failing to be faithful to the basic tasks of their public vocation.[48] Regardless, when faithful to the Word, Luther wrote, "the mouth of every pastor is the mouth of Christ."[49]

Luther spoke and wrote highly, then, about the work and witness of the minister. The Reformer made the office of pastor one of the essential marks of the church, along with the Word, baptism, Eucharist, and penance, without which there would be no church, or at least one lacking an inherent and fundamental element. For the sake of order, Luther wrote, this public work "must be entrusted to one person, and he alone should be allowed to preach, to baptize, to absolve, and to administer the sacraments. The others should be content with this arrangement and should agree with it."[50] The power of ordination, then, comes through the Word by the divine call of God and the confirmation of the church.

Luther's Rejection of Ordination as a Sacrament

Based on his positive framework and purpose for ordination and the ministerial vocation, one may readily deduce why Luther rejected the medieval notion of ordination as a sacrament. According to Luther, the Scriptures nowhere support the idea that a divine promise is conveyed in ordination, that one's character is "indelibly impressed,"[51] and that the ordinand is now the

---

45. Ibid.

46. LW 40:36. In another work titled *That a Christian Assembly or Congregation Has the Right and Power to Judge All Teaching and to Call, Appoint, and Dismiss Teachers*, the Reformer called the pastoral office of preaching "the highest office in Christendom." LW 39:314.

47. LW 40:18.

48. LW 39:306.

49. WA 37:381.13–14.

50. LW 41:154.

51. As previously observed, Luther here was arguing against the Catholic notion of *character indelebilis*, which conveys the notion that an indelible mark is received through ordination by the new priest as a divine gift. This marking of the soul creates an alteration in those ordained

conduit through which God's grace might be meted out through the sacraments. Ordination was, instead, simply an ecclesial ceremony that marked the consent and blessing of the congregation and bishop on an individual called as a teacher of the Word. Again, as with many of the practices eventually promoted to sacraments, Luther maintained, "I do not hold that this rite, which has been observed for so many centuries, should be condemned; but in sacred things I am opposed to the invention of human fictions. And it is not right to give out as divinely instituted what is not divinely instituted."[52] If the Scriptures do not support this practice as a sacrament, the church cannot make it one. "That is to say, it is the promises of God that make the church, and not the church that makes the promises of God."[53] The church, then, cannot institute a sacrament. Only God can do so through the Scriptures. Hence, Luther provocatively concluded, "I refuse to place a man-made fiction among divine things."[54]

Luther reasoned that much of what had become the customary observance regarding the sacraments was in error because councils themselves were prone to mistakes. Serious theological resolutions, he pointed out, were established with relatively few bishops and scholars present; thus without the approval of the universal church beyond Rome, the Roman hierarchy could be amiss. Consequently, the 1414–18 Council of Constance, which condemned any alternate ways of considering the sacraments, was groundless in its decrees.[55] Scripture nowhere supports the notion that a promise is conveyed through this ritual. If any custom could willy-nilly be deemed a sacrament by the church, Luther asked rhetorically, why stop at seven? Why not, for instance, make funeral processions a sacrament? "There will then be as many sacraments as there have been rites and ceremonies multiplied in the church."[56] When

---

to the priesthood, to distinguish them from others. Thus Catholic authorities argued, "Once a priest, always a priest." *Character indelebilis* received its official status through the bull *Exultate Deo* in 1439. See LW 36:111n201. However, in Canons on the Sacraments in General, a document written in 1547 by the Council of Trent, the Catholic Church argued that baptism, confirmation, and ordination each imprint on the soul a certain character, "a spiritual and indelible mark," in such a way that all three sacraments cannot be repeated for any one person. See *Canons and Decrees of the Council of Trent*, trans. H. J. Schroder (Rockford, IL: Tan Books, 1978), 29–46.

52. LW 36:107.
53. Ibid.
54. Dillenberger, 340; cf. LW 36:107.
55. LW 36:108. In condemning Wycliffe and Hus, for instance, the council declared: "Priests who live in vice in any way pollute the power of the priesthood, and like unfaithful sons are untrustworthy in their thinking about the church's seven sacraments, about the keys, offices, censures, customs, ceremonies and sacred things of the church, about the veneration of relics, and about indulgences and orders." See "Condemned Articles of J. Hus," part 8; see also DS 213.
56. LW 36:110.

anticipating a Catholic rebuttal that utilized the foundational work on holy orders of Dionysius the Areopagite, whose *Ecclesiastical Hierarchy* helped established the sacramental nature of ordination in the Western church, Luther was quick to point out that Dionysius himself only allowed for six sacraments and excluded marriage. "Whence do such ideas come, I ask? By what authority, with what arguments, are they established?"[57] The theologians of the church can assert what they please, but a faithful Christian should instead only be bound to the heavenly and divinely established ordinances.

Beyond eschewing the sacramentality of holy orders, Luther astutely observed how the medieval development fostered a culture of clerical hegemony and abuse. The argument that ordination contained a sacramental character conveying an indelible and irremovable mark on the soul, with celibacy, elevated the clergy to a spiritual class above all other people:

> They have sought by this means to set up a seed bed of implacable discord, by which clergy and laymen should be separated from each other farther than heaven from earth, to the incredible injury of the grace of baptism and to the confusion of our fellowship in the gospel. Here, indeed, are the roots of that detestable tyranny of the clergy over the laity. . . . They not only exalt themselves above the rest of the lay Christians, who are only anointed with the Holy Spirit, but regard them almost as dogs and unworthy to be included with themselves in the church. Hence they are bold to demand, to exact, to threaten, to urge, to oppress, as much as they please. In short, the sacrament of ordination has been and still is an admirable device for establishing all the horrible things that have been done hitherto in the church, and are yet to be done.[58]

It is little wonder that Luther believed the reform of ordination was key to the amelioration of the church. Such ideas of character, indelible marks, and elevated status were mere fictions and fruitful grounds for the clergy's manipulation of the laity. Instead, a pastor is one who is called to preach, "and if he does not preach he is as much a priest as a picture of a man is a man."[59]

Nevertheless, Luther did not intend to obliterate such an important ecclesial practice: "I therefore admit that ordination is a certain churchly rite, on a par with many others introduced by the church fathers."[60] The Reformer then walked the fine line of maintaining this ceremony as still very important to the life and practice of the church, but one without what he perceived were unnecessary superstitions, invented "characters," clerical elevation, and pomp.

57. LW 36:109, 111.
58. LW 36:112.
59. LW 36:115.
60. LW 36:108.

Its sole purpose was as a pragmatic matter, an honorable ceremony that ratified the call of someone to the holy Word of the gospel.[61]

One significant implication for Luther's radical redefinition of ordination was a shift in the locus of power within the two sacraments that continued to be practiced by the German church.[62] In the case of baptism and Eucharist, the authority of the rite did not emanate from its administrator. This notion was in contradistinction to the Roman Catholic Church, which had generally accepted the teaching called sacerdotalism, an idea in which a priest, by virtue of his ordination, is granted the ability not only to administer the sacraments but also to dispense grace through them. Thus, for the late-medieval Westerner, a person not properly ordained by the church (i.e., not in direct line with apostolic succession) who nevertheless tried to administer the sacraments would render them impotent and invalid.

For Luther, however, the rite of ordination did not provide a sacramental potency to the ordinances. Arguing in the case of baptism, for instance, Luther declared,

> We can clearly see the difference in baptism between man who administers the sacrament and God who is its author. For man baptizes, and yet does not baptize. He baptizes in that he performs the work of immersing the person to be baptized; he does not baptize, because in so doing he acts not on his own authority but in God's stead. . . . Ascribe both to God alone, and look upon the person administering it as simply the vicarious instrument of God, by which the Lord sitting in heaven thrusts you under the water with his own hands, and promises you forgiveness of your sins, speaking to you upon earth with a human voice by the mouth of his minister.[63]

Instead, the minister is a designated person "placed in the church for the preaching of the Word and the administration of the sacraments."[64] Ordination is nothing more than the designation of those who are to serve these purposes.

The Catholic Church indeed responded to Luther's charges and reforms, especially at the Council of Trent. Held in three periods that spanned from 1545 to 1563, Trent regarded the new Protestant teachings as "innovations"

61. LW 36:116.

62. Luther writes: "For Christ established the sacrament on himself and not on the person of the minister. It rests on the Word. Accordingly, when there is a confession of the Word, no matter what kind of knave the minister may be, this detracts not at all from the sacrament." LW 54:101.

63. LW 36:62–63. For further study on this topic, see Hans-Wilhelm Kelling, "Martin Luther: The First Forty Years in Remembrance of the 500th Anniversary of His Birth," *Brigham Young University Studies* 23 (Spring 1983): 131–46.

64. LW 54:100.

and reaffirmed not only the hierarchical priesthood of seven orders (bishops, priests, and deacons being the most essential) but also the notion that ordination was sacramental, a rite that conferred a special status on the individual. David Steinmetz observed: "Unlike Luther, Trent taught that priesthood is not merely a vocation like any other and priests are not laity on special assignment. Ordination effects an ontological change in the one ordained. No layperson, however gifted and pious, can confect a valid eucharist, but any priest, however limited and unworthy, can."[65] The sacramental nature of ordination for Catholicism imprints the soul of the priest, granting him not only authority but also power to dispense grace to the laity.

Subsequent Protestant Reforms of Ordination

John Calvin, whose Reformation in Geneva followed Luther's in Germany, concurred with Luther that the purpose of the pastoral office was primarily for preaching the Word. However, Calvin's argument also included some sense of an ontological means to carry out the practical ends: "Through the ministers to whom [God] has entrusted this office *and has conferred the grace to carry it out*, he dispenses and distributes his gifts to the church."[66] Utilizing Isaiah 52:7 ("Beautiful are the feet and blessed the coming of those who announce peace"), Calvin argued for a certain "prestige" of those who are called and appointed to the preaching office. While each pastor is bound to his own congregation, he can, on occasion, then be useful to other churches in times of emergency or when outside advice might be needful, an honor granted by means of his ordination.

Yet the tenor of Calvin's writings certainly elevated pastors not only for what they do but also for who they are: dispensers of God's revelation. Likening the ministry of the ordained pastor to the apostolic ministry and authority of Peter and Paul, Calvin argued for the uniqueness of the apostles then and today by virtue of the fact that Christ entrusts to them God's teaching to humanity. God still entrusts the divine message of the gospel to the modern-day apostle or pastor just as God commended his word to Paul, said Calvin, "that very Paul whom he had determined to catch up into the third heaven and make worthy to receive a wonderful revelation of things unspeakable [2 Cor. 12:2–4]. Who, then, would dare despise that ministry

65. David C. Steinmetz, "The Council of Trent," in *The Cambridge Companion to Reformation Theology*, ed. David Bagchi and David C. Steinmetz (New York: Cambridge University Press, 2004), 242–43.
66. Calvin, *Inst.* 4.3.2; LCC 21:1055, emphasis added.

or dispense with it as something superfluous, whose use God willed to attest with such proofs?"[67] Calvin then argued that while significant for the church and perhaps a rite that granted respect and elicited honor, ordination was still not a sacramental ceremony because it was "not ordinary or common with all believers."[68] Additionally, priests are not given special powers to convey the Holy Spirit into others, nor are they capable of instituting a sacrifice through the Mass; thus "there is no reason why the papist priests should be proud."[69]

With this balanced argument for both honor and humility in the pastoral office, Calvin echoed Luther's theme of a universal priesthood of believers. The church continues to be called upon to institute a sacrifice, though not through a eucharistic transubstantiation. Instead, as Christ serves as all Christians' pontiff, every Christian offers to God a sacrifice of praise: "From this office of sacrificing, all Christians are called a royal priesthood [1 Pet. 2:9]." Through the altar who is also Christ (Heb. 13:10), the Christian can acknowledge that Jesus "has made us a kingdom and priests unto the Father [Rev. 1:6]."[70]

Beyond the magisterial Reformers, the early Anabaptists were known for "one of the first patterns of lay organization in Christian history."[71] So strongly did these radical Reformers hold to Luther's concept of the priesthood of all believers that it is likely ordination was not a part of the first Anabaptist congregations. Conrad Grebel, for instance, was probably never ordained, and early Anabaptists eschewed the notion of a professional class of clergy, especially those who received salaries from the state-church system.[72] Likewise Balthasar Hubmaier likely viewed his baptismal pledge within the Anabaptist congregation as replacing his former priestly vows, rendering a clerical ordination as superfluous.[73]

At the same time, sixteenth-century Anabaptist theology was somewhat nebulous, particularly regarding the notion of ordination. Menno Simons and other second-generation Anabaptists in northern Holland enjoyed a greater sense of distinction between clergy and laity and depended upon "a small circle

67. Calvin, *Inst.* 4.3.2; LCC 21:1056.
68. Calvin, *Inst.* 4.19.28; LCC 21:1476.
69. Ibid.
70. Calvin, *Inst.* 4.18.17; LCC 21:1444–45.
71. Frank Littell, *The Anabaptist View of the Church* (Boston: Starr King, 1958), 94.
72. One example of this rejection of professional clergy can be seen in Conrad Grebel's September 5, 1524, letter to Thomas Müntzer inquiring whether the latter "still accepted a salary"; here via C. Penrose St. Amant, "Sources of Baptist Views on Ordination," *Baptist History and Heritage* 23, no. 3 (July 1988): 8.
73. See Brewer, *A Pledge of Love*, 40, 188.

of elders" to carry out baptisms and do other ministerial tasks.[74] Likewise, the Hutterite Peter Riedemann wrote in 1542:

> It is not for all and sundry to take upon themselves such an office, namely that of teaching and baptizing; as James declares, saying, "Dear brothers, let not each strive to be a teacher, for we all sin much, and shall then receive all the greater condemnation." For which reasons none must take upon himself or accept such power, unless he be chosen properly and rightly by God in his church and community. . . . [Just as] "Christ glorified not himself to be made a high priest" [cf. Heb. 5:5], thus his ministers likewise must not press themselves forward and come to the fore, but wait until God draws them out and chooses them.[75]

On the other hand, Mennonites in the southern region of Holland and what is today Belgium continued to maintain authority within the congregation as a whole. Baptisms were performed by the unordained, and the ban, the act of disciplining unfaithful members, was carried out not by any particular group of presbyters but by the entire congregation. Only later, by the seventeenth century, did these congregations begin to imitate their northern counterparts and attach a greater significance to ordination.[76]

Thus, while early Anabaptists, undoubtedly due to more pressing matters of controversy, placed little emphasis on ordination practices in their theological writings and rejected its sacramentality,[77] probably by virtue of their great emphasis on the universal priesthood of all Christians, later Anabaptists varied in practice, while seeming to elevate the pastorate to a position not only of responsibility but also of distinction, power, and honor. Anabaptist churches that practiced ordination did so on the congregational level, and most churches maintained a pastor, even if he was not ordained. Regardless, in all three Reformation traditions—Lutheran, Reformed, and Anabaptist—a greater emphasis on lay participation was underscored as all believers began to take on roles that heretofore in the Western church's tradition had been reserved exclusively for the clerics.

74. See St. Amant, "Baptist Views on Ordination," 8–9.
75. Peter Riedemann, "The Manner of Baptizing," in *Account* (1542), 79–81; here via *Anabaptism in Outline*, ed. Walter Klaassen (Scottdale, PA: Herald Press, 1981), 129–30.
76. St. Amant, "Baptist Views on Ordination," 9.
77. Although the urgent crisis of martyrdom itself presented the early Anabaptists with procedures for expeditiously replacing their leaders. For instance, the 1527 Schleitheim Confession described their practice: "But if the shepherd should be driven away or led to the Lord by the cross, at the same hour another shall be ordained to his place, so that the little folk and the little flock of God may not be destroyed." In Michael Sattler, *The Legacy of Michael Sattler*, trans. and ed. John H. Yoder (Scottdale, PA: Herald Press, 1973), 36–42; via Janz, *A Reformation Reader*, 210.

The Church of England also attempted to reform some of the abuses of the Catholic notion of sacramental ordination while still maintaining its ecclesial structure and trifold hierarchy of bishop, priest, and deacon. Conservative in its approach, the Anglican Church under Cranmer reduced many of the Catholic elements within the rite for holy orders but underscored the imperative formula in its 1550 ordinal: "Receive the Holy Ghost" for retaining and forgiving sins, proclaim "the Word of God, and [distribute] his holy Sacraments"[78]—a commission apparently retaining a hint of the Catholic along with its Protestant understandings of the ministerial task. Regardless, the latter task of preaching was the dominant feature within the prayers and litanies of the ordinal, evidenced in the original 1550 language of the bishop's charge to the ordained: "Take thou aucthoritie to reade the Gospell in the Church of God, and to preache the same, yf thou bee thereunto ordinarely commanded."[79]

Contemporary Appropriations of Luther's Ordination Reforms

When Luther reformed ordination some five hundred years ago, his intent was to liberate the laity to join in the ministry and to simplify and clarify the high purpose for ordaining individuals to the gospel ministry. An irony of this modification is that many Protestant traditions are now uncertain what ordination is and, in at least some free-church circles, whether it is even necessary to continue its practice. Furthermore, the trajectory of Luther's egalitarian priesthood has disenfranchised many pastors and left congregations uncertain about the degree to which a church can or should accept pastoral authority in its leadership. When ordination services are held, both Protestant clergy and laity alike are often uncertain what to say is taking place through the ceremony. If it is not a sacrament, why retain it at all?

Protestants often utilize the phrase "setting someone apart for ministry" to describe ordination's purpose. Yet the service and its outcome are still confusing to many because it is not altogether clear what the act of setting someone apart for ministerial office means for Protestants. In searching for a biblical precedent, it is not unusual to look to types for this setting-apart practice in Old Testament stories, like Jacob (instead of his older brother) receiving the blessing from Isaac or Samuel anointing first Saul and later David in order to grant them God's leadership over the chosen people. But these biblical types ultimately break down in that a pastor is seen as a servant, not as an estate

---

78. Gibson, *First and Second Prayer-Books of King Edward VI*, 311; here via White, *Sacraments*, 133.

79. Gibson, 301.

holder or a monarch. Thus Protestants instinctively desire to make ordination a special service, yet one that is not too special!

What lies behind this circumspection is Luther's theology of the "priesthood of all believers" that Protestants hold dear: everyone who is baptized in Christ is now ordained to carry out the call to ministry. Protestants acknowledge and even celebrate that as Christians they are not required to go to a specially ordained person to confess their sins; instead, they are to confess them to one another. They should not expect the pastor necessarily to arrive first at their bedside at the hospital or to help them through a difficult spot. Every Christian is called to do that for others. But this question then remains: What do Protestants expect of the clergy that they do ordain?

In asking this collective question on behalf of contemporary Protestants, we recognize that the tradition has accentuated one of Luther's doctrines to the detriment of another. The modern Protestant church has often emphasized the universal priesthood to the extent that Luther's calling for the minister is eclipsed; that is to say, although all Christians are called to be "priests" in their vocation and home life, at least one person still needs to be called as the priest or pastor to the church itself. If God does call persons to be a doctor, farmer, homemaker, or paralegal and to practice ministry in their respective vocations, then the same God calls someone to carry out the functions of pastor in the vocation of the church. In Luther's 1539 order "The Ordination of Ministers of the Word," he wrote, "We bishops—i.e., presbyters and pastors—are called not to watch over geese or cows, but over the congregation God purchased with his own blood that we should feed them with the pure Word of God . . . [which] is why he calls it a good work."[80]

Although Protestants acknowledge that all Christians are ordained by their baptisms, someone needs to be ordained to do the baptizing. While all are ordained to spread the good news of the gospel, someone needs to be ordained to equip Christians and unfold the mysteries of the faith by preaching the Word to the holy priesthood so they may be prepared to carry out their own ministries. So, for the sake of good order and because of God's distribution of gifts, each is to carry out the specific ministry received from God. Luther emphasized a common right of all Christians collectively as the church, such that no one Christian may arise by his or her own authority and assume alone that which belongs to the entire church. Instead, each congregation should choose faithful individuals who are able to teach and should entrust to them the responsibility of carrying out these priestly functions on behalf of all. This is precisely what makes ordination special to Protestants. It is an

80. LW 53:125.

acknowledgment of a community's discernment that found a person worthy and able to fulfill this representative calling.

But this idea, the Reformers still emphasized, is not a simple exchange between an individual and a selecting church. Luther stressed that the minister has no sacerdotal power or indelible character by which he generates anything through himself: "Men are not ordained in order to make or produce anything, but to administer what they find in the church, for they do not produce or make baptism or the Word but are to give and administer these."[81] The gifts of grace through Word and sacrament are already made through the accomplished work of Christ. As the apostle Paul wrote, "Therefore, since it is by God's mercy that we are engaged in this ministry, we do not lose heart. . . . For we do not proclaim ourselves; we proclaim Jesus Christ as Lord and ourselves as your slaves for Jesus' sake" (2 Cor. 4:1, 5).

Luther repeatedly emphasized that the ministry was to the Word and sacrament. The minister thus is called by God and congregation to participate not in the minister's own, or even the church's own, but in God's ministry to the congregation. Hence the real power of ordination for Protestants is not found in an indelible mark conveyed to the ordinand but in the divinely called, representative power that the pastor possesses. Now, while standing in the pulpit to admonish, discipline, or inspire, the pastor brings God's Word to the people as the representative of the congregation behind that pulpit. When the pastor prays at the hospital bedside of a parishioner, the prayers are powerful not only because the pastor is praying as a faithful individual (James 5:15) but also because the prayers are said on behalf of the congregation that the pastor represents and in some sense even embodies in that room. Weddings, funerals, and pastoral counseling also reflect the representative character of the pastor's office. Ordination grants pastors authority not on their own but because of God's gifting as prayerfully discerned and commissioned through the church. Luther then concluded: "By prayer and the laying on of hands let them commend and certify these [selected for ministry] to the whole assembly, and recognize and honor them as lawful bishops and ministers of the Word, believing beyond a shadow of doubt that this has been done and accomplished by God. For in this way the common agreement of the faithful, those who believe and confess the gospel, is realized and expressed."[82]

81. LW 54:119.
82. LW 40:37.

5

Extreme Unction

"Anointing the Sick"

The good Instructor, the Wisdom, the Word of the Father, who made the human, cares for the whole nature of his creature; the all-sufficient Physician of humanity, the Savior, heals both body and soul.

Clement of Alexandria

If ever folly has been uttered, it has been uttered especially on this subject.

Martin Luther

THERE IS LITTLE QUESTION THAT LUTHER consistently and vehemently objected to the premise of the last rites or extreme unction throughout his adult life and in his Protestant writings. Curiously, apocryphal stories have spread in some contemporary circles that the Reformer repented of at least some of his Protestant convictions and asked for last rites on his deathbed in Eisleben. Such reports of an eleventh-hour recantation seem only scuttle-butt and a canard when held against Heiko Oberman's detailed account of Luther's death:

> "Reverend father, will you die steadfast in Christ and the doctrines you have preached?" "Yes," replied the clear voice for the last time. On February 18, 1546, even as he lay dying in Eisleben, far from home, Martin Luther was not

to be spared a final public test, not to be granted privacy even in this last, most personal hour. His longtime confidant Justus Jonas, now pastor in Halle, having hurriedly summoned witnesses to the bedside, shook the dying man by the arm to rouse his spirit for the final exertion. Luther had always prayed for a "peaceful hour": resisting Satan—the ultimate, bitterest enemy—through that trust in the Lord over life and death which is God's gift of liberation from the tyranny of sin. It transforms agony into no more than a brief blow.

But now there was far more at stake than his own fate, than being able to leave the world in peace, and trust in God. For in the late Middle Ages, ever since the first struggle for survival during the persecutions of ancient Rome, going to one's death with fearless fortitude was the outward sign of a true child of God, of the confessors and martyrs. The deathbed in the Eisleben inn had become a stage; and straining their ears to catch Luther's last words were enemies as well as friends.

As early as 1529, Johannes Cochlaeus, Luther's first "biographer," had denounced Luther in Latin and German as the seven-headed dragon, the Devil's spawn. Slanderous reports that he had died a God-forsaken death, miserable and despairing, had circulated time and again. But now the end his friends had dreaded and his enemies had longed for was becoming reality. Who now would lay claim to Luther and fetch him, God or the Devil? While simple believers imagined the Devil literally seizing his prey, the enlightened academic world was convinced that a descent into Hell could be diagnosed medically—as apoplexy and sudden cardiac arrest. Abruptly and without warning, the Devil would snip the thread of a life that had fallen to him, leaving the Church unable to render its last assistance. Thus, in their first reports, Luther's friends, especially Melanchthon, stressed that the cause of death had not been sudden, surprising apoplexy but a gradual flagging of strength: Luther had taken leave of the world and commended his spirit into God's hands. For friend and foe alike his death meant far more than the end of a life.

Shortly after Doctor Martinus died at about 3:00 A.M. on February 18, Justus Jonas carefully recorded Luther's last twenty-four hours, addressing his report not to Luther's widow, as one might expect, but to his sovereign, Elector John Frederick, with a copy for his university colleagues in Wittenberg. Had Luther—born on November 10, 1483, as a simple miner's son—died young, history would have passed over his parents' grief unmoved. But now his death was an affair of state. The day after his birth—the feast of St. Martin—he had been baptized and received into the life of the Church as a simple matter of course, but now there was open dispute over whether, having been excommunicated by the pope, he had departed from this world a son of the Church.

In the last days before his death Luther had been the cheerful man his friends knew and loved. He had successfully completed a difficult mission: a trip from Wittenberg to Eisleben to mediate in a protracted quarrel between the two counts of Mansfeld, the brothers Gebhard and Albert. Hours had been spent sitting between the parties, listening to the clever reasoning of administrative lawyers—a breed he had despised ever since his early days as a law student in Erfurt. After two tough weeks of negotiation, the parties had narrowed their differences and a reconciliation had finally—though only temporarily—been achieved. So there was reason to be cheerful. Luther had suspected that he would die in Eisleben, the place of his birth. But this did not worry him, although he was quite sure he had little time left: "When I get home to Wittenberg again, I will lie down in my coffin and give the worms a fat doctor to feast on." By highlighting the skeleton within the human body, late medieval art had urgently reminded everyone that health, beauty, and wealth were only a few breaths away from the Dance of Death. The "fat doctor" was well aware of this, not as a moralistic horror story, but as a reality of life poised on the brink of eternity.[1]

Likewise, the other two major Protestant Reformers—who, like the father of the Reformation, rebuffed this practice as sacrament in their writings—when facing their own deaths, also declined extreme unction. It was reported that, while dying at the Battle of Kappel in 1531, Ulrich Zwingli was approached by a Catholic soldier. Zwingli was said to have "opened his eyes and looked round. Then he was asked if he wished to confess his sins. He shook his head and indicated that he did not wish to do so."[2] Heinrich Bullinger related that strangers approached the wounded Zwingli "since he was so weak and close to death (for he had fallen in [the] combat and was stricken with a mortal wound), [to inquire] whether a priest should be fetched to hear his confession. Thereat Zwingli shook his head, said nothing, and looked up to heaven." The Catholic soldiers were said to have implored him to confess while he still had breath, to call on the Mother of God and "the beloved saints to plead to God for grace on his behalf. [But] again Zwingli shook his head and continued gazing straight up to heaven."[3]

As a second-generation Reformer in Switzerland, John Calvin did not face the same burden of testing his faithfulness to Protestant theology or of recanting and receiving last rites at the end of his life as did Luther and Zwingli at the outset of the Reformation. Instead, while on his deathbed in

---

1. Heiko A. Oberman, *Luther: Man between God and the Devil* (New Haven: Yale University Press, 2006), 3–5.

2. From "a Catholic version" of Zwingli's death; here via Potter, *Huldrych Zwingli*, 143; earlier from Johannes [= Hans] Salat, *Chronik der schweizerischen Reformation: Von deren Anfängen bis und mit Ao. 1534*, in *Archiv für die schweizerische Reformationsgeschichte* 1 (Freiburg im Breisgau, 1869): 310.

3. "Bullinger's narrative" of Zwingli's death via Potter, *Huldrych Zwingli*, 144; earlier from Heinrich Bullinger, *Reformationsgeschichte nach dem Autographon*, ed. J. J. Hottinger and H. H. Vögeli (Fauenfeld: C. Beyel, 1840), 3:166–68.

April and May of 1564, the Genevan Reformer's dying at peace was recorded as fitting for one who "had been preparing for death all his life."[4] Resolute in his convictions, Calvin wrote his final testament in late April of that final year: "I testify what I have in my soul, that I will live and die in this faith which He has given me: for I have no other hope but that which rests on his free election, the only foundation of my salvation: and with my whole heart do I embrace the mercy which Christ has prepared for me, that all my sins may be buried through the merits of his death and sufferings."[5] Calvin, like Luther and Zwingli before him, then died without equivocating concerning his beliefs, recanting, or receiving last rites.[6]

As King Henry VIII lay dying in January of 1547, this man who had instigated the English Reformation sent for the archbishop of Canterbury, the Reformer Thomas Cranmer, to be by his bedside as he faced death. Cranmer reached the king's bedroom in the early hours of the morning and found the monarch no longer able to speak.[7] Foxe later recorded Cranmer's deathbed ministry to Henry: "Then the archbishop, exhorting him to put his trust in Christ, and to call upon his mercy, desired him, though he could not speak, yet to give some token with his eyes or with his hand, that he trusted in the Lord. Then the King, holding him with his hand, did wring his hand in his as hard as he could."[8] In his biography of Cranmer, Diarmaid MacCulloch observes: "Quietly playing out his calling as royal chaplain, Cranmer had won a final victory in his years of argument with the King on justification. No last rites for Henry; no extreme unction: just an evangelical statement of faith in a grip of the hand. Thus ended the most long-lasting relationship of love which either man had known."[9]

Why did the great Protestant theologians universally reject what had become not just a custom but also a sacrament of the Western church, anointing the

4. Bruce Gordon, *John Calvin* (New Haven: Yale University Press, 2009), 335.

5. The words of Calvin's final will and testament via Paul Henry and Henry Stebbing, *The Life and Times of John Calvin, the Great Reformer* (New York: Carter, 1859), 425.

6. Gordon (*John Calvin*, 333–34) adds: "That Calvin died peacefully was a sign that he had died well. Similarly, in 1546 a death mask of Martin Luther had been produced to demonstrate that his end had not been marked by screaming as his soul was taken away by demons, as Catholic opponents had predicted. To die well meant to have sufficiently prepared for one's end by prayer and repentance, and all confessions, Protestant and Catholic, looked to the good death."

7. Dairmaid MacCulloch, *Thomas Cranmer: A Life* (New Haven: Yale University Press, 1996), 360.

8. John Foxe, "The Death of King Henry the Eighth, with the Manner Thereof," in *The Acts and Monuments of John Foxe*, ed. Stephen Reed Cattley (London: R. B. Seeley and W. Burnside, 1834), 5:689; here via MacCulloch, *Thomas Cranmer*, 60.

9. MacCulloch, *Thomas Cranmer*, 60.

sick and dying? Why would the arguments to support this rite be viewed by Luther as "folly" or "nonsense,"[10] its practice be construed by Calvin as mocking souls and a mere "smear[ing] of their grease . . . [on] half-dead corpses"?[11] To understand the Reformers' opposition to extreme unction, one must first perceive how the rite developed in the course of Christian history and how it was defined and refined by medieval theologians into the shape it took at the advent of the Reformation.

A Brief History of Extreme Unction

The use of oil in sacred ceremonies preceded the Christian movement. Anointing with oil was a practice found in ancient Mesopotamia, Greece, and Rome. Among the Hebrews, various types of oil were used in the sanctuary in worship as a tithe of firstfruits, as something to be consumed ritually by worshipers, as a fuel for the menorahs of the ancient temple, as a way to consecrate objects as holy and set apart, to ordain priests and install prophets, and as a royal unction for anointing kings.[12] But of particular interest to this study is the Hebrew use of oil as a balm for wounds (Isa. 1:6) and a means for bestowing strength and healing (Lev. 14:15–18). The ancient Israelites, and the first-century-AD Jews after them, as opposed to those following Enlightenment ideas, did not completely differentiate between ministering to the physical and the spiritual well-being of a person. Thus at the advent and development of the Christian tradition in the first century AD and following centuries, the physical or the spiritual alternatively eclipsed the other in pastoral care.

James 5:14–15 has played a central role as a, if not the, scriptural basis for the development of what ultimately became extreme unction: "Are any among you sick? They should call for the elders of the church and have them pray over them, anointing them with oil in the name of the Lord. The prayer of faith will save the sick, and the Lord will raise them up; and anyone who has committed sins will be forgiven." When taken together, these two verses appear to validate the ancient propensity to associate, if not adjoin, body and spirit; physical healing and spiritual forgiveness appear to have some

10. Luther, *Babylonian Captivity*, LW 36:118. While Martin Steinhäuser translated Luther as calling the sacrament "folly" in LW, Dillenberger (351) renders this "nonsense."

11. Calvin, *Inst.* 4.19.21; LCC 21:1468.

12. See J. Roy Porter's concise but thorough essay "Oil in the Old Testament," in *The Oil of Gladness: Anointing in the Christian Tradition*, ed. Martin Dudley and Geoffrey Rowell (Collegeville, MN: Liturgical Press, 1993), 35–45; and Charles W. Gusmer, *And You Visited Me: Sacramental Ministry to the Sick and Dying* (New York: Pueblo, 1984), 5–6.

relationship in this passage, even if Jesus himself at times seems to disassociate the two in the Gospels (e.g., "Neither this man nor his parents sinned; he was born blind so that God's works might be revealed in him," John 9:3).[13] Richard McBrien observes: "Sickness . . . was attributed to sin, as in the Old Testament and contemporary Judaism, and so it posed a problem for the early Church."[14] While undoubtedly unencumbered by the subsequent medieval Scholastic attempts at explaining the potential power of the oil, the necessary sacerdotal powers of the cleric, or the question of the requisite faith of the recipient, James 5 at least demonstrates the practice of pastoral visitation to the sick by the presbyters, with the intended purpose of restoring "the sick member not only to physical health but also to spiritual health within the community of faith."[15]

In the Old Testament, Psalm 103:3 credits God as the one "who forgives all your iniquity, who heals all your diseases"; and in the New Testament, Mark 6:13 testifies to the physical-spiritual ministry of healing. Jesus sent out the disciples in pairs: "They cast out many demons, and anointed with oil many who were sick and cured them." It should come as no surprise, then, that the church began to associate anointing the sick with the discipline of penance. And as the church began insidiously to postpone penance to the final days of one's life, as a onetime postbaptismal management for sin, so the ministry of healing and anointing the sick also became a transitional rite of passage from this life to the next.

A thorough search through the history of Christian pastoral care to the sick and anointing of the ailing demonstrates that initial manifestations of the ministry of healing were intended to restore both body and soul. This is evidenced by the prayers of Serapion of Thmuis in the fourth century, which consecrated oil for the purpose of restoring health by the Spirit;[16] a letter by Innocent I in the fifth century, insisting that bishops be the normative individuals who "anoint with holy chrism";[17] Bede the Venerable's commentary

13. Note, however, that Jesus uses the same pronouncement to say both "Your faith has made you well [from your disease]" and "Your faith has saved you [from your sins]": *Hē pistis sou sesōken se* (Mark 5:34; Matt. 9:22; Luke 7:50).

14. Richard P. McBrien, "The Sacraments of Healing: Penance and Anointing of the Sick," in *A History of Pastoral Care*, ed. G. R. Evans (London: Cassell, 2000), 408.

15. Ibid.

16. See Sarapion of Thmuis, *Prayer-Book*, in *The Prayers of Sarapion of Thmuis: A Liturgical, Literary, and Theological Analysis*, trans. Maxwell E. Johnson (Rome: Pontificio Istituto Orientale, 1995), 67.

17. See *The Letter of Pope Innocent I to Decentius of Gubbio* 8 (416), in *Church and Worship in Fifth-Century Rome: The Letter of Innocent I to Decentius of Gubbio*, trans. Martin Connell (Cambridge: Grove Books, 2002), 46; here via Johnson, *Sacraments and Worship*, 287.

on James in the eighth century, where he claims that the presbyter's anointing the infirmed for the purpose of healing was already a long-standing custom originating from apostolic times;[18] and a highly developed ninth-century Carolingian ritual of anointing with blessed water, the sprinkling of salt, and the articulation of prayers and psalms over the infirm Christian, which beseeches God to "heal him [or her] with spiritual medicine, that, restored to former health, he may return thanks to Thee in soundness of health."[19]

Ultimately, however, through wars and pestilence, the prayers and ultimate anointing by the faithful seemed to channel little divine power to affect the fleshly nature, thus leaving little more than the promise of spiritual provision *ad tempus mortis*: if the body could not be saved, a believer's soul may, at least, be prepared for eternity. Bishop Theodulf of Orléans, an early ninth-century theological adviser to Emperor Charles the Great, instructed the clergy in his diocese to apply holy oil to fifteen places on the infirmed person's body. Then he significantly added: "When the sick man has been anointed in the way that has been set forth, let him be enjoined by the priest to say the Lord's Prayer and the Creed, and to commend his spirit into the hands of God, and to fortify himself with the sign of the cross, and to bid farewell to the living. Then let the priest communicate him."[20] Theodulf's emphasis on the rite as spiritual preparation for death gradually became the predominant view in the Middle Ages.

By the twelfth century, Hugh of Saint Victor argued that unction was instituted with apostolic authority for the purpose of remitting sin and alleviating sickness but centered this healing balm spiritually as alleviating the "sickness" of the soul. Physical healing was an indirect and only secondary outcome of the rite. Master Herman, disciple of the twelfth-century French Scholastic philosopher Peter Abelard, in turn made unction the final Christian ritual of a believer, describing it as "the last of all and, so to speak, the final consummation. . . . Every Christian is anointed three times: first, for his inception, namely in baptism; secondly, in confirmation, where the gifts of grace are conferred; thirdly, on departing *in exitu*, where if sins are present, they are

18. Though Richard McBrien ("Sacraments of Healing," 409) observes: "Nowhere in the early tradition does one find mention of the Anointing as a sacrament of preparation for death."
19. See "A Carolingian Rite of Anointing the Sick" (ninth century), in *Sacraments and Forgiveness*, vol. 2 of *Sources of Christian Theology*, ed. Paul F. Palmer (Westminster, MD: Newman, 1959), 294–95; here via Johnson, *Sacraments and Worship*, 288–89.
20. See F. W. Puller, *The Anointing of the Sick in Scripture and Tradition, with Some Considerations on the Numbering of the Sacraments* (London: SPCK, 1910), 194; here via William A. Clebsch and Charles R. Jaekle, *Pastoral Care in Historical Perspective* (New York: Jason Aronson, 1964), 35.

remitted in whole or in major part."[21] The Christian practice of anointing the sick had incrementally been replaced with last rites.[22]

Thus by the High Middle Ages, anointing the dying had become an accepted sacramental practice in the Western church and was increasingly referred to as *sacramentum exeuntium* (the sacrament of the departing) or what Peter Lombard successfully termed *extrema unctio* (last anointing), numbering it among his list of seven sacraments.[23] To be fair, Lombard still maintained a connection between the rite and "the relief of bodily infirmity," but only "provided it is expedient that [the sick] be relieved in both [spiritual and physical senses]. But if perhaps it is not expedient for him to have bodily health, he acquires in this sacrament that health which is of the soul."[24] So strong was the association between the ceremony and death that apparently by the late medieval period many believers hesitated to receive unction lest the service be the certain cause of and not the spiritual security in one's death.[25]

In the thirteenth and fourteenth centuries, various Scholastic theologians and schools disputed among themselves the exact effect of what had become a widely accepted sacrament. While both Franciscan and Dominican schools concurred that the rite remitted iniquity, the Franciscan school of Bonaventure and Scotus perceived extreme unction as forgiving even venial sins, while the Dominican school of Albert the Great and Thomas Aquinas saw the ritual as remitting any and all remaining sin that might prevent a soul from heavenly bliss.[26] Aquinas explained:

21. See Master Herman, *Epitome*, PL 178:153; here via Palmer, *Sacraments and Forgiveness*, 328; and Gusmer, *And You Visited Me*, 29.

22. J. Steven O'Malley outlines the diminution of both faith among Christians in a God who heals the body and the corresponding truncation of the church's role as divine agent in physical healing, with the ultimate result that the church relegated "Holy Unction to become extreme unction. It became a last rite to prepare one for a good death, instead of an occasion for the healing power of God to come to His people." O'Malley traces the abatement of faith in healing in "dispensations" from (1) Cyprian's claim in the second century that "the sins of Christians have weakened the power of the church," to (2) a subsequent development of belief that illness was God's punishment for iniquity, to (3) the church's repudiation of the science of medicine, and finally to (4) the Christian dualism of ceding the art of healing to the medical sciences while maintaining the cure of souls within the church's domain, thus explaining the medieval transition of the healing sacrament to last rites to ensure a spiritual transition to the next life. See J. Steven O'Malley, "Probing the Demise and Recovery of Healing in Christianity," in *Pneuma* 5, no. 1 (1983): esp. 46–50.

23. McBrien, "Sacraments of Healing," 409.

24. See Lombard, *Sentences* 4; here via Johnson, *Sacraments and Worship*, 289.

25. See Ronald K. Rittgers, *The Reformation of Suffering: Pastoral Theology and Lay Piety in Late Medieval and Early Modern Germany* (New York: Oxford University Press, 2012), 21.

26. Gusmer, *And You Visited Me*, 31.

Since a sacrament causes what it signifies, the principal effect of a sacrament must be gathered from its signification. Now this sacrament is conferred by way of a kind of medicament, even just as Baptism is conferred by way of washing, and the purpose of a medicament is to expel sickness. Hence the chief object of the institution of this sacrament is the cure of the sickness of sin. . . . Consequently we must say that the principal effect of this sacrament is the remission of sin as to its remnants, and consequently even as to its guilt, if it find it.[27]

Unction then destroyed the "remnants" of sin in Dominical thought and served as a final provision for and conduit of divine grace to overcome sin in ordering one's earthly life for a Christian's ensuing death, judgment, and life to come.[28]

Interestingly, the Franciscan school required the priest to anoint the infirm person, as Bonaventure articulated, only "where danger of death is imminent" and only to those "who are as it were in transit to another state,"[29] for, as Scotus logically concluded, the sacrament is appropriate exclusively for "a sick person who is no longer capable of sinning and who is in danger of death."[30] Thus the thirteenth and fourteenth centuries saw the service of unction completely transform to a rite of dying for the primary purpose of sin management. As McBrien explains of the Western church tradition of this time, "To die immediately after extreme unction . . . guaranteed an unimpeded journey to God."[31]

That the rite of unction served as last rites was finally codified in the fifteenth century in the Council of Florence's Decree for the Armenians (1439), which stated that "this sacrament shall not be given to any except the sick who are in fear of death."[32] The decree outlined that the dying be anointed on the eyes, ears, nostrils, mouth, hands, feet, and loins accompanied by a prayer for sins committed by each portion of the body. Despite the promises that this ritual would remove all barriers to heaven, as the church posited, many laypeople chose not to receive extreme unction. The rite was expensive, and, given the requirements that the sacrament be withheld until death was nigh, the gravely ill often waited too long, expiring before a priest could attend to the person.[33]

27. See Thomas Aquinas, *"Summa theologica" of Thomas Aquinas*, Suppl. 30, 3:2671–72; here via Johnson, *Sacraments and Worship*, 290.

28. Kelly, *Sacraments Revisited*, 122.

29. See Bonaventure, *Breviloquium* 6; here via Palmer, *Sacraments and Worship*, 334; and Gusmer, *And You Visited Me*, 32.

30. Scotus, *In 4 Sent.* (*Opus Parisiense*) d. 23. q. unica; here via Palmer, *Sacraments and Worship*, 335; and Gusmer, *And You Visited Me*, 32.

31. McBrien, "Sacraments of Healing," 410. Additionally, White called this "a kind of eternal fire insurance" (*Sacraments*, 125).

32. See The Decree for the Armenians, Council of Trent, *DS* 1324.

33. Kelly, *Sacraments Revisited*, 123.

In the early sixteenth century, Johannes von Paltz, an Augustinian monk and professor of theology at Erfurt, recorded various superstitions that had developed among Germans regarding pilgrimages to unapproved sites, alchemy, astrology, and magic. To the point of this study, while serving as an indulgence preacher in the region, Paltz noticed a certain belief among the people that had developed regarding the reception of extreme unction, a superstition that Luther, a fellow Augustinian theologian and professor, later drew from in his reformatory writings. Paltz observed that the people feared the rite would be the cause or at least the catalyst of death rather than a blessed sacrament to ready the dying for the next life. In one case, as Paltz reported, a pregnant woman who had recovered after receiving last rites was required to abstain from sex for one year. The lives of pregnant women who received extreme unction were thought to be even more endangered if they survived to give birth. For his part, Paltz worked to demythologize these superstitious beliefs, associating them with the devil, and he preached to counter such popular apprehensions by claiming that extreme unction could provide salvation to even the greatest of sinners.[34]

Not So Extreme: Luther's Rejection of the Rite

After the Council of Florence officially declared extreme unction to be one of the church's seven sanctioned sacraments, priests throughout Western Europe settled into this appointed convention. As a son of the church, Luther is recorded as writing constructively about extreme unction as late as November of 1519. At the request of his friend George Spalatin, who served as the secretary to Prince Frederick of Saxony, Luther published a sermon in response to one of Frederick's court counselors named Mark Schart, who apparently was anguished and tormented by the idea of dying. As Martin Dietrich observed, "The entire writing echoes [Luther's] experience as a pastor and confessor constantly in contact with men and women who were terrified by the maze of popular customs and practices observed by the church in connection with death."[35] Among his twenty points of advice, the German Reformer counseled:

> Anyone who is granted the time and the grace to confess, to be absolved, and to receive the sacrament [of the Lord's Supper] and Extreme Unction before his

34. Scott H. Hendrix, *Recultivating the Vineyard: The Reformation Agendas of Christianization* (Louisville: Westminster John Knox, 2004), 12; cf. Christoph Burger, "Volksfrömmigkeit in Deutschland um 1500 im Spiegel der Schriften des Johannes von Paltz OESA," in *Volksreligion im hohen und späten Mittelalter*, ed. Peter Dinzelbacher and Dieter R. Bauer (Paderborn: Schöningh, 1990), 311–13.

35. Dietrich, "Introduction [to a Sermon on Preparing to Die]," LW 42:98.

death has great cause indeed to love, praise, and thank God and to die cheerfully, if he relies firmly on and believes in the sacraments. . . . In the sacraments your God, Christ himself, deals, speaks and works with you through the priest. His are not the works and words of man. In the sacraments God himself grants you all the blessings . . . with Christ. God wants the sacraments to be a sign and testimony that Christ's life has taken your death, his obedience your sin, his love your hell, upon themselves and overcome them. . . . You thereby enter into the true communion of saints so that they die with you in Christ, bear sin, and vanquish hell.[36]

Already one may readily see Luther's maturing notion of faith being what makes the sacrament effective,[37] as the dying person receives and appropriates the words of comfort from the priest as a promise from God himself. Those then who die in Christ can say with confidence:

God promised and in his sacraments he gave me a sure sign of his grace that Christ's life overcame my death in his death, that his obedience blotted out my sin in his suffering, that his love destroyed my hell in his forsakenness. This sign and promise of my salvation will not lie to me or deceive me. It is God who has promised it, and he cannot lie either in words or in deeds.[38]

Trusting in the promise found in the sacraments should serve as a great source of comfort and assurance.

Although Luther wrote positively and even pastorally about the practice of extreme unction and other sacraments in November, by December of 1519 he appears to have had a change of heart regarding the sacramentality of extreme unction along with three other rites, now accepted by the church as sacraments, by not addressing them in his sacramental sermons.[39] By the fall of 1520, Luther wrote his most comprehensive treatise on sacramental theology in his *Babylonian Captivity of the Church*. Regarding the ceremony of anointing the sick, the Reformer critiqued its metamorphosis into extreme unction, a ceremony exclusively for those on death's door. He also reproved

36. Luther, "A Sermon on Preparing to Die," LW 42:108.
37. Indeed, Luther later reiterated this theme of personal appropriation in his "Treatise on the New Testament": "Just as I cannot give or receive the sacrament of baptism, of penance, of extreme unction in any one's stead or for his benefit, but I accept for myself alone the blessing therein offered by God." LW 35:94.
38. LW 42:109.
39. In December of 1519 Luther wrote a letter to George Spalatin explaining that he was preaching on the three sacraments of baptism, penance, and the Lord's Supper but not on the others, since Luther had begun to question their legitimacy as "sacraments" of the church. See WA Br 1, no. 231.19–24; see also E. Theodore Bachmann, "Introduction [to 'The Sacrament of Penance']," LW 35:5.

the church's move to make anointing into a sacrament. Admitting that his opponents could cite James 5 as the scriptural authority for both the promise and sign of this sacrament, in keeping with the Reformer's own definition of "sacrament," Luther used the same passage now against the sacramental convention, countering:

> For the apostle [James] did not desire it to be an extreme unction or administered only to the dying, but he says expressly: "Is any one sick?" He does not say: "Is any one dying?" . . . The apostle's words are clear enough, on which he as well as they rely; but they do not follow them. It is evident, therefore, that they have arbitrarily and without any authority made a sacrament and an extreme unction out of the words of the apostle which they have wrongly interpreted.[40]

Luther, moreover, mocked the church's conclusion, using Thomistic logic against itself, that a sacrament causes what it signifies. As an "effective sign," the anointing referred to in the text seems to promise healing and strength to the ailing, as James professes: "The prayer of faith will save the sick, and the Lord will raise them up." Luther now goes for the jugular: "But who does not see that this promise is seldom, if ever, fulfilled? Scarcely one in a thousand is restored to health, and when one is restored nobody believes that it came about through the sacrament, but through the working of nature or of medicine. Indeed to the sacrament they ascribe the opposite effect."[41] Thus, Luther rhetorically deduced, either anointing is not a sacrament or the apostle James is a fraud. If only this case were not so dire as affecting life and death, Luther commented, the scriptural exegesis and application would be humorous. As it stands, the new convention of the church "affirms what the Scriptures deny, and denies what the Scriptures affirm." Then, in now familiar polemical prose, the Reformer stated, "If nonsense is spoken anywhere, this is the very place,"[42] and mockingly asked: "Why should we not give thanks to these excellent masters of ours? Surely I spoke the truth when I said that they never uttered greater folly than on this subject."[43]

Here Luther even questioned the genuine authorship of the epistle as coming from the original apostle, but he conceded that regardless of its apostolic authority, a sacrament cannot be instituted by an apostle by his own authority but only by the commission of Christ. In support of this claim, Luther observed that when writing on the words of the Supper in 1 Corinthians 11,

40. Luther, *Babylonian Captivity*, LW 36:118–19.
41. LW 36:119–20.
42. Luther citation via Dillenberger, 351; cf. LW 36:118.
43. LW 36:119.

Paul clearly stated that he "received from the Lord what" he passed on to the church (v. 23);[44] James instead appears merely to give good pastoral advice.

But beyond overlooking the ancient and traditional use of oil by the church for healing and the promise conveyed in the passage, Luther also pointed out that James did not attribute the physical restoration of the patient to the unction but to the prayers made in faith by the "elders." While it is incumbent upon a recipient always to believe in the "promise and institution of God" for a genuine sacrament to be made effective, Luther underscored that in this case it is the faith of the minister(s) that brings about what is promised. But in the case of the church's practice of last rites, the priests do not expect the ailing person to revive and be healed; instead, they anticipate the sickly believer to die.[45] Of further note, Luther submitted that the passage is unclear whether the "presbyters" who are said to pray for the sick are even to be taken as clergy or, rather, as what might be more readily translated as "older, graver men in the church" who would have benefit of "age and long experience" in the spiritual life. The latter seemed more likely, as Luther saw it, given that James begins his epistle by admonishing the church to "let him ask in faith, with no doubting" (cf. 1:6); James encourages the church, "Confess your sins to one another" (5:16); and Christ himself confirmed this sentiment: "Whatever you ask for in prayer, believe that you have received it, and it will be yours" (Mark 11:24).

Luther concluded this rousing section of his treatise by again rejecting what he saw as the permutation of religious advice from a traditional epistle and thereby inventing a "brand-new sacrament" for the dying; he admitted only that the ritual is akin to other church practices like "blessing and sprinkling salt and water."[46] Yet the Reformer conceded that, regardless of the unnecessary ceremony associated with the rite, those dying who believe in the promise of God would still receive the forgiveness of God and find peace at life's conclusion because of the trust the ailing place in the blessings granted to them,

for the faith of the recipient does not err, however much the minister may err. . . . How much more will one who administers extreme unction confer peace,

44. LW 36:118.

45. Austra Reinis, *Reforming the Art of Dying: The* ars moriendi *in the German Reformation (1519–1528)* (Burlington, VT: Ashgate, 2007), 82.

46. LW 36:122–23. On this point Luther later wrote, in his *Lectures on Genesis*, that "the pope invented holy water, extreme unction, and many similar things to which he has ascribed forgiveness of sins. Always consider here whether God has added His command and promise. If there is no promise and command of God, decide at once that it is idolatry and a desecration of the name of God" (LW 1:229); by 1530 he listed extreme unction with such common church customs as indulgences, poltergeists, soul baths, and altar dedications as practices in the "pretended church." See Luther, *Exhortation to All Clergy Assembled at Augsburg*, LW 34:54–55.

even though he does not really confer peace so far as his ministry is concerned, since there is no sacrament there! The faith of the one anointed receives even that which the minister either could not give or did not intend to give. It is sufficient for the one anointed to hear and believe the Word.[47]

Luther was now using the theme of last rites as a seventh verse to repeat his new theological chorus of "faith alone" as making any promise, sacrament, or blessing effective for justification and salvation, for "all things can be done for the one who believes" (Mark 9:23; cf. Matt. 8:13). The subjective appropriation of faith by the laity is credited unto righteousness even as the clerics may distort and mislead through what Luther viewed as superstitious ceremonies.

Protestant Pastoral Care: Luther's Positive Replacement for Last Rites

It would be unfortunate if Luther's assessment of the convention of extreme unction were completely disannulling. Fortunately, Luther also attempted to give productive counsel on how the minister and other members of the congregation might rightfully care for the indisposed, even while he wrote in the context of his blistering critique of the present state of sacramental theology and practice in his *Babylonian Captivity*. In this case, Luther proposed what he viewed as a better interpretation of James 5, particularly where the elders of the church are advised to pray for and anoint the sick. Luther again underscored that it was the faithful prayers of the righteous, not the unction itself, that brought healing by the power of God. A ministry enshrouded by faith is key. Luther wrote wistfully: "There is no doubt at all that, even if today such a prayer were made over a sick man, that is, made in full faith by older, graver, and saintly men, as many as we wished would be healed. For what could faith not do?"[48]

Thus, while the present state of extreme unction, given as last rites to the dying, may still be of some benefit to those near death, especially as they believe in God's Word and promise, all the more are the prayers effective if truly made in faith not only for the dying but more generally for those at all seasons of life and illness. And this ministry is not a onetime, final rite but an ongoing, daily unction and ministry of pastoral and priestly care made by those more mature in the faith to those at various stages of infirmity. Its purpose is to bring both spiritual and bodily healing by the power of the Holy Spirit and the prayers

47. LW 36:122.
48. LW 36:121.

made in faith. Said Luther, "If [this ministry of prayer] had remained a practice of daily occurrence, especially if it had cured the sick, even without taking away sins, how many worlds, do you think, would not the pontiffs have under their control today?"[49] But by converting this simple yet powerful ministry of the faithful to one another into a sacerdotal and sacramental ritual for the dying, the popes and clerics "despise the prayer of faith" and commandeer the common and honorable pastoral ministry of the church.[50]

Although Luther's thoughts in his 1520 treatise on the topic of extreme unction are relatively brief, they importantly serve as the groundwork for the developing structure of his notion of prayer ministry. His early writings that led up to this seminal document and also much of what develops later give the reader a fuller picture of Luther's aspirations regarding pastoral and congregational care to the sick as the proper restoration of and replacement for what the church had relatively recently contrived as a "sacrament."

Most studies into Luther's development of pastoral care have approached his work from his personal theological crisis: The young priest could not find rest for his own conscience, spiritually wrestling with the demands of the law and the Righteous Judge until he believed he discovered a new soteriology of the promise of God's Word of grace alone. Such a new Word served as a balm to the disturbed conscience, initially for Luther himself and eventually for the German nation, which in large measure followed him. Thus it is now commonplace to argue that "Luther's efforts to reform the church began with an attempt to reform the care of souls, above all, the care of his own soul."[51] Luther's twin notions of sola gratia and the universal priesthood of believers, then, bring theological structure to the church's ministry to the sick and dying, replacing the false security (or fears à la Paltz) of superstitions associated with last rites. Naturally, for the theologian and preacher in Luther, the primary mode of pastoral care came through the proclamation of the gospel as a pastor, and secondarily through correspondence, while most day-to-day ministry of visiting the sick and poor in spirit was delegated to deacons,[52] although Luther is recorded as having periodically visited and corresponded with the grieving and spiritually and physically afflicted himself.[53] These episodes serve as intriguing examples of Luther's intention for such pastoral work.

49. LW 36:123.
50. Ibid.
51. Ronald K. Rittgers, "How Luther's Engagement in Pastoral Care Shaped His Theology," in Kolb et al., *Oxford Handbook of Martin Luther's Theology*, 462.
52. Martin Brecht, *Martin Luther*, vol. 3, *The Preservation of the Church, 1532–1546* (Minneapolis: Fortress, 1993), 252–53.
53. Veit Dietrich, Luther's onetime personal secretary, e.g., wrote of a pastoral visit Luther made to Benedict Paul following the accidental death of his son: Luther encouraged the man

It is safe to say that the Protestant ministry to the sick and dying was part and parcel of Luther's overarching project of the priesthood of all believers. Already in his *Babylonian Captivity*, he had emphasized that baptism serves as the ordination to the priesthood for all Christians, wherein believers bear the ministry of the Word to one another.[54] Luther wrote: "If we lay bare to a brother what lies on our conscience, and in confidence unveil that which we have kept hidden, we receive, through the mouth of a brother, a comfort which God has spoken."[55] Thus all Christians are charged with preaching the gospel, caring for the poor, and praying for their ailing brothers and sisters in the faith. Each Christian must bear witness to this word to reassure the others of God's promises.

But what underscores the divine promises is not any unction in itself but the faith exercised through prayer, as James 5 outlines. Conrad Cordatus recorded his observations of Luther's bedside manner in his pastoral visits:

> When [Luther] approaches a sick man he converses with him in a very friendly way, bends as close to him as he can with his whole body, and first inquires about his illness, what his ailment is, how long he has been sick, what physician he has called, and what kind of medicine he has been using. Then he asks whether the sick man has been patient before God . . . [and] is prepared to die in God's name, if this be his will. . . . Luther [then] commends such faith to others, at the same time admonishing the sick man to continue steadfast in his faith and promising to pray for him.[56]

While we do not have a multitude of examples of Luther's own pastoral care, those examples we do have remain consistent with how the Reformer understood James's injunction for caring for the sick, through the prayers of faith.

In one spellbinding episode, perhaps both figuratively and literally, a clergyman in Frankfurt on the Oder named Andrew Ebert asked Luther for advice regarding a young girl named Matzke Fischer, who was purportedly possessed by the devil and afflicted by mental illness. Ebert conveyed to the Wittenberg theologian that the girl had begun speaking in a German dialect to which she had never been exposed and had also been observed procuring small coins,

---

to focus on God's gifts of his Word, Christ, and a good conscience. Luther also recorded his pastoral care for John Agricola's wife, writing a letter to Agricola in which Luther assessed Elsa's malady as more spiritual than physical. Here via Rittgers, "Engagement in Pastoral Care," 466; cf. LCC 18:68 and 83.

54. LW 36:112–13.
55. Here via Dillenberger, 319; cf. LW 36:86.
56. Luther, "Table Talk Recorded by Conrad Cordatus"; here via LCC 18:36–37; cf. WA Tr 2, no. 2194b.

placing them in her mouth, and then chewing and swallowing them. Her desperate family had called upon a Catholic priest in an adjacent town, who came armed with consecrated herbs and holy water but failed in his attempts the exorcize the demon from the girl. Ebert asked Luther for his counsel.

The Reformer received Ebert's inquiry soberly, and he carefully responded, first with commentary that such events may be a sign of God's judgment upon certain princes who abuse their power and rob the people of their wealth. Specifically regarding the girl, however, Luther, once again, gave advice consistent with his interpretation of James 5:

> We must first of all pray earnestly for the girl who is compelled to suffer such things on our account. In the second place, this spirit must in turn be ridiculed and derided, but he must not be attacked with any exorcisms or serious measures, for he laughs at all these things with diabolical scorn. We must persevere in our prayer for the girl and our contempt of the devil until finally, Christ permitting, he lets her alone.[57]

What is particularly concordant with his 1520 interpretation of James 5 in this example is that, now some sixteen years later, Luther still gave priority and power to the work of prayer as effective for spiritual and even physical transformation and did not consign ontological power to the outward ceremonies, consecrated objects, unctions, holy water, or any other entity that might distract from the genuine spiritual work of pastoral care for the sick and afflicted. The girl's only hope, it would seem, came in the form of prayers said in faith.

Among the collection of other letters of comfort to the sick and dying from Luther's pen over the course of his life, a letter written in June of 1545, less than a year before his own death, demonstrates Luther's lifelong consistency of critiquing last rites in his early career and counterproposal for Protestant pastoral care. In this case, the Reformer was giving advice to Severin Schulze, a pastor in Prettin, a village near Wittenberg, who apparently had welcomed counsel from Luther on how to handle a case of mental illness in his village. Luther's response is telling:

> I know of no worldly help to give. If the physicians are at a loss to find a remedy, you may be sure that it is not a case of ordinary melancholy. It must, rather, be an affliction that comes from the devil, and this must be counteracted by the power of Christ and with the prayer of faith. This is what we do, and what we have been accustomed to do, for a cabinetmaker here was similarly afflicted with madness and we cured him by prayer in Christ's name.

57. Luther, "To Andrew Ebert: August 5, 1536," here via LCC 18:44–45.

Accordingly you should proceed as follows: Go to him with the deacon and two or three good men. Confident that you, as pastor of the place, are clothed with the authority of the ministerial office, lay your hands upon him and say, "Peace be with you, dear brother, from God our Father and from our Lord Jesus Christ." Thereupon repeat the Creed and the Lord's Prayer over him in a clear voice, and close with these words: "O God, almighty Father, who hast told us through thy Son, 'Verily, verily, I say unto you, Whatsoever ye shall ask the Father in my name, he will give it you'; who hast commanded and encouraged us to pray in his name, 'Ask, and ye shall receive'; and who in like manner hast said, 'Call upon me in the day of trouble: I will deliver thee, and thou shalt glorify me'; we unworthy sinners, relying on these thy words and commands, pray for thy mercy with such faith as we can muster. Graciously deign to free this man from all evil, and put to nought the work that Satan has done in him, to the honor of thy name and the strengthening of the faith of believers; through the same Jesus Christ, thy Son, our Lord, who liveth and reigneth with thee, world without end. Amen." Then, when you depart, lay your hands upon the man again and say, "These signs shall follow them that believe; they shall lay hands on the sick, and they shall recover [cf. Mark 16:17–18]."[58]

Luther recommended that this pattern of visitation and prayer be repeated twice more on successive days, adding: "Meanwhile let prayers be said from the chancel of the church, publicly, until God hears them," while he personally affixed his own commitment to prayers for the afflicted man at the letter's conclusion.

Without question, one may see how much faith Luther placed on the work of prayer for the sick and dying. Yet the Reformer repeatedly underscored that it is not the pattern, wording, laying on of hands, anointing, or any outward rite that brought the promise of healing. God's promise of restoration came exclusively through the faith of those ministering and through the work of prayer. The faithful prayers of the elders, Luther maintained, were the best mechanism for unleashing God's promise of healing, and prayer remained the foundation to his Protestant project of pastoral care.

History has often portrayed Luther as a fiery, temperamental, polemical theologian who was absorbed in his preaching and theological writing. Caricatures, though distortions, are often still recognizable sketches of the authentic subject. More recent scholarship, however, has taken up the neglected, softer, pastoral side of Luther's reforms and ministry.[59] Through his

58. Luther, "To Severin Schulze (June 1, 1545)," here via LCC 18:51–52; cf. WA Br 11:111–12.
59. For examples, see Neil R. Leroux, *Martin Luther as Comforter: Writings on Death* (Leiden: Brill, 2007); Dennis Ngien, *Luther as a Spiritual Adviser: The Interface of Theology and Piety in Luther's Devotional Writings* (Milton Keynes, UK: Paternoster, 2007); Timothy J.

Table Talk and personal correspondence, one may gain a fuller picture of
the pastor and preacher who wished to revisit the traditions of the Western
church. He advised fellow pastors on how to stand at the bedside of their
parishioners, pray for and touch them, and communicate God's presence to
them as representative agents of their congregations.[60] Luther complained
that physicians, although useful agents of healing, often missed the underlying causes of their patient's issues, for they were trained to treat medical
symptoms and not, as Luther saw it, the spiritual source of the disease. Said
Luther, "Satan is sometimes the instigator of the material cause of disease;
he can alter the causes and diseases at once, and he can turn fever into chills
and health into illness. To deal with Satan, there must be a higher medicine;
namely, faith and prayer."[61] Thus, for Luther, the spiritual leaders of the
congregation must attend to these broader, transcendent issues, since their
prayers for comfort and divine intercession for the patient may serve as the
real antidote to the ailment.

In a particularly tumultuous time in August of 1527, a case of the bubonic
plague was discovered in Wittenberg. The university was closed, and students
returned to their homes. Yet it is notable that Luther "remained in the city
and was busy with the pastoral and practical care of the sick."[62] He ultimately
responded to a query by a pastor in Breslau who inquired what a responsible
Christian was to do during such a crisis: flee the city or minister to the sick?
Luther replied by means of a public letter, arguing that doctors, government
officials, and pastors all bore an ethical vocational responsibility to stay behind and care for those afflicted. Yet, importantly, Luther again underscored
the notion of the priesthood of every Christian to care for those who did not
otherwise have help. The Reformer wrote provocatively:

Wengert, ed., *The Pastoral Luther: Essays on Martin Luther's Practical Theology* (Grand Rapids:
Lutheran Quarterly Books / Eerdmans, 2009).

60. O'Malley, "Probing the Demise and Recovery of Healing," 57.

61. Luther is here cited in LCC 18:46–47; cf. WA Tr 4, no. 4784. Although Luther primarily attributed suffering to the devil, one of his more notable disciples, the Nuremberg
preacher Veit Dietrich (1506–49), developed an important pastoral guide, Liturgy Booklet
for Pastors in the Countryside (1543), wherein sickness was attributed to divine punishment
or at least the side effect of unconfessed sin. Dietrich directed pastors to approach their
sick congregants and ask: "What do you answer me? Do you acknowledge that you are a
poor sinner and have spent your days in both intending and doing much evil against God,
his Word, and your own conscience? Does this cause you sorrow in your heart so that you
wish you have not done it, and that if God should grant you further life do you resolve not
to do it any longer, but to follow God's Word and will more dutifully?" Only afterward
is the pastor to comfort the sick person with the good news of the gospel. See Rittgers,
Reformation of Suffering, 172.

62. Lull (479) makes this observation in his introduction to this letter by Luther.

This I well know, that if it were Christ or his mother who were laid low by illness everybody would be so solicitous and would gladly become a servant or helper. Everyone would want to be bold and fearless; nobody would flee but everyone would come running. . . . If you wish to serve Christ and to wait on him, very well, you have your sick neighbor close at hand. Go to him and serve him, and you will surely find Christ in him. . . . Whoever wants to serve Christ in person would surely serve his neighbor as well.[63]

Luther additionally gave advice for spiritually preparing the very sick for the time of death in case a pastor is not able to be present during a patient's passing, while exhorting families and neighbors to err in calling for pastors too early rather than too late in such cases. Regardless, the pastor would hear one's confession of faith, hear repentance from sin declared, and also provide communion to the dying, but each friend and neighbor must also supply help if the pastor cannot be present.[64] Citing Matthew 25:41–46 ("I was . . . sick . . . and you did not visit me"), Luther added, "We are bound to each other in such a way that no one may forsake the other in his distress but is obliged to assist and help him as he himself would like to be helped."[65] All Christians, to some degree and in particular situations, especially of emergencies, should perform the ongoing work of pastoral care for and to one another, acting both as nurses for the physical ailments and priests for the connectedly spiritual needs of one another.

Just as he related the ordination of all Christians to their baptisms, so Luther demonstrated that baptism is a believer's dying in solidarity with Christ. The work of pastoral care to one another requires risk to one's own health: "No neighbor," Luther wrote, "can live alongside another without risk to his safety, property, wife or child. . . . [But] anyone who does not do that for his neighbor, but forsakes and leaves him to his misfortune, becomes a murderer in the sight of God."[66] Luther reminded all Christians of the reality of their own mortality, saying: "Death is death no matter how it occurs. . . . [So] let him who has a strong faith wait for his death."[67] Thus all people are ordained to this work of the church in serving one another through the external sign of dying to sin and being resurrected with Christ in the waters of baptism, a sacrament that Christians live out until their bodily deaths. "Therefore," Luther concluded elsewhere, "the life of

63. Luther, "Whether One May Flee from a Deadly Plague," LW 43:130–31.
64. LW 43:134–35.
65. LW 43:122.
66. LW 43:126.
67. LW 43:124.

a Christian, from baptism to the grave, is nothing else than the beginning of a blessed death."[68]

The ministry of prayer, by neighbors and especially by pastors and "elders" of the church, remained integral to Luther's philosophy of pastoral care and his interpretation of James 5. Ultimately, however, Luther did not completely dismiss the ceremony of unction, even last rites, in conjunction with such pastoral work. In 1539, a new church order for Brandenburg, mostly written by Jacob Stratner, court preacher in Berlin, was presented to Luther, Melanchthon, and Justus Jonas for comment (or approval). The order detailed instructions for how pastors were to train parishioners for bedside ministry, even making provisions for training laypeople to recite the words of institution to the sick and dying, yet without the use of consecrated eucharistic elements, so that the infirm might partake of God's Word by faith and participate in the Supper spiritually.[69] Notably, however, the 1540 Brandenburg Church Ordinance revived the use of extreme unction as last rites for the dying. Luther warranted the use of extreme unction in the ordinance with the condition that the gospel must also be proclaimed, that no one was to refer to it as a "sacrament," and that the ritual be done "without superstition."[70] The word of promise and the prayers of faith for the sick and dying remained primary to pastoral care for the Wittenberg theologian.

It is, nevertheless, both interesting and informative that Luther did not necessarily decry the ritual use of oil for the sick and dying among his evangelical pastors, even when, years earlier, the Reformer had rejected extreme unction as a sacrament and its theological justification as "folly." It is also fascinating that Luther, who had once famously referred to the Epistle of James as a "book of straw"[71] and had placed it last, after Revelation, in his German New Testament, located the proper ministry to the sick in its fifth chapter.

A final story from Luther's Table Talk is revealing. In the spring of 1543, near the end of his life, Luther was asked whether one person could secure salvation for another. Perhaps surprisingly, Luther was recorded as responding:

By all means! In fact, the faith of one person may obtain another's whole conversion. Accordingly it's said that Paul was converted and saved by Stephen's

68. LW 35:31; WA 2:728.27–29. See also Lohse, *Martin Luther's Theology*, 129.
69. See Rittgers, *Reformation of Suffering*, 170–71.
70. See WA Br 8, no. 3420, 623.38–57; Denis R. Janz, "Extreme Unction," in *Westminster Handbook to Martin Luther*, 54.
71. Luther made this comment only once, in his 1522 "Preface to the New Testament," LW 35:362. But Luther also is recorded in mid-1542 as saying: "We should throw the Epistle of James out of this school [i.e., the university in Wittenberg], for it doesn't amount to much. It contains not a syllable about Christ." See Luther, Table Talk, LW 54:424, no. 5443.

prayer. However, Paul wasn't accepted on account of Stephen's faith, but Stephen's faith obtained faith for Paul from God and by this faith he was saved in God's sight. Many people have been preserved by prayer, as we prayed Philip [Melanchthon] back to life. Ah, prayer accomplishes much.

. . . It's impossible that God shouldn't hear a prayer of faith. Whether he always does is another matter. God doesn't give according to the prescribed measure, but he presses it down and shakes it together, as he said [cf. Luke 6:38].

. . . So James said well, "Pray for one another," etc., for "the prayer of a righteous man has great power in its effects" [cf. 5:16]. This is one of the best verses in that epistle. Prayer is a powerful thing, if only one believes in it, for God has attached and bound himself to it [by his promises].[72]

Luther, then, did not reject the priestly ministry to the sick and dying altogether, even in its ritual use of unction, nor did the Reformer completely disregard the Epistle of James, which the church had used to justify the ceremony as a sacrament. Instead, from the words of his 1520 *Babylonian Captivity* at the outset of the Reformation to a letter to a pastor regarding visiting the sick in 1546—the final year of Luther's life—the Reformer consistently exhibited a deep concern for those who suffered; for the work of the pastor, "elders," and laity in ministering to the sick; and for James's emphasis on the efficacy of prayer as the foundation of pastoral care. Through his stormy repudiation of last rites as a sacrament, Luther provided the silver lining in developing a Protestant ministry to the sick and dying: "For what could faith not do?"[73]

Subsequent Protestant Rejections of Extreme Unction as a Sacrament

Although the Lutheran tradition demonstrated some openness to extreme unction as a part of pastoral care to the sick, the Reformed tradition was generally blunter in its rejection of the rite. One document of the early reforms in Zurich in June 1524 recorded the efforts to remove relics and organs from the area churches and reported:

The magistrates at Zürich ordered that there should be no more playing of organs in the city and in the churches; no ringing for the dead, and for and against the weather; no more blessing of palms, salt, water, and candles; and no more bringing to any one of the last baptism or extreme unction; but that

72. Luther, Table Talk, LW 54:453–54, no. 5565.
73. LW 36:121.

all such superstitions should cease and be clean put away, inasmuch as they are all at variance with the clear word of God.[74]

Extreme unction fared no better in Geneva under Calvin's reforms a generation later. Calvin attacked the logic of attributing the anointing found in James as an ongoing sacrament of and for the church, referring to it as a haphazard selection from miracles described in the New Testament: "Why not let them lie upon dead men, since Paul raised a dead child by lying upon him? Why is not clay made of spittle and dust a sacrament?"[75] Therefore Calvin rejected extreme unction, calling it instead a "fictitious sacrament."

Calvin defined a sacrament as a ceremony appointed by God with an accompanying divine promise. The age of apostolic healing, he maintained, had passed. Physical healing through the divine work of the first preaching of the gospel served as an analogy for the healing from iniquity that one receives through the gospel. This apostolic healing, by definition, then was arguably once a sacrament for the early church but, after the first two centuries, no longer serves its analogical purpose as the spiritual work of God. Such divine work may now be apprehended more directly. Since "the gift of healing was temporary," the Genevan Reformer contended, "the sign of it ought not to be deemed perpetual."[76]

This is not to say that Calvin eschewed the notion of divine healing in his own day: "The Lord is indeed present with his people in every age; and he heals their weaknesses as often as necessary no less than of old; still he does not put forth these manifest powers, nor dispense miracles through the apostles' hands. For that was a temporary gift, and also quickly perished partly on account of men's ungratefulness."[77]

But Calvin argued still further against a Romanist interpretation of James 5 as instituting a sacrament to be dispensed by the priest to the dying, finding this idea to be a complete misinterpretation of the epistle's witness. The use of oil was to demonstrate that it was not the presbyter but the Holy Spirit who effected the healing, and only those who had been given the gift of healing in that day were to carry out God's work in this matter, not contemporary clerics, whom Calvin called "butchers who are more able to slay and hack than to heal."[78] Additionally, Calvin pointed out that James admonished these

74. Document no. 203, "The Putting Down of Relics and Organs, June 1524," in *Documents Illustrative of the Continental Reformation*, ed. B. J. Kidd (Oxford: Clarendon, 1961), 442–43.
    75. Calvin, *Inst.* 4.19.19; LCC 21:1467.
    76. Calvin, *Commentaries on the Epistle of James*, on 5:14; *Calvin's Commentaries* (Edinburgh: Calvin Translation Society; Grand Rapids: Baker, 1999), 22:356.
    77. Calvin, *Inst.* 4.19.19; LCC 21:1467.
    78. Calvin, *Inst.* 4.19.20.

elders to pray for the sick in order that they might be healed, but the priests of his day "smear with their grease not the sick but half-dead corpses when they are already drawing their last breath, or (as they say), *in extremis*."[79] The oil, then, is not to be seen as a kind of medicine, consecrated by the bishop, "warmed with much breathing, mustered over with long incantations, and saluted with nine kneelings."[80] It was, much more straightforwardly, a common oil used to accompany the faithful prayers of multiple church leaders,[81] by which one may receive both physical restoration and also release from the guilt of sin, which potentially prompted the illness.[82]

Like Luther and his magisterial contemporaries, leading theologians of the nascent and second-generation Anabaptist movement also repudiated last rites as a church sacrament, but their reasoning did not necessarily follow that of their magisterial cousins. One articulate theologian of the first generation of the Anabaptists, Balthasar Hubmaier, as a former Catholic scholar and priest, maintained a greater appreciation for traditional rituals than many of his Anabaptist contemporaries. Hubmaier wrote *A Brief Apologia* while in exile in Nikolsburg in an effort publicly to clarify his theological convictions; in this text he addressed an array of Reformation doctrines against both Catholic and magisterial Protestant opponents. As a radical Reformer, Hubmaier, not surprisingly, called extreme unction "not only a mockery, yea also an idolatry, for to it is ascribed forgiveness for sins."[83] But even passing Luther in proposing a positive replacement for the ceremony, Hubmaier found a continuing use not only for the pastoral prayers of the elders around the bedside but also even for at least the figurative and spiritual use of the oil in a deathbed rite. The Reformer of Waldshut wrote: "However, the spiritual anointing which Christ announced to us, Luke 10:34 and also James 5:14, I esteem highly and am quite satisfied to have it called the last baptism."[84] For Hubmaier, a believer should anticipate receiving three baptisms: the spiritual baptism of conversion, the water baptism of confession of faith and initiation

---

79. Calvin, *Inst.* 4.19.21.

80. Ibid.

81. Calvin's commentary on James 5:14 records the Reformer as underscoring that "pastors were not alone called presbyters or elders, but also those who were chosen from the people to be as it were censors to protect discipline. For every church had, as it were, its own senate, chosen from men of weight and of proved integrity." *Commentaries on the Epistle of James*, 356.

82. For further development of Calvin's view of healing and its association with sin, see *Commentaries on the Epistle of James*, 357–59; Pavel Hejzlar, "John Calvin and the Cessation of Miraculous Healing," *Communio Viatorum* 49, no. 1 (2007): 31–77.

83. Balthasar Hubmaier, "A Brief Apologia," here via Pipkin and Yoder, *Balthasar Hubmaier*, 300.

84. Ibid., 301.

into the church, and the third baptism, or baptism of blood, which culminates in martyrdom or one's deathbed,

> for which we are indeed in need of the spiritual wine and oil which the Samaritan poured into the wounds of the injured man, Luke 10:34. . . . This is indeed precisely the third baptism or last baptism in which people should indeed be anointed with the oil of the holy and comforting gospel (in order that we may be meek and ready to suffer). Thus the illness is lightened for us, and we receive forgiveness of sins, James 5:14ff. But those whom James calls priests, whom the sick person should have to minister over himself, Christ calls servants, that is, preachers and pastors, who attend to the sick sinner with the Word of God.[85]

For Hubmaier, the "sacrament" of baptism was the pledge of love and confession of faith in Christ and to the church. Interestingly, then, though he rejected last rites as a separate sacrament of the church, Hubmaier recategorized it as one of three forms (or stages) of the sacrament of baptism. One's life of suffering and dying with Christ, most highly exemplified in martyrdom, served as the highest level of such a confession, a position that did not eliminate the rite but only reframed unction as a "third baptism," or "baptism of blood." Suffering with Christ in death, especially martyrdom, served as the ultimate experience of solidarity with Christ, one initially represented in being symbolically buried and raised in the waters.[86]

The following year, in May of 1527, Michael Sattler, who became a prominent early Anabaptist martyr, was placed on trial in Rottenburg am Neckar by Archduke Ferdinand of Austria. Among the charges leveled against him and his radical companions was that "they have rejected the sacrament of unction."[87] To this charge, Sattler retorted: "We have not rejected oil, for it is a creature of God. What God has made is good and not to be rejected. But what pope, bishop, monks, and priests have wanted to do to improve on it, this we think nothing of. For the pope has never made anything good. What the Epistle of James speaks of is not the pope's oil."[88] For this sentiment, along with eight other charges, Sattler was tortured and burned. Later Anabaptists, like Menno Simons, rejected "holy oil" along with the other four sacraments generally abnegated by Protestants.[89] It was not until the late nineteenth cen-

85. Ibid.
86. Brewer, A Pledge of Love, 130–31.
87. See Michael Sattler, The Legacy of Michael Sattler, trans. and ed. John H. Yoder (Scottdale, PA: Herald Press, 1973), 70.
88. Ibid., 71.
89. Menno Simons, "Why I Do Not Cease Teaching and Writing," in The Complete Writings of Menno Simons, 301.

tury that Mennonites recovered a rite for anointing the sick with oil for the purpose of healing.[90]

Finally, the first edition of the Book of Common Prayer showed, for the English Reformation, Cranmer's original instinct to retain not only an office for the Visitation of the Sick but also unction to be dispensed by the priest as an outward anointing and combined with prayers for the inward anointing of the Holy Ghost. Although no longer presenting unction for "last rites," Cranmer's 1549 prayer book demonstrates the ongoing use of oil in the now Protestant Church of England. The liturgy begins with the recitation of Psalm 143 ("Heare my prayer. . . . And entre not into judgemente with thy servaunt"), the Lord's Prayer, and a priestly exhortation to the sick person to bear up under the circumstances of the illness as divine testing of one's patience or a testing of one's faith. Next, the priest prompts prayers of confession of and for the sick person so that the individual's life might be amended or strengthened and be prepared for ultimate judgment.[91] Only after this thorough exhortation and confession does the office move to anointing. Here the rubric instructs: "If the sicke person desire to be annoynted, then shal the priest annoynte him upon the forehead or breast only, making the signe of the cross."[92] Absent is any instruction for the laying on of hands. Finally, if the visitation falls on a day on which the Eucharist is observed by the congregation, the priest is instructed to reserve a portion of the elements to be delivered to the sick. If the sick person is unable to partake of the elements due to severe illness, the rubric affirms that the person "doth eat and drink spiritually."[93] While technically not last rites and seemingly a more Protestant pastoral visitation and prayer for healing, the service, observes Linda Malia, seems "on the whole . . . hardly an encouraging one."[94] Indeed, Cranmer's introduction to the office might belie its purpose of healing or simply reflect a lingering medieval tradition of *ars moriendi* by preparing for the inevitable in all of life: the priest is instructed to establish that the sick "may be always in a readiness to dye whensoever it shall please almighty God to call them."[95] In the 1552 prayer book, now consistent with other Protestant traditions, anointing is altogether omitted in the healing office, and the elements of

---

90. See Mark R. Wenger, "The Origins and Development of Anointing among Nineteenth-Century Mennonites," *Mennonite Quarterly Review* 79 (January 2005): 19–50.

91. See *First English Prayer Book*, 69–72; Linda M. Malia, *Healing Touch and Saving Word: Sacraments of Healing, Instruments of Grace* (Eugene, OR: Pickwick, 2013), 84–89.

92. Here cited in Malia, *Healing Touch and Saving Word*, 87.

93. Gibson, *First and Second Prayer-Books of King Edward VI*, 268.

94. Malia, *Healing Touch and Saving Word*, 87.

95. Originally cited from the 1549 BCP: "Visitation of the Sick"; here via Malia, *Healing Touch and Saving Word*, 87.

the Eucharist were to be consecrated in the recipient's presence and not at a previous congregational service.[96]

Recovery of Protestant Pastoral Care to the Sick and Dying

New pastors periodically go to the hospital or deathbed to visit sick and dying parishioners and are not only anxious but also uncertain what to do. Reading a psalm, following the words of a prayer book, and saying a prayer may be the most they feel equipped to do and say. Following the complete rejection of unction as a sacrament, many Protestant circles either provide no specific instructions on how to be of spiritual assistance to the sick, or each tradition, church, or clergyman is left to "reinvent the wheel" in developing a particular version of pastoral care.

Even if the Protestant tradition manifested an aversion to all ceremonies that might be deemed extrabiblical and superstitious, Protestant pastors and laypeople for centuries have continued with commitment to the good work of visiting the sick and dying. Various denominations have even provided services, liturgies, and prayers for the sick. Such orders are undoubtedly helpful and in keeping with a simple version of the Protestant interpretation of the injunction in James 5: "Are any among you sick? They should call for the elders of the church and have them pray over them," and so forth. Additionally, the Protestant reframing of the definition of "sacrament" has brought clarity to the rites instituted by Christ for his church and militated against fallacious and illusory beliefs regarding elements and services rendered to naive laypeople. James 5 does not describe a service of last rites as a transitional sacrament of preparing for death but a "priestly act" of Christian leaders for a fellow Christian and a powerful work of God demonstrated through the effectiveness of their faithful prayer.

Nevertheless, the rite of anointing with oil, though not "sacramental," may serve as a synecdoche for all Protestant sacramental revisionism of the sixteenth century. In this case, because of the development of medieval superstition regarding the use of a physical element, Protestants tended to diminish or, more often, omit the use of material. At the time, such a move seemed a reasonable corrective for believers to depend exclusively on the promise of God as found in Scripture. Centuries later, some Protestants are recognizing what has been lost in perhaps overcorrecting this rite. While anointing is rightly a recessive and symbolic work representing the healing power of the

---

96. White, *Sacraments*, 126.

Holy Spirit through the prayers of the elders, it is nevertheless an important complementary element that has now been excluded. Provided that the recipient understands the oil as accompanying the spiritual work of prayer by the elders and, more importantly, the imperceptible work of God in the life of the ailing person—then the use of oil is not only a tangible reminder of this divine work but also one that is biblically consistent: "Pray over them, anointing them with oil in the name of the Lord" (James 5:14).

Luther's cautious but more mature moderation on this issue may serve as a guide for contemporary Protestants: unction might appropriately be used if preceded by the pastor's teaching the congregation that it represents an important work of faith and that it is not a ritual performed with superstition or with a "magical" element. More importantly, the oil is used in association with the promise of God's Word and the prayers of the faithful church leader(s). Moreover, the Anabaptist Balthasar Hubmaier might also be of assistance to contemporary Protestants. In more liturgical churches that have reintroduced the use of oil in conjunction with the initiatory sacrament of baptism, the unction of healing, when encompassed by theologically rich words of comfort and prayer, might be used to echo the promise of God's salvific gift and as a reassuring sign to accompany the divine Word in times of weakness and before death. The Protestant objection to the oil's "magical" qualities may still remain intact while, at the same time, the oil is used as part and parcel of the faithful prayers that beseech God's intervention.

Contemporary Protestants, both high and low church, historically magisterial and free church, need not reinvent the simplicity of this pastoral visit by overcomplicating pastoral care with rigid and pretentious liturgies. Nor should they redesign that beautiful lucidity of James's directive: pray for and anoint the sick. The spiritual potency of mature believers visiting others in their time of weakness, praying over and anointing them, cannot be overestimated. Such anointing, when combined with the strong injunction of the early Protestant Reformers' instructions for and personal examples of pastoral care, emulates the biblical picture of spiritual care for the sick.

6

Baptism

The "Untouched and Untainted" Sacrament

Blessed be God and the Father of our Lord Jesus Christ, who according to the riches of his mercy has preserved in his church this sacrament at least, untouched and untainted by the ordinances of men, . . . and has not permitted it to be oppressed by the filthy and godless monsters of greed and superstition.

Martin Luther

Deo gratias. The truth must once again come to light. If baptism is truly a sign of commitment through the sign of water, then one must have expressed the commitment before the sign is attached to him.

Balthasar Hubmaier

BAPTISM HAS SERVED AS A RITE OF INITIATION into the Christian faith and into its community through the sign of water since the first century. Because baptism and the Lord's Supper are the only two ordinances Luther eventually determined to retain as "sacraments," they are treated here in the final chapters of the book. Luther wrote more on baptism than on any other church practice next to the Eucharist. Even though he saw baptism as the only "unspoiled and unspotted sacrament," a ceremony not distorted by the church for the purpose of greed or perverted by false delusions, the Reformer still had much to say to help Protestants restore and enhance its theology and practice.

Baptism in the Early Church

Although baptism was administered by the first apostles in the earliest period of Christianity, with Jewish roots in cleansing rituals and the immediate precedent of a sign of repentance as performed by John the Baptist in anticipation of the coming of the Messiah, the Christian rite of initiation underwent much development in the first centuries of Christianity, a process that has continued through the last two millennia. An ordinance that, according to the apostle Paul, was intended to unite Christians ("one Lord, one faith, one baptism," Eph. 4:5), baptism has proved more often to divide them theologically. The New Testament itself has given a multidimensional significance to baptism as each Christian's self-identification with the death, burial, and resurrection of Christ (Rom. 6:3–5); as one's incorporation into the body (1 Cor. 12:13; Gal. 3:27–28); as an act of repentance (Acts 2:38; 22:16); as a prerequisite for entrance into the kingdom of God (John 3:5; Titus 3:5); as the proper act immediately following confession of belief (Acts 8:36–38); as part of the Christian commission to make disciples (Matt. 28:19); and as an ordinance associated with or as a means of salvific grace (Mark 16:16; Titus 3:4–5).

The earliest Christians baptized in natural bodies of water through immersion (the Greek word βαπτίζω [baptizō] literally means to "dip" or to "immerse") in the name of the Trinity (Matt. 28:19) or Christ (Acts 2:38; 10:48; 19:5), but by the late first to early second century, Christian documents evince a malleability in its form given the geographic circumstance: "Baptize 'in the name of the Father and of the Son and of the Holy Spirit' in running water. But if you have no running water, then baptize in some other water; and if you are not able to baptize in cold water, then do so in warm. But if you have neither, then pour water on the head three times 'in the name of the Father and Son and Holy Spirit.'"[1] The baptism of adult converts appears to have been the normative practice until sometime in the fourth century.[2]

By the second century, the church developed prerequisites for the rite and an understanding that, following appropriate instruction, baptism would follow as a means of grace. Justin Martyr, for instance, wrote (ca. 155) that

> those who are persuaded and believe that the things we teach and say are true, and promise that they can live accordingly, are instructed to pray and beseech God with fasting for the remission of their past sins, while we pray and fast along with them. Then they are brought by us where there is water, and are

1. *Didache*; here via Holmes, *Apostolic Fathers*, 153.
2. Everett Ferguson, *Baptism in the Early Church: History, Theology, and Liturgy in the First Five Centuries* (Grand Rapids: Eerdmans, 2009), 631–32.

reborn by the same manner by which we ourselves were reborn, for they are then washed in the water in the name of God the Father and Master of all, and of our Saviour Jesus Christ, and of the Holy Spirit. . . . This washing is called illumination, since those who learn these things are illumined within.[3]

At the beginning of the third century, Clement of Alexandria and Tertullian both described the power of baptism in initiating a neophyte in the faith. Like Justin Martyr, Clement affirmed, "This is what happens with us, whose model the Lord made himself. When we are baptized, we are enlightened; being enlightened, we become adopted sons; becoming adopted sons, we are made perfect; and becoming perfect, we are made divine."[4] The ceremony, for Clement, was a "free gift," "enlightenment," a means to perfection, and a cleansing. For his part, Tertullian declared that when God's name is invoked, the Spirit descends and sanctifies the waters, and "thus sanctified they absorb the power of sanctifying."[5] Inasmuch as Tertullian's words appear to describe the waters as holding divine power objectively, the Latin father also eschewed what appears to have been a new trend of baptizing infants: "It follows that deferment of baptism is more profitable, in accordance with each person's character and attitude, and even age: and especially so as regards children."[6] Here it should be noted that Tertullian was not questioning the validity of paedobaptism but merely the wisdom of its timing. Instead, Tertullian viewed baptism as a once-in-a-lifetime ritual that washed away accumulated sins. It would be superfluous and even foolish, then, to baptize those who had not yet committed volitional sins but would undoubtedly still do so as they grew into adulthood. Thus Tertullian insisted that, as a strategy for sin management, baptism be delayed until the young could be taught the substance of the faith.[7]

Tertullian also detailed certain features the church added to the original baptismal rite as practiced in North Africa: "When on the point of coming to the water we then and there, as also somewhat earlier in church under the bishop's control, affirm that we renounce the devil and his pomp and his

3. Justin Martyr, *First Apology* 61, 65; here via Edward Rochie Hardy, trans., in LCC 1:282, 285.

4. Clement of Alexandria, *The Teacher* 1.4.26; here via E. C. Whitaker and Maxwell E. Johnson, eds., *Documents of the Baptismal Liturgy*, 3rd ed. (Collegeville, MN: Liturgical Press, 2003), 247.

5. Tertullian, *Baptism*; here trans. Ernest Evans, *Tertullian's Homily on Baptism* (London: SPCK, 1964), 11.

6. Tertullian, *Baptism* 18; here via Whitaker and Johnson, *Documents of the Baptismal Liturgy*, 10; cf. Ernest Evans, ed., *Tertullian's Homily on Baptism*, 39.

7. See Brian C. Brewer, "'To Defer and Not to Hasten': The Anabaptist and Baptist Appropriations of Tertullian's Baptismal Theology." *Harvard Theological Review* 106 (July 2013): 287–308.

angels. After this we are thrice immersed, while we answer interrogations rather more extensive than our Lord has prescribed in the gospel."[8] Following the baptisms, the baptizants are given a compound of milk and honey and are to abstain from bathing for a week following baptism. Although he noted the bishop's administration of the rite, the bishop's presence was only ideal; Tertullian recorded that, with episcopal sanction, a presbyter or deacon might preside. In the case of great need, any confessing male would be able to baptize, but women should be prohibited from doing so regardless.[9] However, in the first several centuries, female deacons were known for assisting with female baptizants, especially in communities where candidates were baptized without clothes.[10]

Counter to Tertullian's desires but affirming his observation of his time, the third-century document *Apostolic Tradition of Hippolytus* reports the church's acceptance of the baptism of children but also provides liturgies that presume the candidate to be of an age capable of responding and confessing appropriately. It also reveals that catechesis then extended to three years, with the church observing how candidates preserved their good conduct during that period of preparation. Although Cyprian, the bishop of Carthage (d. 258), was a proponent of paedobaptism,[11] and Origen (d. 254) even argued that the apostles themselves administered infant baptism,[12] believer's baptism must have still been practiced regularly alongside infant baptism through the fourth century, as evidenced by the fact that Basil, Gregory of Nyssa, Gregory of Nazianzus, John Chrysostom, Ephraem the Syrian, Jerome, Rufinus, and Augustine all were not baptized until at least adolescence. Scholars presume, then, that until the fifth century, paedobaptism was not the general pattern but only administered as a spiritual safeguard against infant mortality.[13] Writing on the question of whether to baptize infants, Gregory of Nazianzus (d. 390) acknowledged: "Certainly if danger threatens. For it is better to be sanctified unconsciously than to depart from this life unsealed and uninitiated."[14]

---

8. Tertullian, *The Crown* 3; ANF 3:94; also in Johnson, *Sacraments and Worship*, 112.

9. Tertullian, *Baptism* 17; ANF 3:677.

10. See, e.g., DS 146–47.

11. Cyprian, *Epistles* 58; here via ANF 5:353–54.

12. Origen, *Romans Commentary* 5:9; see Origen, *Commentarii in Epistulam ad Romanos*, ed. Theresia Heither (Freiburg im Breisgau: Herder, 1992), 2:290–91.

13. See Ferguson, *Baptism in the Early Church*, 379; and Everett Ferguson et al., eds., *Encyclopedia of Early Christianity* (New York: Garland, 1990), 133.

14. Gregory of Nazianzus; here via Alec Gilmore, *Christian Baptism: A Fresh Attempt to Understand the Rite in Terms of Scripture, History, and Theology* (London: Lutterworth, 1959), 210.

Augustine's Explication of Baptism

At the close of the late Roman Empire and the advent of the early medieval period, Augustine, bishop of Hippo (d. 430), helped solidify much of the disparate baptismal theologies of previous fathers. Not only did he give the church a working definition of "sacrament," which became a succinct refrain in the medieval church as *invisibilis gratiae visibilis forma* ("the visible form of invisible grace");[15] Augustine also provided a developed doctrine of original sin, which in turn gave theological rationale for the then-already-established practice of infant baptism. Augustine's importance in shaping the theology of baptism for Christianity, particularly in the West, can hardly be overstated.

Augustine argued that, following the fall of humanity, each person is born tainted by sin, a deformity and brokenness that is present in the soul at birth. Infants then appear innocent only because of the "fragility of their frame" but have otherwise inherited the sins of their parents just as they inherited their physical characteristics. In his *Confessions*, Augustine prayed: "For before Thee none is free from sin, not even the infant which has lived but a day upon earth."[16] Consequently, young children who are unbaptized would still die already "poisoned by the serpent's bite" just as unbaptized adults who are condemned for their own accumulated sins.[17] Baptism serves as the amelioration of the sinful condition for both young and old and becomes obligatory for all Christians. It is not surprising that infant baptism became the normative practice by the end of the fifth century. As parents began to have their children baptized often immediately after birth, the practice of awaiting the Easter vigil for the rite, along with most forms of the catechumenate, became inconsequential, and all forms of prebaptismal teaching ultimately dissipated.[18] Although the Eastern church maintained immersion, with the hegemony of paedobaptism, affusion (i.e., pouring water on the head of the baptizant) was deemed more practical and became the common mode of baptism in the West.

15. Augustine wrote: "The signs of divine things are, it is true, things visible, but . . . invisible things themselves are also honored in them." *Catechizing the Uninstructed* 26.50.

16. Augustine, *Confessions* 1.7.11; NPNF[1] 1:48.

17. Augustine, *Guilt and Remission of Sins* 1.32.61; NPNF[1] 5:39.

18. A document written by John the Deacon of Rome to Senarius in ca. 500 described infants as still being "scrutinized" before the Pascha and how catechesis and exorcisms apparently continued for a time. Clarifying how this could still be, John wrote: "I must say plainly and at once, in case I seem to have overlooked the point, that all these things are done even to infants, who by reason of their youth understand nothing. And by this you may know that when they are presented by their parents or others, it is necessary that their salvation should come through other people's profession, since their damnation came by another's fault." Hence baptism is the antidote to original sin, and proxy faith is appropriate because of the proxy fall through Adam. See Johnson, *Rites of Christian Initiation*, 166–67.

For Augustine, a real, effectual nature of divine grace was conveyed in the sacrament, combined with its visible, exterior component. Christ provided the sacraments by first serving as the sacrament of the church through the incarnation. In response, the faithful come to God through the sacrament of the church. Irrespective of the spiritual condition of the administrator, baptism served as the rite that incorporated the believer into the church, and its effectiveness cannot be denied. Nevertheless, Augustine also stressed that grace was not conveyed mechanically through the rite, and he correspondingly underscored the importance of both faith and the Word in establishing baptism's effectiveness. "If anyone, receiving it at the hands of a misguided man, yet does not receive the perversity of the minister, but only the holiness of the mystery, being closely bound to the unity of the Church in good faith and hope and charity, he receives remission of his sins . . . by the sacraments of the gospel flowing from a heavenly source."[19] Regarding the Word-and-sign relationship, for example, Augustine wrote: "The Word comes to the element; and so there is a sacrament, that is, a sort of visible word."[20] Baptism, like every sacrament for Augustine, then had two components: the physical, meaning the sign (*signum*), and the invisible reality (*res*), that which is signified and proclaimed. In baptism, the element of water signifies the inward reality of the word of justification (which also designates one's incorporation into the church). The sign is inextricably linked to the word in baptism such that

> the cleansing, therefore, would on no account be attributed to the fleeting and perishable element, were it not for that which is added, "by the word" [Eph. 5:26]. This word of faith possesses such power in the Church of God, that through the one who believes, presents, blesses and baptizes, [the word] cleanses even a tiny infant, although itself unable as yet with the heart to believe unto righteousness, and to make confession with the mouth unto salvation. All this is done through the word, whereof the Lord said: "Now you are clean through the word that I have spoken to you" [cf. John 15:3 KJV].[21]

Thus Augustine saw salvation as exclusively possessed in and through the church, based not simply on the sacrament of baptism itself nor on personal ethics but instead on the unity of the church through faith and love, promised through God's Word in Scripture and the sacraments, of which the

19. Augustine, *Baptism* 4.12.19; NPNF[1] 4:455. Both this notion and the association of the sacrament with the Word are theological themes from which Luther drew.
20. Augustine, *Tractates in the Gospel of John* 80.3; NPNF[1] 7:344.
21. Augustine, NPNF[1] 7:345; CCSL 36:529.

latter, Peter Leithart affirms, are "congruent with the fulfillment of what is promised."[22]

Baptism in the Middle Ages

By the sixth century, Emperor Justinian made baptism required of all citizens by the legal code Corpus Juris Civilis. Rebaptism, an issue especially among Donatists in the fourth century, was also prohibited as a capital offense. Infant baptism became normative. Although the Roman rite never settled on a uniform pattern throughout Europe during the Middle Ages,[23] many of the medieval theological interpretations of baptism were based on at least a caricature of Augustine's foundational thoughts. Often suppressing the bishop of Hippo's counterbalancing emphases of faith and the Word conveyed in the baptism, the sacrament instead was a conduit of grace objectively, ex opere operato, regardless of the spiritual condition of either the officiant or the baptizant. What had once been years of catechetical preparation for baptismal candidates had now been truncated to a series of questions asked of the parents, sponsors, or godparents on behalf of the infant during the rite.[24]

Although it was carried out in various ways through regions of Western Europe, the basic service for baptism included the preparation of the candidate, the blessing of the font, and the baptismal order itself. The child and sponsors would be met at the church doors, where the priest would say a series of prayers, exorcisms, and blessings over the child—often including a ritual of the priest spitting into his own hand and then touching the ears and nose of the child in order to make the child more open and responsive to the Word.[25] Upon entering the sanctuary, the priest would prepare the baptismal waters by saying a series of prayers over the font, invoking the name of the Trinity and mixing oil into the water. At the time of the actual baptism itself, the godparents would be called upon to renounce the devil, and all those gathered would affirm the creed. The priest would then dip the child's head three times into the waters of the font, and, upon completion, the infant would be wrapped in a white robe, anointed with chrism, and presented with a candle.

22. Peter J. Leithart, "Augustine's Visible Words," *First Things*, February 5, 2011, https://www.firstthings.com/blogs/leithart/2011/02/visible-words.

23. On this point, James F. White observed that liturgical centralization would not be feasible until the invention of the printing press. See White, *A Brief History of Christian Worship* (Nashville: Abingdon, 1993), 78–79.

24. Johnson, *Rites of Christian Initiation*, 230.

25. See Susan C. Karant-Nunn, *The Reformation of Ritual: An Interpretation of Early Modern Germany* (New York: Routledge, 1997), 48.

As a required step for attaining salvation, the baptism of young children placed them in an enviable position. As Mark Tranvik observes, "In earthly life no person approached the lofty status of a baptized infant. Cleansed from the stain of Original Sin and yet free from the guilt of actual sin, a newly baptized infant hovered near the portals of heaven."[26]

The objective power of baptism was conveyed by God through the Word and by the work of Christ. By the twelfth and thirteenth centuries, Scholastic theologians articulated the theological substance, symbolism, and power of baptism at great length. Hugh of Saint Victor (d. 1142) described baptism as "water sanctified by God's word for the blotting out of sins."[27] Though water could not wash spiritually on its own, the use of water for this holy purpose could. Many Scholastic thinkers discussed the form and matter of baptism as dual themes. Aquinas explained that the matter of the sacrament was water while the form was the trinitarian formula used by the priest. The dual consequences of baptism were that baptizants had a sacramental character imprinted on their souls that, second, strengthened them to rise above their human conditions to live Christlike lives in faith, hope, and love. However, Aquinas also stressed (1) the ongoing responsibility of the Christian henceforth to strive to live a holy life; (2) that while baptism empowered, it also required human cooperation; and (3) that baptism was only effective through the faith of an adult baptizant or of the parents on behalf of their baptized child.[28] Both original and actual sins could not be forgiven, Aquinas argued, without faith in the power of Christ's passion.

Although these ideas remained holy mysteries and items of nuance and debate among medieval Scholastic theologians—whether the sacraments contained and conferred saving grace or whether they only provided an assisting grace for humans to overcome their sinful ways—most laypeople appropriated the objective work of baptism superstitiously as if the water had an almost magical character. Regardless, they also understood that baptism's effect was foundational and essential to salvation but was not entirely sufficient. The souls of the baptized were placed on the long road to salvation by incorporating them into the saving church. After the rite, as a person matured in years, "the force of baptism [was] effectively exhausted in the initial entry

26. Mark D. Tranvik, "Baptism: Popular Practices," in Hillerbrand, *Oxford Encyclopedia of the Reformation*, 1:115.

27. Hugh of Saint Victor, *Sacr.* 2.6.2; PL 176:443. See also Paul Rorem, *Hugh of Saint Victor* (Oxford: Oxford University Press, 2009), 97–99.

28. Thomas Aquinas, *Summa theologica* 3:68–69; see esp. 68.8; here via James J. Cunningham et al., eds., *Summa theologiae* 57: "Baptism and Confirmation" (New York: Blackfriars / McGraw-Hill, 1975), 103–11.

into grace and the removal of original sin."[29] But the objective work for the infant was secured through the waters of initiation. By the late medieval period, the Council of Florence seemed to codify many of the objective effects of baptism. In its 1439 Decree for the Armenians, the council stipulated that baptism was the "doorway to the life of the Spirit," must be performed by a properly ordained priest "competent to baptize,"[30] and must utilize the appropriate trinitarian formula. Its effect was the remission of all sins and all punishments due to its guilt.[31]

At the advent of the Reformation, much of the robust rite of initiation found in the first several centuries of the church had undergone insidious changes and condensing. What was once a three-part initiation of catechumens (baptism, confirmation, and first Eucharist)—a unity still preserved in the Eastern church—had been separated into three different rites held at various stages of faith and maturity. Second, the Western church had all but discontinued both baptizing through the mode of immersion and even of dipping the head of the child in the font. In their place, the priest sprinkled an infant's head with a small portion of water from his hand. Also lost was the initial connection the church had made between baptism and the paschal season as baptizants had once demonstrated their solidarity with Christ through his death, burial, and resurrection, reenacted through baptismal waters at Holy Week.[32] Such an association with the Messiah's work, even if no longer observed by the timing of the Christian calendar, was lost in medieval Europe when the untrained peasantry would not directly associate baptism with faith in Christ's work over sin and death but instead merely as an ecclesial release from eternal punishment and as a supernatural remedy for heaven through numinous waters. During the Middle Ages, the baptism of infants became customary for the vast majority of Europeans (for every non-Jewish or non-Muslim citizen), and, as with many acts that make that subtle move to the perfunctory, many of the original, powerful intents were abbreviated, clouded, and ultimately lost to the contemporary participants.

The Early Development of Luther's Baptismal Theology

Martin Luther was born into such a world of obligatory and even mechanical practice of baptism as an antidote to original sin and damnation in the

---

29. Jonathan Trigg, "Luther on Baptism and Penance," in Kolb et al., *Oxford Handbook of Martin Luther's Theology*, 310.

30. Although three years later, the Decree of the Jacobites permitted "a layman or a woman" to baptize if a child was in imminent peril. See Kelly, *Sacraments Revisited*, 43.

31. See The Decree for the Armenians, DS 333–34; here via White, *Documents*, 164–65.

32. White, *Sacraments*, 32–33.

case of infant mortality. Luther was likely born an hour before midnight on November 10, 1543, in Eisleben and was baptized the following day at the Church of Saints Peter and Paul. Luther's parents had the boy named for the saint whose feast day Luther shared as his date of baptism, Martin of Tours.[33]

As his thoughts developed as a young monk, and he experienced his "Reformation breakthrough" regarding justification, grace, and the nature of God's passive righteousness, Luther eventually turned his gaze toward reforming the sacraments through which God's grace could be conveyed. Much of his earliest work on the sacraments, beginning with penance, pertained to their definition, proper use, and relation to divine grace. By 1519 he had already established that a sacrament was an external sign signifying a divine promise made effective through faith.

In his 1519 treatise *The Holy and Blessed Sacrament of Baptism*, Luther asserted that for those plunged into and drawn from the waters, the token of water baptism was intended to represent their death to sin and resurrection to and through the grace of God. Citing Paul's phrase, a "washing of regeneration" (Titus 3:5 KJV), Luther maintained that through the physical act, where faith is present, spiritual grace is conferred: one's iniquity is drowned and is replaced with righteousness, albeit as a first installment awaiting the complete eradication of sin at death. Luther also presented apparent paradoxes regarding baptism's effects: once raised, he argued, baptizants are then pure and sinless, yet still burdened by the fleshly bent toward subsequent sin and the ongoing need for penance. Hence, those raised are simultaneously both pure and still lamenting the sinful appetites of the flesh in this life.[34] "He can be called pure only in the sense that he has started to become pure and has a sign and covenant of this purity and is ever to become more pure."[35] Because the human body is perpetually mired in sin in the postfallen world, only death itself completes what was initiated in baptism.[36] More precisely, resurrection at the eschaton concludes what was signified through baptism, being raised to new life; while we are still in this mortal existence, baptism may only provide foretastes of that accomplished task.[37] Stated positively, baptism provides an initial grace, after which the Christian experiences increasing grace and righteousness through the remainder of life.

33. Scott H. Hendrix observes that while historians mark November 10 as Luther's date of birth, the Reformer's grave marker at the Castle Church in Wittenberg lists his days, months, and years living as suggesting his birth in December instead. See Hendrix, *Luther: Visionary Reformer*, 17–18.
34. Compare Luther's points 7 and 8 in the treatise, in LW 35:32–33.
35. LW 35:35–36.
36. Luther, *The Holy and Blessed Sacrament of Baptism*, LW 35:30–31.
37. LW 35:35.

While utilizing Augustine, Luther goes beyond the Latin father's infused righteousness by arguing that God dismisses and will ultimately destroy the sins of those who are baptized and that God makes the faithful pure not by their own virtue but by "the gracious imputation of God." Such a notion presages what Luther later called *simul justus et peccator*. Baptism thus serves both as an anthropological confession and a divine gift, both as one's own pledge to surrender one's sinful self to God through repentance, to die, and to be made clean on the last day, and also God's acceptance of the penitent believer and corresponding promise to grant grace now and in the time to come.[38]

What may be surprising to those unfamiliar with Luther's writing on this topic, but is fitting to what has just been outlined, is that Luther admonished the church, both in this treatise and in *The Babylonian Captivity* in the following year, to return to the mode of immersion for all baptisms. Since both the Greek and the Latin words for baptism mean "to plunge" and even the German word for it, *Taufe*, is derived from the German adjective *tief* (deep), not only would immersion best represent what is to be conveyed theologically through the sign of water (i.e., one's death, burial, and resurrection with Christ), but the form also more precisely matches the biblical and historic words used for the rite. Only immersion can fully represent the dying and drowning of the old sinful self and the raising and resurrecting of the new— and symbolically emulate the flood of Noah and God's wrath now through a new flood and God's mercy.[39] Since divine promises are accompanied by signs, it follows that the signs should best represent the substance of God's promise. To be clear, Luther wrote in *The Babylonian Captivity* that immersion should not be compulsory, but "it would be well to give to a thing so perfect and complete a sign that is also complete and perfect. And this is doubtless the way in which it was instituted by Christ."[40]

Although both the sign and that which is signified are essential to the making of a sacrament, Luther repeatedly underscored that the signs do not work mechanically or by virtue of the celebrant's spiritual traits. Here Luther took pains to reject both medieval theories of ex opere operato (literally, "from the work worked") and ex opere operans ("by virtue of the worker"). Baptism is effective neither because of the consecrated water nor because of the sacerdotal power conveyed through the officiant. Instead, Luther contended, "faith is of all things the most necessary." In this case, perhaps drawing on a much neglected concept of Aquinas, faith is a necessary component in Scripture in

38. LW 35:33.
39. LW 35:29–32.
40. Luther, *Babylonian Captivity*, LW 36:68.

the promise that "the one who believes and is baptized will be saved" (Mark 16:16). If Christians lean on the assurance by faith that through baptism the process of purification has begun, their baptisms can be a source of spiritual encouragement throughout life.[41] Penance, which in 1519 Luther still retained as a sacrament, was inextricably linked to baptism, since its promise of forgiveness sprang from the initial divine testament in baptism. Following this process of reconciliation, Luther stated, "You now come again into that which baptism is and does. Believe, and you have it. Doubt, and you are lost."[42] Faith, then, is the only contingency upon which this or any sacrament is maintained or is mislaid.

For Luther, then, baptism conveyed the substance of the gospel as a divine gift and not a human accomplishment. He admonished Christians: "Beware, therefore, that the external pomp of works and the deceits of man-made ordinances do not deceive you, lest you wrong the divine truth and your faith. If you would be saved, you must begin with the faith of the sacraments, without any works whatever."[43] But Luther accused Rome of burying the people beneath the "flood of their tyranny" in order to lead them astray from this good news. Rather than allowing the sacraments to nourish faith, the church had robbed Christians of their assurance. For Luther, this was the "Babylonian Captivity" with regard to baptism: the church had destroyed baptism, which is the "chief glory" of people's conscience, and in its absence had replaced it with satisfactions, contritions, good works, and anxiety.[44] Baptism cannot be annulled by sin but only by doubt, and faith is no work produced in humanity but comes only as an unmerited heavenly gift. Provided each person believes in the promise of baptism, its initiating grace, because of Christ's previous work on their behalf, is thus fulfilled in each of them. Thus Luther cites the saying: "Not the sacrament, but the faith of the sacrament, justifies," and specifically for baptism it is the faith in the word of promise to which the sign of baptism is attached.[45] Consequently, those who fall into the trap of attempting to ameliorate their sins through works of satisfaction deny and blot out the power of their baptisms.[46] Instead, Luther implores Christians to remember their baptisms and to rejoice that, because of God's ongoing promise, they remain "within the fortress of salvation."[47]

41. See LW 35:36 and LW 36:58.
42. LW 35:38.
43. LW 36:62.
44. LW 36:61.
45. LW 36:66.
46. LW 35:37.
47. LW 36:59.

In these nascent years of the Reformation, it is abundantly clear that Luther considered baptism to be a legitimate sacrament, one of two he ultimately retained. The biblical evidence and even the church's tradition regarding this rite, he thought, categorically fit Luther's own trifold sacramental framework of sign, promise, and faith.[48] Although he cited his concerns regarding what he perceived as Rome's distortions of the sacrament, nevertheless, because the church had not applied it as a human work on the disturbed consciences of adults—but at least preserved something of its purity in still performing the rite on infants, who, as a beautiful sign of divine grace, do nothing on their own but completely depend on others—baptism remained the "untouched and untainted" ordinance. Luther's rhetoric in 1519–20 was squarely addressed to those on his right in Rome; unforeseen to the Wittenberg Reformer was a subsequent attack on his baptismal theology from radicals on his left. His words used here would vex him later.

Luther on Infant Baptism and Faith

Although he was harshly critical of Rome's handling of this rite, Luther affirmed the retention of the sacramental nature and practice of infant baptism as an act of God, who "has not permitted it to be oppressed by the filthy and godless monsters of greed and superstition."[49] Yet Luther's dual insistence on the necessity of faith in order to make a sacrament effective and that faith must precede the sign led him down a serpentine path of nuanced explanations regarding the nature of faith's presence in this rite. More precisely, in discussing the effectiveness of sacraments in general, Luther continued to insist that each recipient must possess faith in order for the sacrament to be made effective in that person. To that point, in his treatment of the Supper in *The Babylonian Captivity*, Luther underscored that "nothing else than faith is needed for a worthy observance of the mass."[50] Several paragraphs later, it is clear that Luther required individuals to believe for themselves. Here Luther compared the Lord's Supper to baptism, maintaining that baptism was not a good work or an offering to God but that both rites were sacraments and testaments passively received from heaven. Then Luther, arguing against the practice of private masses, concluded rhetorically:

48. Luther repeatedly cited Augustine's formula *accedat verbum ad elementum et fit sacramentum* (the Word is added to the element and makes a sacrament). See, e.g., *Die Bekenntnisschriften der evangelisch-lutherischen Kirche* (Göttingen: Vandenhoeck & Ruprecht, 1982), 449.18; 694.29; 709.37. See also Jonathan D. Trigg, *Baptism in the Theology of Martin Luther* (Leiden: Brill, 2001), 72–73.

49. LW 36:57.

50. Here cited via Dillenberger, 275; cf. LW 36:40.

Who can receive or apply, in behalf of another, the promise of God, which demands the personal faith of each one individually? Can I give to another the promise of God, even if he does not believe? Can I believe for another, or cause another to believe? . . . But if it is true that I can [apply the Mass to another], then I can also hear and believe the gospel for another, I can be baptized for another, I can be absolved from sins for another, I can also partake of the Sacrament of the Altar for another and—to go through the list of their sacraments also—I can marry a wife for another, get ordained for another, be confirmed for another, and receive extreme unction for another![51]

Clearly, in this passage Luther intended to require each person to believe and appropriate the promise granted in any sacrament in order for its particular grace to be acquired in that person. The notion of proxy faith was then untentable.

In the following section on baptism in the same treatise, the Reformer again underscored the need for faith. The sacraments are signs of justification whose "whole efficacy, therefore, consists in faith itself, not in the doing of work. Whoever believes them, fulfills them, even if he should not do a single work. . . . For the power of baptism depends not so much on the faith or use of the one who confers it as on the faith or use of the one who receives it."[52] Yet Luther maintained infant baptism as the "untouched and untainted" sacrament. Anticipating his detractors, Luther subsequently wrote:

In contradiction to what has been said, some might cite the baptism of infants who do not comprehend the promise of God and cannot have the faith of baptism; so that therefore either faith is not necessary or else infant baptism is without effect. Here I say what all say: Infants are aided by the faith of others, namely, those who bring them for baptism. . . . So through the prayer of the believing church which presents it, a prayer to which all things are possible [Mark 9:23], the infant is changed, cleansed, and renewed by inpoured faith.[53]

A close reading of Luther's words here likely elicits questions from most any researcher. First, why is baptism apparently different from any other sacrament in that the proxy faith of others is sufficient for the rite to be exercised on an infant? Second, is it through the vicarious faith of the parents or the congregation that an infant receives what is promised? To complicate matters further, still within the same 1520 work, Luther already left early intimations of his later developed notion of infant faith. First, in the passage cited above,

51. LW 36:48.
52. LW 36:65–66 and 36:64.
53. LW 36:73.

Luther described an "inpoured," or infused, faith given through baptism. He also emphasized the saving nature of baptism through the promise of faith. But without faith, he conceded, unless it is "conferred in baptism," the sacrament is superfluous.[54] The potential that the sign of baptism itself may convey faith would be an approach inconsistent with what Luther had previously articulated regarding the prerequisites for and effects of the sacraments vis-à-vis the medieval ordinances.

In 1521, Luther still maintained the necessity of the surrogate faith of parents or sponsors as meeting the qualification for faith to precede the sign for their child.[55] But by the following year, Luther seemed resolved that each person is baptized for his or her own faith. Therefore, newborns already possess faith, or baptism serves as the means for faith's infusion.[56] By 1523, Luther had become embroiled in attacks from his left against his defense of infant baptism. Radicals such as the Zwickau prophets, Thomas Müntzer, and even Luther's own former Wittenberg professor and colleague Andreas Karlstadt, all began to recommend the cessation of baptism until baptizants manifested to the church a commitment to the faith.

Though Luther's previous words were directed toward Catholicism's ex opere operato sentiments, the unanticipated assault on his left flank apparently caused the Reformer to double down on his previous rhetoric and claim that infants possess faith. In a 1523 treatise addressed to the Bohemian Brethren, Luther critiqued their practice of baptizing infants based on their future faith. "For you hold (as they tell me) that the young children do not have faith; nevertheless you baptize them." At this juncture, Luther began to repeat a refrain he would use frequently in years to come: "On this point I have said it would be better not to baptize any children anywhere at all than to baptize them without faith."[57] To be clear, Luther's point was not that of his radical counterparts but the opposite. Because he posited the purity of infant baptism, Christians should understand its meaning; to administer baptism without an association with faith would be unwarranted and even injurious. But he reasoned that if infant baptism has been properly exercised through the centuries of the church and the promise of Christ holds true (i.e., "The one who believes and is baptized," etc., Mark 16:16), then faith must be nigh. In the case of paedobaptism, "through the faith and prayer of the church young children are cleansed of unbelief and of the devil and are endowed

54. LW 36:59.
55. LW 32:14.
56. WA 10/3:310.15–17. Here noticed in Janz, "Baptism," in *Westminster Handbook to Martin Luther*, 11.
57. Luther, *The Adoration of the Sacrament of the Holy Body of Christ*, LW 36:300.

with faith, and thus are baptized."[58] Here the vicarious faith of the church is prerequisite to the infusion of faith into the infant through the rite. On this point, Denis Janz rightly observed: "The logic of Luther's insistence on the centrality of faith for the sacrament had driven him to this position. Yet one senses that he did not relish defending it."[59] By the mid-1520s, Luther may well have theologically painted himself into a corner, defending his initial words against inspiring what became the nascent Anabaptist movement on the one hand, and subsequently eliciting their criticisms of his new conclusions on the other.

Luther and the Anabaptists

Contemporary scholars, though broadly classifying miscellaneous dissenting religious groups as "radical Reformers," have carefully identified evangelical spiritualists, Waldensians, mystics, rationalists, and certain other sectarian groups and differentiated them from the Anabaptists, in all their own geographic and theological assortment. Luther was at least less careful in his day, if not obtuse to their distinctions, pejoratively labeling any group to his left as *Schwärmer/Schwärmgeister* (fanatics/enthusiasts) for appealing to the Holy Spirit in mystical ways beyond his comfort, as Sacramentarians for denying Christ's bodily presence in the Eucharist, or as *Wiedertäufer* (rebaptizers). Receiving most of his information about them secondhand, Luther did not personally meet an Anabaptist until late in life, in 1541. It is not surprising that his most extensive treatment of them, *Concerning Rebaptism*, written as a letter to two pastors at the close of 1527 and beginning of 1528, demonstrated something of his admitted ignorance of them.

At the outset of the letter, Luther acknowledged that the South German Anabaptist theologian Balthasar Hubmaier had credited Luther with sharing if not also inspiring the Anabaptists' own beliefs. For his part, Luther quickly dismissed such a notion. Though registering his objections to the executions of Anabaptists in other territories, the remainder of his treatise refutes their attempts at disavowing the long-established tradition of infant baptism and argues that practicing rebaptism is an even greater grievance. Luther affirmed that he had already clearly published his support of paedobaptism.[60]

---

58. LW 36:301. Later, in a 1525 sermon, Luther contradicted this notion, refuting this position as that of Rome. Instead, it is the faith of the sponsors, not the church, that should be relied upon for proper intercession and in order for God to bring the promise of faith to the child. See WA 17/2:78.30–79.3.

59. Janz, "Baptism," 11.

60. Luther, *Concerning Rebaptism*, LW 40:229.

The treatise then serves as an apology for continuing its practice as the best expression of the sacrament's promise. Infant baptism, he argued, "derives from the apostles" and was practiced in the earliest of days by Christians. If it were heretical, Luther reasoned, God would have intervened centuries prior to alter the practice (perhaps an ironic line of argumentation from a fellow Reformer of the church). Instead, infant baptism is a "miracle of God," and its continued existence proves its orthodoxy. As evidence for this supposition, God has used saints of the church in past ages for divine purposes, still bestowing spiritual gifts upon them, though they too were baptized as children. If paedobaptism were illegitimate, there would have been no baptism for a millennium in the church, and without true baptism, there has been no historic Christianity.

Additionally, Luther detailed scriptural proofs that Jesus welcomed children (Matt. 19:14), the apostles baptized entire households (Acts 16:15), and that John the Baptist obviously possessed faith by leaping in his mother's womb (Luke 1:41). Such passages, Luther submitted, should justify its practice. Beyond deductive logic and scriptural support, Luther adjoined the pattern of the covenants of the Old Testament to that of the New, observing the universal nature of God's promises. The gospel is then common to all people, including children, and the common gospel means a common baptism. Baptism is a means of planting and watering but leaving the growth to the Lord.[61] Although he conceded that there are no passages commissioning infant baptism directly, Luther retorted that "they on their side have just as little of Scripture which bids us baptize adults."[62] He concluded by ironically arguing that Anabaptists have "no substantial or certain arguments" for their position, while again admitting, "I am not sure what they do believe."[63] Denis Janz's critique of the treatise is not an overstatement: "Hurriedly written, repetitious, and disorganized, it is not one of Luther's finer literary efforts."[64]

Despite its weaknesses, the 1528 publication is nevertheless an interesting window into Luther's developing concept of and, ultimately, honest uncertainty regarding infant faith. Because Luther's notion of the sacramental promise conveyed in baptism is salvation through faith (Mark 16:16), substantiating that young children possess faith or have it imputed to them through the rite was at one point central to his argument against the Anabaptist rationale for baptism's delay. If, as he held, within each person is performed the "work of God" by which one is baptized and "reckoned among Christians," faith must be substantiated, even within the young. That those who later manifest

61. LW 40:254–58.
62. LW 40:258.
63. LW 40:258, 261.
64. Janz, "Baptism," 12.

faith were first baptized as infants seems to support baptism's role in faith's development in each person. Without faith in the objective working of God, anyone would be prone to doubt its effects. Furthermore, if Anabaptists argue for requiring proof of faith before a candidate can be properly baptized, they have fallen prey to "a great presumption," for no one human can genuinely discern the authenticity of the faith of another. Such matters are left to God and the individual alone. Hence, if Anabaptists were true to their own convictions, he argued, they would never be able to baptize because they could never have certainty of anyone's faith. Confession and belief are not the same, according to Luther: "Even if you baptized a person a hundred times a day you would not at all know if he believes."[65] This line of argumentation may be among the strongest parts of his thesis against rebaptism.

Here Luther seems to argue against the simplicity of faith found in his earlier writings and instead to acknowledge its enigmatic qualities, that "often he who claims to believe does not at all believe; and on the other hand, he who doesn't think he believes, but is in despair, has the greatest faith."[66] Thus belief cannot be left either to another's reading or even to the subjective experience of the self but only to divine determination, for believing and knowing one believes are not the same. Furthermore, because "no one can prove with good reasons that [children] do not have faith," the long-held custom of baptizing infants should not be altered. For the tradition to be changed, the burden of proof must be on the Anabaptists. For no one can prove that children cannot believe, and no Scripture denies this as a possibility. The incapacity to speak or understand does not necessarily negate the potential for faith to still be present. Since both the Old Testament and the New describe the sacrifice of "innocent children," Luther reasoned, their innocence must have involved both spirit and faith in order to make them so blessed. And since Christ said that the "kingdom of heaven belongs to children" (Matt. 19:14) and John leapt in his mother's womb, faith must be present in the smallest of humans.[67]

Undoubtedly recognizing these passages as stretching the limits of his argument, Luther again called on the Anabaptists instead to demonstrate where Scripture disproves his theory that children can believe. Yet the Reformer finally conceded, "On the other hand we cannot prove that children do believe with any Scripture verse that clearly and expressly declares in so many words, or the like, 'You are to baptize children because they also believe.'"[68] At this point Luther had apparently abandoned his previous polemic for the proxy faith of the parents

65. LW 40:240.
66. LW 40:241.
67. LW 40:242.
68. LW 40:254.

or the church. Instead, he argued that it is simply better to err on the side of the potential benefit of the faith being granted to children by the rite: "For if, as we believe, baptism is right and useful and brings the children to salvation, and I then did away with it, then I would be responsible for all the children who were lost because they were unbaptized—a cruel and terrible thing."[69]

Irrespective of whether infants can or cannot believe, Luther never entertained reforming baptism's timing: "You say it is not a proper baptism. What does it matter, if it is still a baptism? It was a correct baptism in itself, regardless of whether it was received rightly. For the words were spoken and everything that pertains to baptism was done as fully as when faith is present." Faith should never serve baptism, but baptism is to serve faith. "When faith comes, baptism is complete. A second baptism is not necessary."[70] Provided the child manifests faith later in life, Luther argued, baptism has served its divine purpose.[71] The further Luther considered the topic in this treatise, the more it seems that he was increasingly uncertain of the reasons for his position. It was not until the following year, 1529, that Luther arrived at greater clarity and his final position on the matter.

Luther's Mature Baptismal Theology

Many of Luther's theological treatises were polemical; thus his positions were often configured to and arguably exaggerated by the particular rival he was addressing. Although Luther was still undoubtedly conscious of his detractors, his 1529 Large and Small Catechisms took on a more proactive and arguably constructive quality than many of his other writings. It is here that one can also sense Luther's confidence in arriving at a mature and cohesive position regarding baptism.

Luther first addressed the nature of the sign of water. While Catholicism had emphasized an almost mechanical or magical substance once consecrated, in Luther's mind the Anabaptists had overstated the ordinariness of the element.[72] Luther attempted to carve out a middle position, drawing upon something of both but also eschewing both poles as extreme. First and foremost, the Scriptures witness to the fact that baptism is not a human ordinance but a

69. Ibid.
70. LW 40:246.
71. At this juncture, Luther appears to be proposing the very argument he refuted as "Waldensian" some three years earlier; cf. WA 17/2:81.8–18.
72. Balthasar Hubmaier, e.g., baptized some three hundred parishioners from a milk pail filled with well water; following the service, he had the baptismal font thrown into the Rhine lest it become a papal relic. See Brewer, *A Pledge of Love*, 39.

sacrament instituted by God (Matt. 28; Mark 16). Christians are commanded to be baptized and should attend to this rite with solemnity and reverence. Although water is external and physical, its use in this case is holy because of the divine command to baptize and its performance in and through God's name.[73] Water is no longer common water when combined with the Word since it is divinely used as a means of grace.[74] In response to the third question of the Small Catechism, "How can water do such great things?" Luther responded, "Clearly the water does not do it, but the Word of God, which is with and alongside the water, and faith, which trusts in this Word of God in the water. For without the Word of God the water is plain water and not a baptism."[75]

Consequently, Zwingli and the radicals were wrong to separate faith from the external sign. Water and faith are instead intentionally connected by God for the sake of humanity: "Yes, it must be external so that it can be perceived and grasped by the senses and thus brought into the heart, just as the entire gospel is an external, oral proclamation."[76] Just as in the hearing of the gospel, Luther asserted that baptism is useless unless it is received in faith: "Just by allowing the water to be poured over you, you do not receive or retain [divine] baptism" but a bath-keeper's baptism at best. This water is superfluous to its recipient. Only when baptism is accepted as God's command and ordinance and through the name of Christ can one receive the promise of salvation. Consequently, it is not the hand or body that receives the promise through the exterior sign but only the believing heart.[77] Regardless, undoubtedly relating baptism to the resurrection to come, Luther posited that both soul and body will be saved through baptism and abide in eternity—the soul because it has believed in God's Word, the body because it has received the water and is inextricably tied to the soul.[78]

Luther also argued against the medieval notion of baptism being the first installment or an initial form of grace. Baptism instead conveys grace to the Christian in toto with all its benefits: "Victory over death and the devil, forgiveness of sin, God's grace, the entire Christ, and the Holy Spirit with his gifts. In short," Luther added, "the blessings of baptism are so boundless that if our timid nature considers them, it may well doubt whether they could all be true."[79] The sign of baptism both represents and conveys the

73. Luther, Large Catechism, BC 456–57.
74. See WA 42:10.3–10; and Trigg, "Luther on Baptism and Penance," 312.
75. See BC 359; also Peters, Commentary on Luther's Catechisms, 90–94.
76. BC 460.
77. BC 461.
78. BC 462.
79. BC 461.

accomplished reality of the slaying of the old Adam and the raising of the new—an inexorable process that Christians pursue throughout this earthly life by decreasing daily in their corruptions. "Thus a Christian life is nothing else than a daily baptism, begun once and continuing ever after."[80] As such, baptism, once performed, can perpetually assuage the guilty conscience haunted by sin throughout life and become a source of strength, encouragement, and comfort for each believer.[81]

In the Large Catechism, Luther maintained the legitimacy and importance of infant baptism as blessed by God—again evidenced by the fact that God made "many holy who have been thus baptized and has given them the Holy Spirit,"[82] which Luther interpreted as the sign of the divine confirmation of their baptisms. Here the Reformer conceded that the infant may not believe, but asserted that such a point is irrelevant to baptism's validity. Provided that baptism combines both Word and water, it is effective once faith is first exercised. When the candidate does not at first possess faith, the rite should not be repeated at the point of believing; instead, its original promise is finally realized as the Christian now draws upon the initial promise of God's Word through the rite. Luther then cited a traditional maxim: *Abusus non tollit, sed confirmat substantiam* (misuse does not destroy the substance, but confirms its existence). In other words, the simple fact that one may not utilize God's offer of grace does not nullify the legitimacy of the divine overture. Without faith, the offer is valid but is left as an "empty symbol" or an "unfruitful sign"[83] to the recipient. But when faith is added, before, during, or following the rite, baptism's promise is realized and appropriated. At this juncture Luther no longer pursued the timing of faith relative to the sacrament but simply posited that baptism is performed with the hope that its recipient would believe. Once faith is recognized, God's promise through the sacrament has been made effective.[84] Just as Christ's work on the cross was the product of no human work but a divine treasure offered through the Word to be received by each person in faith, so the regenerative power of baptism is tendered by God, but is fulfilled through each person's response in faith during and following the act and throughout his or her life.[85] Thus, as each person is *simul justus et peccator*, daily repentance is a continual return to baptism.

80. BC 465.
81. BC 462.
82. Ibid.
83. BC 465.
84. Ibid.
85. Trigg, "Luther on Baptism and Penance," 313.

The Sacrament of Baptism among Other Reformers

The Swiss Reformer of the city-state of Zurich, Ulrich Zwingli, differed with his Wittenberg contemporary on the nature of the sacraments. Since his strongly Neoplatonic convictions disentangled all things spiritual from physical matter, Zwingli instead distinguished the sacramental signs as powerful symbols of a genuine inward and spiritual transformation. Consequently, Zwingli unmistakably separated the signs from their spiritual substance far more than did his Wittenberg counterpart. He demurred at the notion that the water of baptism was in any way an effectual emblem. A product of Renaissance humanism, Zwingli found the etymology of the term "sacrament" to be helpful to this partition; an oath taken by a Roman soldier typically before battle, to be faithful to his general, "sacraments" became badges or marks worn to declare one's allegiance. Christian sacraments are outward signs to demarcate one's inner resolve to follow Christ.[86] Nevertheless, Zwingli also underscored, especially following his own heated dispute with Anabaptists, that the baptism of infants was normative to the gospel, identifying baptism as the expression of the new covenant and thus tied, and parallel, to circumcision in the old (e.g., Col. 2:11–12). Baptism thus was reserved exclusively for the children of Christian parents, those already incorporated into the covenant community. Based on the proxy confession of faith by the parents, their children would be incorporated into the community until such time as they could confess faith for themselves.[87] Positively for Zwingli, then, baptism is an "initiatory sign, and those who receive it are dedicated and pledged to the Lord God." Through baptism one is marked as "dedicated to God" and incorporated into the Christian community, with baptism carrying more ecclesiological than soteriological implications.[88]

Defining a sacrament as an outward sign testifying to divine grace, the Reformer of Geneva, John Calvin, rejected the merely symbolic notion of baptism as being akin to a mark or token, viewing it instead as a sign accompanied by a promise from God.[89] Through baptism, one is received into the covenant community and reckoned as a child of God. The sign of water

86. Bryan D. Spinks, *Reformation and Modern Rituals and Theologies of Baptism: From Luther to Contemporary Practices* (Burlington, VT: Ashgate, 2006), 32–33.

87. Ibid., 33.

88. Zwingli, *Of Baptism*, in *Zwingli and Bullinger*, ed. and trans. G. W. Bromiley, LCC 24 (Philadelphia: Westminster, 1953), 146. On this cited passage, James F. White has also commented that Zwingli may be the first theologian to make use of dedication as an aspect of baptism. See White, *Sacraments*, 37.

89. Calvin, *Inst.* 4.15.1; LCC 21:1304.

is a symbol of one's spiritual cleansing and confirmation of the permanent expunging of one's sins (Matt. 28:19; Acts 2:38). Thus, like Luther, Calvin underscored the importance for Christians to remember their baptisms as the source of assurance for ongoing forgiveness. As a multidimensional sign, baptism also was seen as engrafting baptizants into Christ's death in order for them to realize the mortification of their flesh and enjoy the benefits of Christ's own resurrection. Through this spiritual union, the Christian also shares in all the blessings of Christ.[90] Like other Protestant Reformers, although Calvin valued the symbol of water, he perceived that the element itself did not convey the spiritual effects outlined above. Such divine work was left to the promises and "spiritual mysteries" that the ceremony was intended to represent.[91]

Although he appears to move beyond his Swiss predecessor's focus on symbolism, Calvin at the same time affirmed Zwingli's parallel between baptism and circumcision, using their association as a sanction for infant baptism. Perhaps Calvin qualified more of the nuances between the two signs, yet they both still affirmed God's watch-care over his children, the forgiveness of sins, and the promise of eternal life. Just as Abraham received the Old Testament sacrament following his faith and his son Isaac received it preceding his own faith, so offspring of the new covenant may be baptized by "hereditary right" as children of the covenant.[92] Nevertheless, because he did not associate baptism with original sin, Calvin rejected the medieval notion that unbaptized children who died would inevitably be damned.[93] Sacraments were instead the normative instrumental means by which God granted the promises according to God's divine will.[94]

Cranmer's 1549 baptismal rite in the prayer book demonstrated his reliance on Augustine's theology of baptism, underscoring the importance of baptism and its regenerative effects to counter original sin. Cranmer demonstrated no influence from covenantal theology in the Reformed tradition but instead, like Luther, highlighted baptism as conveying God's promise.[95] Likewise, in detailing his mature baptismal theology in article 26 of his Forty-Two Articles, Cranmer argued that the sacraments were no mere badges or tokens but "sure witnesses and effectual signs of grace, and God's goodwill toward

90. Calvin, *Inst.* 4.15.5–6; LCC 21:1307.
91. Calvin, *Inst.* 4.16.2; LCC 21:1325.
92. Calvin, *Inst.* 4.16.24; LCC 21:1346–47.
93. Calvin, *Inst.* 4.16.26; LCC 21:1349.
94. Christopher Elwood, *The Body Broken: The Calvinist Doctrine of the Eucharist and the Symbolization of Power in Sixteenth-Century France* (Oxford: Oxford University Press, 1999), 71; Spinks, *Rituals and Theologies of Baptism*, 41–42.
95. Spinks, *Rituals and Theologies of Baptism*, 67.

us, by which he doth work invisibly in us; and doth not only quicken, but also strengthen, and confirm our faith in him." At the same time, Cranmer made clear that he rejected all ex opere operato interpretations of baptism. It is a sign and seal of a Christian's new birth, a means to engraft the candidate into the church, the promise of forgiveness of sins, and one's adoption as a child of God.[96]

Many of the Anabaptists, influenced by Zwingli, saw baptism as a visible initiatory sign, emblematic of one's response in faith to God as well as incorporation in submission to the confessing community of believers. Baptism served as a doorway to the believers' church, a community distinct from the fallen world. Balthasar Hubmaier undoubtedly wrote forthrightly that Luther's initial writings on baptism inspired Hubmaier's Anabaptist views.[97] As Luther insisted that not the element of water but the faith of the recipient effects the sacrament, Hubmaier and his Anabaptist colleagues heartily concurred, concluding that only those malleable to being taught and capable of confession were proper candidates for the rite. Thus baptism became, for them, a public proclamation of faith:

> After the person has now committed himself inwardly and in faith to a new life, he then professes this also outwardly and publicly before the Christian church, into whose communion he lets himself be registered and counted according to the order and institution of Christ. Therefore he professes to the Christian church, that is, to all brothers and sisters who live in the faith in Christ, that in his heart he has been thus inwardly instructed in the Word of Christ . . . , that he has surrendered himself already to live henceforth according to the Word, will, and rule of Christ, . . . [and] lets himself be baptized with outward water in which he professes publicly his faith and intention.[98]

Baptism thus served for Anabaptists as an outward sign representing the inward obedience and commitment of an adult believer, engrafting the individual into the disciplined community to live a life apart from and in witness to the postfallen world. The symbol of water was normally accompanied by a public vow by the candidate, testifying to the individual's commitment to Christ and the community. Water baptism served as an outward token of this verbal pledge and inward assent.

96. Thomas Cranmer, Forty-Two Articles; here cited from Gordon P. Jeanes, *Signs of God's Promise: Thomas Cranmer's Sacramental Theology and the Book of Common Prayer* (London: T&T Clark, 2008), 137.

97. See Brewer, "Radicalizing Luther," 95–115.

98. Hubmaier, *Summa of the Entire Christian Life"*; here via Pipkin and Yoder, *Balthasar Hubmaier*, 85.

A Contemporary Protestant Appropriation of Baptism

Like the Reformers who followed Luther, contemporary Protestants have much to glean from Luther's baptismal theology in order to understand more fully what the rite is intended to mean and not mean in its performance. Protestants agree, through Luther's initial work on this subject, that baptism does not work mechanically or magically apart from faith. Luther helped bring to the fore, albeit by drawing from Aquinas, that faith is prerequisite for and associated with baptism. Luther also carefully demonstrated that baptism is not merely a sign but a particular use of a common, physical element for a holy purpose. Such a notion helps modern Protestants avoid the pitfalls of a Neoplatonic dualism that separates all things as either physical or spiritual, common or celestial, body or soul. The miracle of the incarnation, the foundation of Christology, is that God became flesh (a topic developed further in chapter 7). A lesson drawn from this larger doctrine should help shape the sacramental ones, which are intended to point to it: God uses the physical, and nothing in God's created order is outside of God's domain. God can then ordain the use of ordinary water to do the supernatural, to be a sign of God conveying grace and a service to incorporate the Christian into the community of faith.

Perhaps one of the most overlooked aspects of Luther's proposed reforms of baptism is the restoration of the mode of immersion for every baptizant. Luther understood that the actual word "baptize," both in Greek and German, meant to dip or immerse. But beyond its linguistic rendering, Luther saw the reestablishment of immersion as of great theological import. Baptism is each Christian's way to demonstrate solidarity with Christ and one another at the outset of the Christian life. Being buried with Christ and raised to walk in the newness of life through the water rehearses the meaning of the death of the old Adam and the raising of the new creation through individual confession on the day of initiation (cf. Rom. 6:4). Additionally, this event spiritually represents the experience of a Christian's ongoing existence through sanctification and, ultimately, what will be actualized through new, incorruptible bodies granted on the day of resurrection. Contemporary liturgical scholars concur with Luther, critiquing the church for often shrinking the baptismal font in the sanctuary and reducing the visibility of elements to the witnessing congregation—moves, they argue, that tend unwittingly to demonstrate a trivial attitude toward the church's powerful symbols and sacraments. Although some traditions will repeat the cliché that immersion is not necessary for a baptism to be effective, the sign of immersion is so powerful, both for the candidate and for the gathered witnesses, that there is no strong justification for retaining mere sprinkling or affusion. Protestant traditions that practice paedobaptism need only refer to the Eastern Orthodox tradition and baptism rituals to see how churches in that tradition have been safely baptizing infants for centuries. Typically, in the Eastern Orthodox tradition, baptism is practiced by partly submerging the child into water and then pouring water over the head so that the entire body is covered in water. In a day when most churches have the capability of enlarging their fonts to full baptisteries, there is little reason not to follow Luther's exhortation to immerse.

There is much, then, to be appreciated in Luther's understanding of baptism. However, the Anabaptists were a particular challenge to Luther's sacramental theology, in part because they exposed a potential Achilles' heel in Luther's otherwise consonant theological logic, a quandary he never fully resolved even in his final remarks on the rite. Integral to Luther's project was the importance of faith preceding the sign in the sacraments, of rejecting the mechanical conveyance of grace; the faith of the recipient was then necessary for the sacrament to be appropriated. But in order to defend the long-held practice of infant baptism, Luther at first had to backtrack on his initial conviction that no one person can believe on behalf of another—at first relying on the surrogate faith of the parents or sponsors, then on the congregation's collective faith, and finally on a kind of dormant faith or infused faith in infants themselves in order to validate the sacrament for children. Ultimately, Luther simply argued that the timing of faith in a child was irrelevant—whether one believed before or after the rite—for faith would activate the offer of forgiveness and salvation granted through the sacrament.

Contemporary Christians are all the more cognizant of childhood education, mental cognition, and nuances in spiritual development than their Protestant forebears were five centuries ago. As products of post-Enlightenment thinking, Protestants of today may be particularly dubious of Luther's claims for the potential of nascent faith in infancy. Yet one must concede that the nature of faith is trusting in that which cannot be perceived, and modern Protestants can at least concur with Luther that God may move beyond human comprehension, especially in soteriological matters. Nevertheless, for all those except the staunchest adherents to Luther's baptismal theology, while utilizing and appreciating the foundation Luther laid for the Protestant understanding of this rite, many Protestants may find more attractive alternatives to consider. Luther's theology here may serve more as a beginning point than a theological destination, establishing baptism's associations with sign, grace, faith, and church.

For free-church Protestants, Anabaptist interpretations may seem to be the logical trajectory of Luther's thought: if faith must precede the sign, then baptizants should possess faith in order to appropriate the promises of God.

The free church viewed this idea as a completion of Luther's basic principle of sola fide, for faith alone is necessary for the sacrament to be performed on each recipient, and without faith, the ceremony may easily slide down the slippery slope of becoming a perfunctory ritual, imbued with the supernatural. Without grasping the confessional nature of the rite—how baptism was performed on new believers as recorded in so many New Testament passages— Protestants will continue to bring their children to be baptized but not return to the church until a wedding, funeral, or the next rite of passage. Believer's baptism, when rightly administered with proper teaching beforehand and by continuing the historic use of catechizing questions regarding the candidate's belief and intent to commit to the communal life during the rite, may teach not only the baptizant but also the congregation the deep ecclesial meaning that baptism can possess. On the other hand, without also considering Luther's claims for the objective working of God in the service, baptism can be reduced to one's own promise and commitment to God, replacing the divine promise with merely an anthropological sentiment.

Alternatively, both the Lutheran and Reformed traditions point out that infant baptism best describes the objective nature of God's grace by normatively performing the sacrament on the most vulnerable and helpless of humanity, those who cannot perform and produce good works but only receive and depend upon others. The Reformed tradition's emphasis on covenantal theology may provide a more understandable and biblical justification for this practice. Provided that the parents are confessing Christians in good standing with the church, they and the congregation can rightly promise to do their parts to bring the children up in the ways of the Lord, and baptism serves as a sign and seal of God's grace to that end. But one is left wondering what becomes of the many baptisms of those who never live into this divine promise and manifest belief for themselves. Do such baptisms become empty signs?

Regardless of which trajectory a Protestant community or tradition may pursue, Luther, surprisingly, may provide some necessary assistance. That is to say, regardless of the ordering and timing of the rite, once faith and baptism have met, God's promises have begun to be realized in the believer. And these promises are not yet fully established, since Christians, like God's creation, groan for their coming redemption (Rom. 8:22). In the meantime, the faithful continue to live *simul justus et peccator*, acknowledging

> what baptism signifies and why God ordained precisely this sign and external ceremony for the sacrament by which we are first received into the Christian community. This act or ceremony consists of being dipped into the water, which

covers us completely, and being drawn out again. These two parts . . . point to the power and effect of baptism, which is nothing else than the slaying of the old Adam and the resurrection of the new creature, both of which must continue in us our whole life long. Thus a Christian life is nothing else than a daily baptism, begun once and continuing ever after.[99]

99. BC 464–65.

7

The Lord's Supper

"The Most Important of All"

But no eating can give life except that which is by faith, for that is truly a spiritual and living eating. . . . For the sacramental eating does not give life, since many eat unworthily.

Martin Luther

When I say: The sacrament of the Lord's body, I am simply referring to that bread which is the symbol of the body of Christ who was put to death for our sakes. . . . Now the sign and the thing signified cannot be one and the same.

Ulrich Zwingli

If it's just a symbol, to hell with it!

Flannery O'Conner

THE COMMEMORATION OF JESUS CHRIST'S FINAL MEAL with his disciples before his arrest and crucifixion (Mark 14:22–26; Matt. 26:26–29; Luke 22:14–20; 1 Cor. 11:23–25) has been practiced by Christians since the time of the early church. As an integral part of Christian worship, the sharing of bread and wine in the Eucharist also took up a central position of debate—regarding its theological meaning, benefits, and the exact form for the liturgical service itself—between Protestants and Catholics during the era of the Reformation and among Protestants themselves.[1] It is a service intended to unite Christians (1 Cor. 10:16–17) but has ironically also been a source of division for centuries.

The Lord's Supper in Scripture and the Early Church

As an eschatological community, it appears that the early church was more intent on faithfully observing the Lord's Supper than on developing a eucharistic theology. The service itself reflected a geographical diversity of liturgical practices. The sharing of a meal (i.e., the "breaking of bread") is found in the earliest descriptions of Christian worship: "They devoted themselves to the apostles' teaching and fellowship, to the breaking of bread and the prayers. . . . Day by day, as they spent much time together in the temple, they broke bread at home and ate their food with glad and generous hearts" (Acts 2:42, 46). The apostle Paul equated the elements for the early church with (at least the ceremonial eating of) Christ's body and blood: "The cup of blessing that we bless, is it not a sharing in the blood of Christ? The bread that we break, is it not a sharing in the body of Christ?" (1 Cor. 10:16). Paul also worded what is often regarded as the first written liturgical formula for the church's eucharistic service (1 Cor. 11:23–26), while also admonishing Christians to repent and thus spiritually and soberly prepare for the meal so as not to eat and drink "unworthily" or "without discerning the body" (1 Cor. 11:27–29).

By the turn of the second century, the *Didache* revealed that Christians were already using the word "Eucharist" (from the Greek *eucharistia*, "thanksgiving"),[2] a word previously used for "giving thanks" in worship but now applied to the Lord's Supper's itself. The document also records a series of prayers preceding and following the service and includes the instructions, which stipulate that only baptized Christians are to partake of the meal.[3]

By the mid-second century, Justin Martyr (d. 165) provided a description of the Lord's Supper as a weekly worship practice for Christians in Rome.

1. B. A. Gerrish probably does not overstate the doctrine's importance to this period: "No theological theme, not even justification, was more keenly debated in the Reformation era than the meaning of the central Christian rite." *Thinking with the Church: Essays in Historical Theology* (Grand Rapids: Eerdmans, 2010), 229.
2. See, e.g., 1 Cor. 10:16, "the cup of thanksgiving" (NIV); 1 Cor. 11:24, "and when he had given thanks," etc. This is also demonstrated in Ignatius, *To the Smyrnaeans* 6.2, here via Ignatius, *Letters*, trans. Cyril C. Richardson, LCC 1:114–15; and Justin Martyr, *First Apology* 66, here trans. Edward Rochie Hardy, LCC 1:286.
3. See *Didache*; here via Holmes, *Apostolic Fathers*, 153–55.

Again, only baptized believers were permitted to participate because the congregation did not receive the elements as common bread and wine but as the Christ, the incarnate Savior: "So also we have been taught that the food consecrated by the word of prayer which comes from him, from which our flesh and blood are nourished by transformation, is the flesh and blood of that incarnate Jesus."[4] This spiritual understanding was characterized only as a divine mystery. After readings from the apostles and prophets, the president gives a "discourse" to encourage faithfulness to what has been read, and the congregation responds by standing for the prayers. The president finally offers a series of extemporaneous prayers before distributing the consecrated elements of bread, wine, and water to those gathered.[5] The service concludes with an offering for the poor, widowed, sick, and orphaned.

The third-century document (ca. 230) *Didascalia Apostolorum*, modeled on the pattern of the *Didache*, made passing comments about the service of the Eucharist. The document stressed the importance of prayer and Scripture in reference to the Holy Spirit during the rite: "For consider and see that prayer is also heard through the Holy Spirit, and the eucharist is accepted and sanctified through the Holy Spirit, and the Scriptures are the words of the Holy Spirit, and are holy."[6]

For the next several centuries, the church was forced to deal with Docetism and other christological issues along with Donatism and other ecclesial issues, all of which affected the practice, participants, and understanding of the Lord's Supper among Christian communities. Nevertheless, the church did not attempt to establish a unified doctrine of the Eucharist until the eighth century.[7] Until then, various patristic sources described the effect of the Supper as a mystery, even as a mystical reality, but also as a means to become united with Christ's body,[8] especially when accompanied by or combined with the

4. Justin Martyr, *First Apology* 66.

5. See Bryan D. Spinks, *Do This in Remembrance of Me: The Eucharist from the Early Church to the Present Day* (Norwich, UK: SCM, 2013), 32–33. James F. White surmised that the elements were selected from the food brought by various members of the church. See White, *Brief History of Christian Worship*, 55.

6. *Didascalia Apostolorum* 6.21, here trans. Sebastian Brock and Michael Vasey, in *The Liturgical Portions of the Didascalia*, Grove Liturgical Study 29 (Bramcote, Nottingham, UK: Grove Books, 1982), 32.

7. Even here, the issue in 787 at the seventh ecumenical council (Nicaea II) pertained to the early iconoclastic controversy by merely denying that the real presence of Christ found in the Supper could be equated with a symbolic presence of Christ in the iconography. The Supper, it argued, is wholly unique since the physical elements are made divine by the descent of the Holy Spirit through the mediation of the priest.

8. See, e.g., Cyril of Jerusalem and Augustine: Cyril of Jerusalem, *The Mystagogical Catecheses* 4.3, in *St. Cyril of Jerusalem's Lectures on the Christian Sacraments*, ed. Frank Leslie

Word.[9] Regardless, the basic form of the service initially developed over the course of the first four centuries of Christianity.

The Development of Eucharistic Theology in the Middle Ages

During the medieval period, the Eucharist gradually became the central act of worship, but it was not embroiled in theological controversy until the High Middle Ages. Building on the foundation of the Fathers, the early medieval church assumed a mysterious sense of the presence of Christ in the Supper without requiring a rigorous theological exactness. But the eucharistic dispute that manifested in the eleventh and twelfth centuries was presaged by a ninth-century difference between two monks in explaining the Eucharist; they were Paschasius Radbertus (d. 860) and Ratramnus (d. 868), both at the monastery of Corbie in Picardy, France. Radbertus advocated for the real presence of the true, historic body of Christ in the elements of the Supper; Ratramnus maintained that the bread and wine served a spiritual service by representing the body and blood of Christ figuratively and in remembrance, pointing to Christ's spiritual presence with the church.[10] Despite the differences of opinion in their writings, there is no historical evidence for strife or disputation between the monastic brothers.

But the eleventh century saw the outbreak of the first significant eucharistic controversy centered on the thought of the archbishop of Angers, Berengar of Tours (d. 1088). Berengar refracted much of the position and observations

---

Cross (London: SPCK, 1951), 68, here via Johnson, *Sacraments and Worship*, 201; and Augustine of Hippo, *Treatise on the Gospel of St. John* 21, in *A History of the Doctrine of the Holy Eucharist*, trans. Darwell Stone (London: Longmans, Green, 1909), 1:93–96.

9. Irenaeus, e.g., argued (ca. 180) that the elements, "having received the Word of God, become the Eucharist, which is the body and blood of Christ"; Clement of Alexandria stated that the "mixture of both—of the water and of the Word—is called the Eucharist, renowned and glorious grace"; and Origen of Alexandria wrote that the "bread which God the Word [*deus verbum*] owns to be His Body, is the Word which nourishes the soul, the Word which proceeds from God the Word [*verbum de deo verbum procedens*]." See Irenaeus, *Against Heresies* 5.2, in *ANF* 1:528; Clement of Alexandria, *Christ the Educator* 2.21, in *ANF* 2:242; and Origen of Alexandria, in *Matthew*, sermon 85, trans. Paul Jacquemont, in *The Eucharist of the Early Christians*, by Willy Rordorf et al. (New York: Pueblo, 1978), 187.

10. Ratramnus observed that the wine remained wine to the senses and in substance: "It is now to the minds of believers not the liquid of Christ's blood" but "Christ's body and blood in a figurative sense." For his part, Paschasius simply maintained that "nothing is possible outside the will of God or contrary to it," for miracles are always beyond what humans believe is possible. See Ratramnus of Corbie, *Christ's Body and Blood* 10, trans. George E. McCracken and Allen Cabaniss, LCC 9:120–21; and Paschasius Radbertus of Corbie, *The Lord's Body and Blood* 1, trans. George E. McCracken and Allen Cabaniss, LCC 9:94; both cited in Johnson, *Sacraments and Worship*, 224.

that Ratramnus made before him, arguing that the elements could not be the historical body of Christ because Christ's presence was not readily perceivable to the senses and because Christ's body, as a physical entity, must take up space, which is now in heaven. Thus Christ is only present spiritually on the altar, and the bread and wine remain as symbols of this presence. Berengar even provocatively asked how Christ could be physically present at numerous altars simultaneously, how Christ could be present physically but not be sensed by anyone, and even what it would mean if the consecrated elements, which his opponents held possessed Christ's historical body, were eaten by pagans and animals. To the latter question, Berengar pointed out that the unholy would then digest and excrete Christ's body.[11]

Berengar's theology was denounced by Pope Leo IX at a synod in Rome in 1050, and Berengar was required in the next three decades to sign three different statements affirming Christ's real presence in the Eucharist. Yet Berengar's piercing questions regarding the sacrament served as a catalyst eliciting a stronger defense of Christ's real presence through what became a highly developed doctrine of transubstantiation in the ensuing centuries.

Hugh of Saint Victor and Peter Lombard proposed that the substance of the elements, that which is truly present, became Christ's body and blood, while the species or accidents of the elements, that which the senses perceive, remained intact. Thus the elements still looked and tasted as before but now were Christ's real body instead. Such an Aristotelian explanation solved the dilemma Berengar presented, for only accidents took up time and space, could desecrate or be digested, while substance could not be readily observed by the senses, and Christ's substance could be ubiquitous. Subsequently, the Fourth Lateran Council in 1215 famously utilized the word "transubstantiation" in its opening creed and affirmed the notion that the elements of the Mass were substantially changed into the body and blood of Christ, a feat accomplished only through a properly ordained priest.[12] Nevertheless, the use of the term was not viewed as a formal endorsement of this theory of Christ's presence.[13] In the following decades, Thomas Aquinas, whose theology became "the standard of orthodoxy"[14] for Roman Catholicism, affirmed and built upon the previously accepted metaphysical construct for

11. Gary Macy, "The Medieval Inheritance," in *A Companion to the Eucharist in the Reformation*, ed. Lee Palmer Wandel (Leiden: Brill, 2014), 23–25.

12. See the Fourth Lateran Council, in DS 260, here via Johnson, *Sacraments and Worship*, 225–26; and Macy, "Medieval Inheritance," 25–26.

13. Here Macy notes that "there was, in fact, still no common understanding of the category of substance, much less agreement on either the use of the term transubstantiation or what the word might have meant when used." "Medieval Inheritance," 26.

14. Ibid., 27.

the Eucharist. Citing Aristotle's claim that "change is the actuation of that which is still in potentiality" (to the final actuation), Aquinas posited that "God is unlimited actuality" in that God's "action reaches out to the whole extent of the being of a thing." It then follows that "the complete substance of the bread is converted into the complete substance of Christ's body, and the complete substance of the wine into the complete substance of Christ's blood. Hence this change is not a formal change, but a substantial one. It does not belong to the natural kinds of change, and it can be called by a name proper to itself—'transubstantiation.'"[15] By the end of the thirteenth century, theological explanations of and quodlibets regarding the presence of Christ through transubstantiation were so complicated that understanding its nuances had become the exclusive domain of theological scholars. Laity only needed to believe that Christ is present in the consecrated host. Gary Macy explains well that "for the ordinary Christian, . . . transubstantiation must have been something like quantum physics for non-scientists today: an amazing thing we trust a scientist to explain."[16]

Aquinas's position ruled the period; yet transubstantiation was not formally codified as the church's official teaching until the thirteenth session of the Council of Trent, ending October 11, 1551. Regardless, Ratramnus and Berengar were not the only dissenting voices over what was developing in the Middle Ages as the church's understanding of Christ's presence in the Supper. Franciscan theologians William de la Mare (d. 1285), John Peckham (d. 1292), and Peter John Olivi (d. 1298) all contested the Thomistic deduction that substantial conversion was the only means God could have used to accomplish Christ's presence in the host. The philosopher-theologian Duns Scotus (d. 1308) defended the Franciscan position, suggesting instead Christ's presence along with the substance of the bread, hence consubstantiation seemed to him a more biblical understanding of the real presence of Christ in the Eucharist. Several decades later, the English Scholastic philosopher and theologian John Wycliffe (d. 1384) generally concurred with this alternative notion.

Another significant medieval theological development was the notion that the Mass became the primary channel for conveying the atoning work of Calvary. The Mass, as a repeatable sacrament, became the conduit to receive God's mercy, through which Christ can make restitution on behalf of sinners, since no human work can satisfy God's justice on its own. The rite thus served as a sacrifice through which Christ was mediated to the worshipers

15. Thomas Aquinas, *Summa theologica*, part 3, q. 75, art. 4; here from *St. Thomas Aquinas: Summa theologiae*, vol. 58, *The Eucharistic Presence*, ed. William Barden (New York: Blackfriars / McGraw-Hill, 1965), 68–73.

16. Macy, "Medieval Inheritance," 29.

and/or sponsors of the Mass.[17] The Council of Florence in 1439 affirmed that the mixing of water and wine and the offering of the cup and bread to God in the Eucharist constituted a sacrifice that effects the union of Christ with his church.[18]

The twin theological developments of the Mass serving as a sacrifice of Christ and as a conduit of Christ's presence through transubstantiation held powerful sway over worship practices in the high and especially late medieval periods. First, the Eucharist became an ocular communion; that is, the viewing of the host in its elevation was of higher import to the participants than hearing the Word or even partaking of the elements themselves. As the Eucharist became the central point of worship, elevation of the host became the highest point of the Eucharist,[19] the point at which Christ would have been transubstantiated, a moment now demarcated for the laity by the ringing of bells to call for their full attention. At this pivotal point, Christ was visibly and physically present. The layperson would await this moment in an attitude of prayer, a spirit of anticipation that transformed the rite from a merely liturgical exercise to a devotional experience. The rituals and readings by the priests in the chancel during the Mass were otherwise superfluous and often seemed only to be clerical preparations to the layperson, a notion reinforced by the church's exclusive use of Latin instead of the vernacular and the often inaudible recitation of the liturgy by the clergy.[20] The Mass was not a service focused on the hearing of the proclaimed Word but of priestly pantomime in order for laity to witness the visible miracle of the Word made flesh, sacrificed on behalf of the faithful.

Predictably, numerous superstitions developed regarding the effects of the Eucharist on those who participated or paid for such rites, notions often not discouraged by the church. Medieval piety transformed the Mass into a channel for a bevy of spiritual benefits and divine blessings and even miraculous healings for one's friends, one's loved ones, or oneself, though church councils repeatedly condemned the use of the Mass for seeking revenge or the death of an enemy.[21] Private masses for the living and the dead became a common means to mitigate the sponsor's suffering while in purgatory. Individuals often left endowments for a Mass to be said following their deaths, and guilds might

17. White, *Sacraments*, 75.
18. See the Council of Florence, Decree for the Armenians, DS 334–35; here via Johnson, *Sacraments and Worship*, 227.
19. See Peter Browe, "Die Elevation der Hostie," in *Die Eucharistie im Mittelalter* (Münster: Lit Verlag, 2003), 487–89.
20. White, *Sacraments*, 74.
21. Ibid., 75.

even sponsor masses for departed members.[22] Since priests were remunerated for such services, the church saw an explosion in the numbers of those ordained, evidenced by the introduction of "chantry priests" in England in the twelfth century, a classification of priests whose sole responsibility was to say Mass for each day's list of intentions.[23]

Accompanying the medieval church's clarifications on the real presence of Christ in the Eucharist was the eleventh-century Gregorian Reform Movement, which strengthened the spiritual authority of the clergy, specifically in its insistence that only a properly ordained priest could preside over the Mass. By virtue of his indelible mark granted in ordination, the medieval priest possessed sacerdotal power to make Christ present in the sacrament. This new understanding gradually separated and elevated the clergy above the laity through the High Middle Ages. Consequently, "the Eucharist became a moment of divine presence and clerical power."[24] Unsurprisingly, the creation of such a disparate spiritual division between these classes, combined with the multiplication of superstitions regarding the Eucharist itself, lent itself to numerous liturgical abuses concerning Mass stipends and the practice of indulgences.[25]

To amplify the medieval rite as only an ocular sacrament by the eleventh century, it became customary for laity to receive the elements at only three feasts of the year: Easter, Christmas, and Pentecost. By 1215, the Fourth Lateran Council made confession a prerequisite for receiving the Eucharist and required the faithful to make confession at least annually and receive Eucharist at least on Easter. What was required as a minimum typically morphed into a maximum for the laity, as Lent became a penitential season in preparation for performing their annual "Easter duty" in order to remain in good standing with the church.[26]

The laity was further distanced from the Eucharist since by the twelfth century they typically no longer had access to the chalice. In centuries prior to this, laity drank from a straw (fistula) or by dipping the bread into the cup (intinction).[27] But, coinciding with a developed doctrine of transubstantiation, a growing concern evolved among the clergy about the risk of spilling the consecrated wine by allowing the laity to partake. The faithful were reassured,

22. White, *Brief History of Christian Worship*, 88.
23. Keith F. Pecklers, SJ, "Eucharist in Western Churches," in *The Cambridge Dictionary of Christianity*, ed. Daniel Patte (Cambridge: Cambridge University Press, 2010), 388.
24. Macy, "Medieval Inheritance," 19.
25. Pecklers, "Eucharist in Western Churches," 388.
26. Macy, "Medieval Influence," 20.
27. White, *Brief History of Christian Worship*, 90.

through the new doctrine of concomitance, that Christ was wholly present in the bread and that the cup was unnecessary for receiving the promised grace. But Jan Hus (d. 1415) was among those who argued for utraquism, that the laity be provided both kinds, which ultimately paved the way for the Christians of Bohemia temporarily to enjoy that privilege following concessions made to them at the Council of Basel in 1533.[28]

The Early Development of Luther's Eucharistic Thought

In 1520 Luther declared that "the church kept the true faith for more than twelve hundred years,"[29] words that related not just to an estimated time of perceived greater purity but also to a time preceding the development of transubstantiation, what he saw as the source of a myriad of Catholicism's unmitigated ethical corruptions and theological distortions of the gospel. Although he repudiated the medieval doctrine as a "pseudophilosophy of Aristotle," Luther never denied Christ's real presence in the Eucharist as a divine mystery, a concept that originally disquieted, mystified, and at times overawed him as a young priest.

As a young theology student, Luther would have been keenly aware of the development of eucharistic theology from patristic to medieval theologians and the periodic decisions of the church's councils regarding this sacrament, and he would have undoubtedly read widely from the complex and sometimes obscure medieval sources of Scholastic theology on the Mass. The degree to which the early Luther accepted the established tradition is uncertain.[30] Luther is said to at least have "adored [the Supper] as divine mystery, not analyzed and defined [it] as was done by the Scholastics."[31] But as the Reformer began to separate justification as a divinely accomplished task from sanctification and advanced a more elucidated conception of

28. White, *Sacraments*, 94.
29. LW 36:31.
30. Joseph Lortz has assessed Luther's early eucharistic thought as congruous with Catholic thought. Erich Seeberg argued that the young Luther held a symbolic view of the Lord's Supper, while Gottfried G. Krodel, drawing upon Luther's first lectures on the Psalms, posited that, while not in conformity with Catholic Scholasticism nor with his mature eucharistic theology in light of his Protestant notion of justification, the early Luther believed in the real presence of Christ in the elements as a divine mystery irreducible to Scholastic speculation. See Lortz, "Sakramentales Denken beim jungen Luther," in *Luther-Jahrbuch 1969*, ed. D. Franz Lau (Hamburg: Friedrich Wittig, 1969), 11; Erich Seeberg, *Luthers Theologie in ihren Grundzügen*, 2nd ed. (Stuttgart: W. Kohlhammer, 1950), 154; and Gottfried G. Krodel, "The Lord's Supper in the Theology of the Young Luther," *Lutheran Quarterly* 13, no. 1 (1961): esp. 29–32.
31. Krodel, "Lord's Supper in the Theology of the Young Luther," 31.

faith, his understanding of the Supper became more aligned with his nascent Protestant principles.

In 1518, Luther wrote a meditation on the Lord's Supper, "Sermon on the Proper Preparation of the Heart for the Sacramental Reception of the Eucharist," admonishing participants on how to prepare spiritually through confession and genuine sorrow in order to receive the sacrament.[32] Luther was attempting to strike a commensurate balance between reverent humility for a sinner before the altar and proper confidence, not simply through one's own faith but especially via the community's collective faith, that the benefits of the Eucharist would be conveyed upon the faithful. Yet the sermon dwelled upon humility as the appropriate spirit for preparation and attitude for receiving the spiritual gift conferred. Each individual's faith would then be strengthened through the Eucharist as it (re)unified the sinner into the "one Lord, one faith" (Eph. 5:1–6) of the communion of saints, Christ's body. The sacrament became the means for an individual's incorporation into the whole, seen visibly through the individual grains made into one loaf and individual grapes into one cup. Not only as a means of reuniting the perpetually wayward Christian into the church body, the Supper correspondingly allowed the individual to participate in and draw upon the church's corporate faith. Therefore, regardless of how fragile one's own faith, how unworthy one may feel, through the aggregate faith of the body, a believer may realize and appropriate Christ's comfortable words and follow with confidence Christ's invitation: *Venite ad me* (Matt. 11:28 Vulg.), "Come to me."[33]

In late 1519, Luther wrote the treatise *The Blessed Sacrament of the Holy and True Body of Christ, and the Brotherhoods*, addressed to laity. This document provisionally develops some of what became Luther's theological structure defining the sacraments as well as the ascending importance for Luther of an individual's faith in order to benefit from the sacrament. At this juncture, the Reformer underscored his reliance on Augustine for his three-part description of a "sacrament" as possessing an outward sign, conveying an inward significance, and needing faith for the sacrament to be effective. Still present is the notion that Christians, heavily burdened by sin, can now lay down the miserable weight of their misdeeds and attend to the altar in the company of the saints.[34]

What is new is the importance Luther placed on the individual's faith at the altar: "See to it," Luther admonished the worshiper, "that here you exercise

---

32. WA 1:329–33.

33. WA 1:331. See also Thomas J. Davis, *This Is My Body: The Presence of Christ in Reformation Thought* (Grand Rapids: Baker Academic, 2008), 20–23.

34. LW 35:53.

and strengthen your faith, so that when you are sorrowful or when your sins press you and you go to the sacrament or hear mass, you do so with a hearty desire for this sacrament and for what it signifies."[35] For this reason, Luther repudiated the medieval Scholastic axiom *ex opere operato*, which made the sacrament effective in itself, irrespective of faith. In its place, Luther underscored the sacrament as *opus operantis* (action of the one acting), "for it was not instituted for its own sake, that it might please God, but for our sake, that we might use it right, exercise our faith by it, and through it become pleasing to God."[36] The church has gone astray by attending more to Christ's natural body than to the spiritual body of the fellowship, Luther argued. But what Christ did at Calvary was an accomplished fact and an objective reality. The service at the altar, then, appropriated that event to the community at present, provided that the recipients believed. This 1519 treatise demonstrates, as Janz put it, that "Luther appears to be groping toward something significantly new."[37]

In July of 1520, Luther brought greater clarity to his evolving eucharistic thought with his *Treatise on the New Testament, That Is, the Holy Mass*. As a precursor to his more noted sacramental writing *The Babylonian Captivity of the Church*, written two months later, here Luther developed[38] his notion of the Lord's Supper as "testament" or will bequeathed to the faithful, as opposed to viewing the sacrament as a sacrifice and a human work performed before God.[39]

Perhaps shaped by his training in the law, Luther interpreted Jesus's words and actions at the Last Supper to be conveying Christ's "testament" as a special vow made visible through the sign of the cup "of the new testament." In support of this notion, Luther looked to Hebrews 9:16–17: "Where a will is involved, the death of the one who made it must be established. For a will takes effect only at death, since it is not in force as long as the one who made it is alive." Hence, Luther here established both a theory of atonement and the means for its bequeathal through the Eucharist. Christ established the New Testament through the cup of his blood for the forgiveness of sins and disannulled the law of Moses in the Old Testament.[40] In order to certify the

---

35. LW 35:61.
36. LW 35:63.
37. Janz, "The Lord's Supper," in *Westminster Handbook to Martin Luther*, 85.
38. Though he more fully developed his notion of "testament" in his *Treatise on the New Testament*, Luther's first mention of this concept in reference to the Supper came as early as 1517, in his lectures on Heb. 8:6: "For one must believe Him who makes the covenant [*testatori*] when he says (Matt. 26:28; Luke 22:20): 'This is the blood which is shed for you and for many for the remission of sins'" (LW 29:209); here via Spinks, *Do This in Remembrance of Me*, 247.
39. LW 35:79–111.
40. LW 35:84.

promise, Christ died so that the will might be granted: "Even as a man who bequeaths something stipulates also [in his will] what shall be done for him afterward—as is the custom at present in the requiems and masses for the dead—so also Christ has made a requiem for himself in this testament."

Yet this requiem, Luther posited, was not a service for the sake of God but for the will's recipients—that is, all those who have faith. The Supper becomes a necessary reminder of the promise established in the upper room and ratified at Golgotha. "We are thereby strengthened in faith, confirmed in hope, and made ardent in love."[41] Just as God used signs in the past to demonstrate and remind believers of divine promises (e.g., the rainbow for Noah and circumcision for Abraham), so the elements of the Table serve this ongoing purpose for the worshiping community. Luther thus maintained the threefold sacramental definition he has previously outlined: sign, promise, and faith. Consequently, he critiqued the medieval notion of the Eucharist as a sacrifice done for God—arguing that "we do not presume to give God something in the sacrament"[42]—but transposed its purpose as a rite done by God for the faithful.

The sacrament should always be exercised in tandem with the corresponding words of Christ's promise. Just as baptism cannot simply be the pouring of water on a child in silence, Luther, in turn, scolded priests who mumbled the words of institution and thereby concealed the promise of the gospel: "Christ has gathered up the whole gospel in a short summary with the words of this testament or sacrament. For the gospel is nothing but a proclamation of God's grace and of the forgiveness of all sins, granted us through the sufferings of Christ."[43]

Luther likewise excoriated the clergy for performing private masses and masses for the dead as a work to lessen the years the namesake would suffer in purgatory and also for their denying the laity access to the cup along with the bread. The Reformer likewise scolded the laity for treating the sacrament superstitiously as a form of magic, as a defense against evil, and for attempting to manipulate the divine promise into a means for worldly prosperity and divine healing.[44] "Yet," he opined, "they all find priests perverted enough to take their money and do their bidding."[45] Rather than depending on the Mass for these perverted purposes, the church should, Luther emphasized,

41. LW 35:85.
42. LW 35:98.
43. LW 35:106.
44. Gordon A. Jensen, "Luther and the Lord's Supper," in Kolb et al., *Oxford Handbook of Martin Luther's Theology*, 324.
45. LW 35:107.

view the rite as the testament for the forgiveness of sin, open to all those genuinely seeking forgiveness. But without faith in God's promised gift, no prayers, good works, or hearing masses could be effective in receiving forgiveness. The Supper, then, is divinely designed for those who apprehend God's promise and believe.[46]

In September of 1520, Luther famously attacked the entire sacramental system of the Western church, ultimately rejecting all but two of the seven rites as sacraments. Even though the Lord's Supper retained its sacramental status and was even touted by the Reformer as "the most important of all,"[47] Luther invested approximately half of this treatise's ink addressing its abuses and his proposed theological emendations for the rite. Still early in the Reformer's career, *The Babylonian Captivity of the Church* became Luther's magnum opus on and the foundation for his Protestant view of the sacraments.[48] Much of what Luther introduced in the *Treatise on the New Testament* is repeated here but expanded with more substantive arguments. Structuring his treatise around "captivities" that the clergy imposed upon the laity, Luther highlighted three captivities pertaining to the Supper: denial of the cup for the laity, denial of the simple faith in Christ's presence and replacing it with transubstantiation, and denial of the divine promise conveyed in the Supper and replacing it with a sacrifice and a human work. Although the first and third "captivities" are already familiar themes in Luther, the Wittenberg professor sharpened his rhetoric in pushing for eucharistic reforms.

Luther, believing the church to be violating the spirit of the Scriptures by serving only bread to the laity, highlighted Christ's injunctive, "Drink from it, all of you" (Matt. 26:27). Such words, Luther stated, were directed not to the clergy alone but must have been addressed to the gathered community of faith. Pushing against the doctrine of concomitance, Luther observed that the priests never partook only of the bread but always of both elements, and he asked rhetorically, "How can it be that the sacrament in one kind is not complete in the case of the priests, yet in the case of the laity it is complete?"[49] And if the church has the authority to withhold one kind from the laity, it follows that the clergy can withhold the other, along with baptism and penance.[50] But Christ clearly taught, Luther insisted, that it is poured out for all:

46. LW 35:111.
47. Translation via Dillenberger, 256; cf. LW 36:19, which merely renders the phrase as an ordering of Luther's outline, the Eucharist being the "first of all" the sacraments that Luther would address.
48. LW 36:11–126.
49. LW 36:22.
50. LW 36:21.

"'For you' [Luke 22:20], he says—let this refer to the priests. 'And for many' [Matt. 26:28], however, cannot refer to the priests."[51] At the end of this section, Luther called for the end of Roman tyranny in this matter, for the laity to seize both kinds by force, and for the priests to henceforth no longer view themselves as lords but as servants of God, bound by duty for the people.[52]

Although the captivity of the cup was bad enough, far worse in Luther's mind was the wicked notion that the Mass was a sacrifice and a good work, such that "the faith of this sacrament has become utterly extinct and the holy sacrament has been turned into mere merchandise, a market, and a profit-making business."[53] Though such traditions of purchasing masses had become common practice, Luther admonished the church to return to the Supper's simplicity: its words of institution that encapsulate the gospel, God's promise of the forgiveness of sins. All candles, vestments, and traditions attached to this simple rite, along with prayers, preparations, and gestures, are merely adjunctive and are human works. Recipients need only faith in the Word of the divine Testament to receive what Christ set forth. Paralleling his understanding of justification, the Supper for Luther is God's work alone for all those who believe.[54]

What has gone undeveloped until this point is Luther's rejection of the theory of transubstantiation, the abuse of what should be a simple understanding of the Mass, which Luther ironically listed as the least important eucharistic "captivity." Yet, through his critique of the medieval teaching, the Reformer provided a very significant theological alternative to explain real presence: Luther's concept of sacramental union. Although he had previously described the Lord's Supper as conferring Christ's "testament" and rejected the notion that the Eucharist was a sacrifice, Luther had yet to denounce the doctrine of transubstantiation directly. There may have been good reason for his initial caution in attacking this Catholic stronghold. Luther's reluctance undoubtedly derived neither from deference to the medieval heavyweights who had developed and endorsed the view, nor from fear of being associated with famous heretics who rejected it,[55] but from his recognition that transubstantiation, even with all its dependence on philosophical constructs, still protected the real presence of Christ in the Eucharist, a safekeeping Luther interpreted to be biblically necessary.

51. LW 36:22–23.
52. LW 36:27–28.
53. LW 36:35.
54. LW 36:36–43; Jensen, "Luther and the Lord's Supper," 325.
55. Instead, Luther willingly conceded: "Here I shall be called a Wycliffite and a heretic by six hundred names." LW 36:28.

What Luther now recognized was that one could hold to a simple view of Christ's real presence in the elements without subscribing to "the Aristotelian church."[56] Luther now saw the medieval concept of transubstantiation as mere theory and opinion instead of biblical or ecclesial doctrine or even sound reason. Luther pointed out that "the church kept the true faith for more than twelve hundred years, during which time the holy fathers never, at any time or place, mentioned this transubstantiation (a monstrous word and monstrous idea), until the pseudophilosophy of Aristotle began to make its inroads into the church in these last three hundred years."[57] Luther asked why it was inconceivable or unacceptable for Christ's body to be present with the elements, using an illustration from the blacksmith's shop: "In red-hot iron, for instance, the two substances, fire and iron, are so mingled that every part is both iron and fire. Why is it not even more possible that the body of Christ be contained in every part of the substance of the bread?"[58] As James F. White has conceded, Luther's comparison may not be good physics,[59] but the picture is certainly easier for ordinary laity to grasp than nuances of Aristotelian philosophy.

Luther further bolstered this notion of the union of the physical with the divine by comparing the eucharistic event to the incarnation: If Christ was born in the inviolate womb of his mother, he rhetorically asked, was Mary's own flesh annihilated such that Jesus was able to overcome his own accidents? Instead, Luther contended, Christ used simple images of bread and wine so that his presence and promise would not be clouded by philosophical Scholasticism but be easily grasped by believers. What is true of Christ's incarnated body must now be true of the bread and wine, as the old axiom puts it: "This man is God; this God is man." What philosophy cannot apprehend, faith grasps nonetheless.[60]

Luther repeated much of his new eucharistic theology in treatises in the following years. In *The Misuse of the Mass* in 1521,[61] he accepted the use of other trappings, signs, and ceremonies accompanying the Eucharist but argued that they are unnecessary and that whether to retain or discard them should be left as a matter of conscience. But holding that the Supper is a

---

56. LW 36:29.

57. LW 36:31; Luther's dating may be more attributable to the popularization of the term, since Hildebert de Lavardin, Archbishop of Tours, in the eleventh century, is often credited with first employing the term "transubstantiation." See John Cuthbert Hedley, *Holy Eucharist* (London: Longman, Green, 1907), 37.

58. LW 36:32.

59. White, *Sacraments*, 76.

60. LW 36:32–35.

61. LW 36:162–98.

sacrifice distorts its meaning and loses its message: the promise of "the body of Christ and the pouring out of his blood for the forgiveness of sins, which is the new testament."[62] Confusing the nature of the Supper with what has been previously established amounts to exchanging God's gift to the recipients with some work that the faithful perform for God: "For a sacrifice and a promise are further apart than sunrise and sunset."[63] In this treatise Luther also argued that the priesthood had abused its status, denying the laity access to prayer and the sacraments by pretending that the clergy are necessary mediators between God and the laity. Instead, Luther contended that all the people are equally priests, for all are one in Christ and have equal access to God. Christ then is the sole mediator between God and humanity.[64] Therefore the administrator of the Supper serves in a place of privilege, but not one of higher spiritual authority.

Luther makes a similar point about free conscience in his 1523 work *The Adoration of the Sacrament*, in this case regarding the veneration of Christ in the sacrament. Whether one should worship the divine presence in the elements "should be left a matter of freedom" since Christ gave no specific command along these lines.[65] Neither those who do nor those who do not adore the sacrament should be condemned by the others: "Free, free it must be, according as one is disposed in his heart and has opportunity."[66] But Luther urged Christians to not miss the point: they should not so much focus on the sacrament itself as on the words of promise, for there, when those words are accompanied by bread and wine, are they reminded not to rely upon their own works but by faith depend solely upon God.

Luther's Liturgical Reforms of the Eucharist

While Luther was living in confinement at Wartburg Castle following the Diet of Worms (1521–22), Andreas Bodenstein von Karlstadt began introducing liturgical modifications to the Eucharist in Wittenberg. As preacher of the Schlosskirche (the Wittenberg Castle Church), Karlstadt, along with other members of the university faculty, was pressed from various constituents to make public reforms in conformity with Luther's theology.[67] Karlstadt altered

---

62. LW 36:169.
63. Ibid.
64. LW 36:139.
65. LW 36:294.
66. LW 36:295.
67. Amy Nelson Burnett, ed. and trans., *The Eucharistic Pamphlets of Andreas Bodenstein von Karlstadt*, Early Modern Studies 6 (Kirkville, MO: Truman State University Press, 2011),

the language of consecration to the vernacular, gave the laity both elements, and on Christmas Day, 1521, without traditional vestments or exacting the traditional requirement of precommunion confession, he administered what may have been the first simplified, evangelical Mass.[68]

Upon his return to Wittenberg in the spring of 1522 and without retracting the new modifications, Luther advised for a more prudent and cautious reform of the Supper, publishing a new treatise, *Receiving Both Kinds in the Sacrament*.[69] For the most part, Luther once again called for freedom in matters of liturgical form. Many of the outward trappings of the service are just that. Opponents of any reform of the Mass "must also admit that the things they emphasize and rage about are mere human regulations."[70] Thus the church should not make requirements out of such trifles as vestments, consecrated vessels, and the like and bind consciences of others to conform or accuse of heresy those who do not. "The conscience must be free to choose either way in this matter, and our liberty must remain unimpaired."[71] Christians should be able to consider receiving the elements with their hands and how often to observe the Eucharist and when to fast and attend to private confession, and priests should be enabled to determine whether to wear vestments, chant in the service, and even, unrelatedly, whether to marry a wife.[72] Regardless, Luther underscored, "It is irksome to God and to men that we begin our Christian life with external matters and pass over that which is really inward,"[73] which is outwardly expressed in love and service to one's neighbor.

By January of 1523, Luther had begun to construct liturgical reforms of worship in which he underscored the priority of the Word over the outward sign by replacing daily masses with morning and evening and even noontime services of prayer and readings from Scripture. The Mass would be available only if desired, since "one cannot make hard and fast rules." Likewise, the sacrament would be given at the Sunday service, which now should be accompanied by the preaching of the gospel.[74] At the close of the year, Luther

---

6–7. E.g., Nelson and Abdel Ross Wentz both point out that students and Wittenberg residents demanded the abolition of the Mass and the free preaching of the gospel, to the point of making demands to the city council and driving off priests. A group of monks led an iconoclastic skirmish in Luther's absence as well. See Burnett, *Eucharistic Pamphlets*, 7; Wentz, "Introduction [to Luther's *Receiving Both Kinds in the Sacrament*]," LW 36:233.

68. Burnett, *Eucharist Pamphlets*, 8.

69. LW 36:237–67.

70. LW 36:243.

71. Ibid.

72. LW 36:244–62; Janz, "The Lord's Supper," 87.

73. LW 36:262.

74. Luther, *Concerning the Order of Public Worship*, LW 58:13.

had finally constructed more specific instructions for the administration of the Eucharist in his outline, An Order of Mass and Communion for the Church at Wittenberg.[75] Retaining his spirit of freedom regarding outward ceremony ("I have used neither authority nor pressure"),[76] Luther recommended conservative reforms, including the use of German both in the singing and in the sermon, and he redacted all language of "sacrifice" from the service. Luther also announced that the time of patience for the ignorant and weak-minded had now passed and that both kinds could now be requested at the altar. Private confession was not required before the service, but partakers of the rite were advised still to prepare through fasting and prayer.[77] For the administrator, Luther recommended serving pure wine instead of mixing it with water, the continuation of chants and collects, provided they are "evangelical," and placing either the Creed or the sermon before the sacrament. But, beyond any possible reforms, "all that matters is that the Words of Institution should be kept intact and that everything should be done by faith."[78]

By 1525, Luther made two required alterations to the Mass: that the language of "sacrifice" be purged from the liturgy and that the priest not whisper (i.e., *Stillmesse*) but proclaim the gospel through the words of institution, which testify to Christ as humanity's only mediator.[79] And in 1526, the Reformer at long last published his own German Mass, although his evangelical colleagues had already been utilizing various services in the vernacular for the past several years. As a scholar, he loved Latin, along with Greek and Hebrew, but Luther acknowledged the need for the Mass to be in German "for the sake of the unlearned lay folk."[80] Regardless, Luther placed the preaching, teaching, and chanting of God's Word as a greater priority.

Luther's Disputes with Karlstadt, Zwingli, and Oecolampadius on Real Presence

Just as was the case with baptism, Luther was forced to shift his rhetoric from dealing with Catholicism on his right in order to address theological attacks on his Protestant left in the mid-1520s. Labeling these new adversaries "fanatics" for rejecting Christ's real presence in the Eucharist, Luther battled the three-headed Chimera of Andreas Karlstadt, Ulrich Zwingli, and

75. LW 53:19–40.
76. LW 53:19.
77. LW 53:34–36.
78. LW 53:31.
79. Luther, *The Abomination of the Secret Mass*, LW 36:311–28.
80. LW 53:63.

Johannes Oecolampadius, who collectively argued instead for various nuances of Christ's figurative, spiritual, or symbolic presence in the elements and advocated for the Supper to be viewed as a memorial for Christ, who is really, physically at the right hand of God in the heavenly realm and thus is necessarily corporeally absent from the bread and cup. Desiring a united Protestant theological front against Rome, Luther was originally opposed to Protestant infighting. But following some twenty-four printed attacks on his understanding of the sacramental union of Christ in and with the host, the Reformer recognized that a public rebuttal was necessary.[81] Luther's response came in four treatises written over four years and sharing a common theme: a lengthy treatise against Karlstadt, *Against the Heavenly Prophets in the Matter of Images and Sacraments*,[82] in 1525; the short treatise or "sermon," *The Sacrament of the Body and Blood of Christ—Against the Fanatics*,[83] in 1526; the more extensive *That These Words of Christ, "This Is My Body," etc., Still Stand Firm against the Fanatics*[84] in 1527; and the prodigious but rambling *Confession concerning Christ's Supper*[85] in 1528.

Zwingli had argued that the sacraments served as a public testimony or a sign of a previously given divine grace. Likewise, Oecolampadius viewed Christ's words of institution as figurative, and Karlstadt had posited that the elements could not possess salvific efficacy, for such a notion would diminish the grace Christ conveyed at Calvary. Karlstadt even accused Luther of teaching that the bread itself forgives sins. Luther recognized from these detractors that he needed to clarify further both the role of the elements in conveying grace and, more importantly, the nature of Christ's real presence in them.

Luther first underscored that it was not the sacramental elements that conveyed grace but hearing the promise of God's Word and apprehending it with faith. "Our teaching is that bread and wine do not avail. I will go still farther. Christ on the cross and all his suffering and his death do not avail, even if, as you teach, they are 'acknowledged and meditated upon' with the utmost 'passion, ardor, heartfeltness.' Something else must always be there. What is it? The Word, the Word, the Word."[86] One cannot simply rehearse this service, Luther argued, preaching remembrance. Even if the preacher were to sweat blood and become feverish, it would not avail but simply be another human work because no gift of God would be conveyed. What Karlstadt and

---

81. Jensen, "Luther and the Lord's Supper," 326; and Janz, "The Lord's Supper," 88.
82. LW 40:79–223.
83. LW 36:335–61.
84. LW 37:13–150.
85. LW 37:161–372.
86. LW 40:212.

Zwingli miss is that Christ urged, "Take, eat, this is the body given for you."
The "for you" part, Luther posited, pertains to the personal appropriation
of the promise through the sacrament. After all, if the Supper were merely
a memorial meal, Luther noted, no gift or Word of God could be divinely
granted to anyone. "It would be as if I had a chest full of gold and great
treasure buried or preserved in a certain place. I might think myself to death
and experience all desire, great passion, and ardor in such knowledge and
remembrance of the treasure until I became ill. But what benefit would all
this be to me if this treasure were not opened, given, and brought to me and
placed in my keeping?"[87]

Thus Karlstadt is only partly right yet comes up dangerously short, contended Luther. Christ did indeed win the victory of salvation on the cross.
But he likewise chose to distribute this grace to believers, continuously, unto
the end of this world, through the sacrament of the altar. Remembrance only
places one in a state of mind. "But I will find in the sacrament or gospel the
word which distributes, presents, offers, and gives to me that forgiveness which
was won on the cross. . . . For while the act has taken place [at Calvary], as
long as I have not appropriated it, it is as if it has not taken place for me."[88]
Thus, for Luther, the focus was not to be on the elements themselves but on
the Word and the grace of forgiveness received through them by faith.

What disturbed Luther most of all in his fellow Reformers' arguments for
only spiritual presence or real absence was how they created what he perceived
as a false dualism between the physical and the spiritual, between the sign and
the thing signified, as if the physical could not be used for spiritual purposes.
"The flesh is of no avail," they pointed out, citing John 6:63 (RSV). Zwingli
and Karlstadt shaped their interpretations of biblical passages pertaining to
the Supper around this verse, whereas Luther framed this verse around the
Supper passages.[89] The flesh not only is of no avail, Luther argued, but is
"poison and death if it is eaten without faith and the Word."[90] Faith, then, is
what effects the sacrament, not the other way around.

Luther perceived that behind much of the "fanatics'" arguments was a
misunderstood and overliteral interpretation of Christology. In the key passage presenting the words of institution, Christ says, "This is my body."
Luther noticed that Zwingli interpreted this to mean, "This represents my
body"; and Oecolampadius rendered it, "This is a sign of my body."[91] This

87. LW 40:213.
88. LW 40:213–14.
89. Jensen, "Luther and the Lord's Supper," 327.
90. LW 37:238.
91. LW 37:34.

must be so to these fanatics, Luther maintained, because of their overliteral-ist interpretation of the ascension of Christ to a place "at the right hand" of God in glory. But this notion misunderstands the expression "at the right hand" as a literal place, as if on a golden throne, and precludes Christ's pres-ence elsewhere.[92] Luther, on the other hand, famously argued for Christ's ubiquity and that the "right hand of God" describes the almighty power of God, "which at one and the same time can be nowhere and yet must be everywhere,"[93] for God cannot be reduced to time, place, and human mea-sure. Instead, God is essentially or substantially present everywhere and in every creature, "even in the tiniest leaf,"[94] for the hand of the Creator is still present in the creation, and yet, mysteriously, God is also nowhere, "above and apart from all creatures."[95] God is free and unbound: "See, the bright rays of the sun are so near you that they pierce into your eyes or your skin so that you feel it, yet you are unable to grasp them and put them into a box, even if you should try forever. . . . So too with Christ: although he is everywhere, he does not permit himself to be so caught and grasped."[96] What makes the sacrament different from everything else is when it is ac-companied by the spoken Word. Through the Word, Christ binds himself to the elements, saying, "Here you are to find me." Believers apprehend this grace only as they attend in faith to the sacrament and likewise say, "Here I have thee, according to thy Word."[97] It is here that God allows himself to be known personally, as the bread is broken "for you."[98] Thus Christians can eat the bread with their mouths and the body with their hearts and partake of Christ and his promise. "So God arranges that the mouth eats physically for the heart and the heart eats spiritually for the mouth, and thus both are satisfied and saved by one and the same food."[99]

If Christ is truly absent from earth and can exclusively be found in the heavenly realm, Luther asked rhetorically, how can we say that Christ enters the hearts of those who believe? And yet, if Christ can enter one's heart "without breaking a hole in it," so through faith Christ enters the bread "without needing to make any hole in it."[100] Just the same way, now draw-ing on William of Ockham's thought, Luther mentioned that Christ was

92. LW 37:57.
93. Ibid.
94. Ibid.
95. LW 37:68.
96. Ibid.
97. Ibid.
98. Ibid.
99. LW 37:93.
100. LW 36:341.

physical, yet, according to Gospel accounts, he appeared and disappeared in his resurrected body in rooms with closed doors.[101] Christ is inseparably both human and divine: thus wherever Christ is one, he is also the other: "Christ's body is everywhere because it is at the right hand of God which is everywhere, although we do not know how that occurs."[102] Hence one cannot so easily divorce the material from the spiritual. Instead, one can find Christ especially where he reveals himself in his Word, and the Scriptures reveal that he can be found in faith through the bread and cup. At most, this could only be understood as synecdoche, an expression where the part is mentioned instead of the whole. The bread and wine also contain Christ's body and blood. But beyond analogies, Luther refused to repeat what he saw as medieval errors of creating out of this understanding a philosophical construct; that is, he refused to explain exactly how Christ accomplishes this sacramental union within the elements.[103] Jensen observes: "He did not want a doctrine or theory about the Lord's Supper to distract from the benefits of the Lord's Supper."[104] Instead, Luther left such divine work to the realm of God's mystery and accepted in faith that Christ was present in the elements.

In an effort to unify German and Swiss Protestant forces, Landgrave Philip I of Hesse asked Luther and Melanchthon to meet with Zwingli and Oecolampadius at Marburg Castle from October 1 to 4, 1529, in order to work out their theological differences, in hope of arriving at consensus. Along with a number of other Reformers, the foursome discussed and found common ground on fourteen points of doctrine. But on the Lord's Supper, they agreed to disagree and so conclude their long debate on the question of Christ's presence. At Philip's behest, Luther carefully crafted the points of discussion into articles. On the fifteenth point, perhaps under Philip's influence, the articles imply that the Reformers all agreed on five of six points regarding the Supper.[105] With artful diplomacy, the last article reads in part:

> We all believe and hold . . . that the sacrament of the altar is a sacrament of the true body and blood of Jesus Christ and that the spiritual partaking of the same body and blood is especially necessary for every Christian. Similarly, that the use

101. Volker Leppin observes of this argument that "there are few places in Luther's theology where one can see so clearly the impact of his learning in the *Via moderna* as in this aspect of eucharistic teaching." See Leppin, "Martin Luther," in Wandel, *Companion to the Eucharist*, 53.

102. LW 37:214.

103. Spinks, *Do This in Remembrance of Me*, 250.

104. Jensen, "Luther and the Lord's Supper," 328.

105. Martin E. Lehmann, "Introduction [to the Marburg Colloquy and the Marburg Articles]," LW 38:12–13.

of the sacrament, like the word, has been given and ordained by God Almighty in order that weak consciences may thereby be excited to faith by the Holy Spirit. And although at this time, we have not reached an agreement as to whether the true body and blood of Christ are bodily present in the bread and wine, each side should show Christian love to the other side insofar as conscience will permit.[106]

Although the letter was signed by all four Reformers along with six others, it is still notable that in a subsequent letter to Jacobus, the provost at Bremen, Luther reflected on how markedly different from the Wittenbergers he believed Zwingli and his companions were in theology because of the latter's rejection of real presence. Luther even referred to his opponents' effort during the colloquy to concede to a spiritual presence of Christ as to "feign harmony," and Luther reportedly retorted, "You have a different spirit from ours."[107]

Luther's Mature Thought and Reforms of the Eucharist

Following Marburg, Luther's project on the Eucharist was, for the most part, complete, and his writings on the topic in his later years revealed little novelty. One can still read angry polemical treatises against both Catholic and Sacramentarian views of the Supper.[108] But his most positive summations of the Lutheran understanding of the sacrament came in his 1529 catechisms. In the Small Catechism, for instance, Luther concisely defined the sacrament of the altar as "the true body and blood of our Lord Jesus Christ under the bread and wine, instituted by Christ himself for us Christians to eat and to drink."[109] The words of institution make clear, Luther posited, that if this bread and cup are "given for you" for the forgiveness of sins, then salvation is given personally to each believer by the sacrament through Jesus's words. And yet, Luther explained, eating and drinking do not effect the promise of

---

106. LW 38:88.

107. See Wilhelm Oechsli et al., *History of Switzerland: 1499–1914*, Cambridge Historical Series (Cambridge: Cambridge University Press, 1922), 116. Additionally, according to "The Report of Osiander," Luther said these latter words to Bucer, adding, "It is clear that we do not possess the same spirit, for it cannot be the same spirit when in one place the words of Christ ["This is my body"] are simply believed and in another place the same faith is censured, resisted, regarded as false, and attacked with all kinds of malicious and blasphemous words." LW 38:70–71.

108. One can read Luther's attack on private masses in *The Private Mass and the Consecration of Priests*, LW 38:147–214; his attack on those who refuse to administer both kinds in "Disputation Theses against the Councils of Constance," WA 39/1:16.20–24; and his attack on Caspar Schwenckfeld's denial of real presence in "Brief Confession concerning the Holy Supper," LW 38:287–319.

109. Luther, Small Catechism, *BC* 362.

forgiveness, but the promise found in Christ's words is effective. Whoever obediently eats and believes receives this grace.[110]

In the Large Catechism, Luther admonished ordinary Christians to know the words of institution by heart so as to acknowledge and believe what is promised at the administration of the sacrament. Here Luther described the presence of Christ in the elements as "in and under" the bread and wine.[111] Hence, the elements, just as with the water in baptism, are not mere bread and wine but are physical elements now paired with and bound to God's Word. The Word distinguishes the elements from their formerly common uses and allows them to be "called and truly [be] Christ's body and blood."[112] The only reason the bread and wine can convey divine forgiveness is the presence of Christ's words. Consequently, the bread and wine become a treasure, a divine gift that now nourishes the soul and gives strength to the new person, provided each recipient accepts Christ's invitation to partake and believes in Christ's solemn promise.[113]

Luther's 1530 devotional work *Admonition concerning the Sacrament of the Body and Blood of Our Lord* also serves as a constructive summation of much of Luther's mature theology of the Eucharist. Here Luther pointed out that now, for Protestant Christians, the Mass is no longer a compulsory ritual done out of deference to the pope but a free gift from God. Christians have all the more reason to understand the rite properly and seek after it with appreciation for God's goodness and mercy.[114] Finally, Luther's 1537 Smalcald Articles offer a helpful distinction between Luther's understanding of the abuses of the Catholic Mass and what he saw as the proper celebration of the sacrament. What is of particular help here is that Luther framed the imparity around his chief article of Christ's person and work on the cross. If Christ alone accomplished the abolition of sin through his atoning sacrifice, then it follows that any attempt to transform the blessed ceremony into a sacrifice for God and a rite that is sold by the church and bought by the faithful is an abomination that possesses "innumerable, unspeakable abuses."[115]

The Sacrament of the Lord's Supper among Other Reformers

Much of Zwingli's eucharistic thought is seen by most students of theology through the caricaturizing lens of Luther's writing. Zwingli did indeed

110. BC 362–63.
111. BC 467.
112. BC 468.
113. BC 369–71.
114. LW 38:97–137.
115. BC 301–2.

generally view a sacrament as "the sign of a holy thing" that testifies to the historical Christ, and he specifically interpreted the sacrament of altar as simply "the symbol of the body of Christ, who was put to death for our sakes."[116] But behind Zwingli's apparent reductions of the sacrament, to be a real absence of Christ's body but an outward token of the historic, spiritual work of Christ, is the corollary concern about those who associate too closely the sign with the thing signified. When kept distinct, the acts of God by means of the cross event and the present work of the Spirit are protected as accomplished divine works in their own right and are not transmitted and reduced to the visible rites, as if granting physical objects inherent divine power. The signs can only point to the former work of God and are, as such, not means of grace but signs of past grace (factae gratiae signum).[117]

Zwingli additionally believed that such an interpretation was scripturally founded, "as Jesus said, 'This is my body,'" while still in his incarnate form. It follows that Jesus was speaking metaphorically rather than literally about the elements of the Supper, and faith does not require a rigid literalism here.[118] If Christ's substance replaced the bread or was in and with the element, Zwingli deduced that, when consumed, it would mean that "he is broken, and pressed with the teeth."[119] Yet even the human senses reject this notion of presence. What should be protected, however, is the notion that Christ bodily ascended into the heavenly realm and the human nature of Christ abides "at the right hand of God" (Mark 16:19). Such deductions required Zwingli to apprehend that the Supper was a memorial meal and a thanksgiving for Christ's sacrifice at Calvary. Here believers may powerfully confess their faith and pledge themselves anew to follow their Savior.[120]

However, what is often missed in Zwingli's Christology as it relates to the Supper is Zwingli's nuance that the ascension pertained to Christ's human nature, while Christ's spiritual nature is one with God and thus remains ubiquitous.[121] Therefore, Christ is not present in the Eucharist corporeally, naturally, or essentially but spiritually. Christians then are invited to eat of Christ spiritually, which is the "equivalent to trusting with heart and soul upon the mercy and goodness of God through Christ, that is, to have the assurance of an unbroken faith that God will give us the forgiveness of

116. Zwingli, *On the Lord's Supper*, here cited in LCC 24:188.
117. B. A. Gerrish, "The Reformation and the Eucharist," in *Thinking with the Church*, 235.
118. Zwingli, *On the Lord's Supper*, LCC 24:195.
119. Ibid.
120. See Peter Stephens, *The Theology of Huldrych Zwingli* (Oxford: Clarendon, 1986), 254; and Spinks, *Do This in Remembrance of Me*, 274–75.
121. Zwingli, *On the Lord's Supper*, LCC 24:212–13.

sins and the joy of eternal salvation for the sake of his Son."[122] It also follows that to eat spiritually is to eat sacramentally "in conjunction with the sacrament." In this sense Christians feed spiritually upon Christ and find their souls strengthened by faith through the outward tokens.[123] While a symbolic memorialism, Zwingli's eucharistic theology perceived the Supper as a common feast of the faithful and underscored the corporate nature of the congregation, which collectively brought its thanksgiving (hence, "Eucharist") to God through this ceremony. But Zwingli remained concerned that its overuse would once again produce a rote and mechanical service in the minds of his congregants; thus he reduced its observance to four times a year (Easter, Pentecost, September 11 in honor of the patron saint of Zurich, and Christmas).[124]

The Anabaptists were generally closer to Zwingli's symbolic memorialism than to Catholicism, Luther, or most other magisterial Reformers. Most early Anabaptists, like Michael Sattler, agreed with Zwingli's Christology that the bodily Christ was risen: "It follows therefrom," Sattler testified, "since He is in heaven and not in the bread, that He cannot be eaten bodily."[125] A number of Anabaptists also concurred with Zwingli's division between Christ's bodily and spiritual presence, but the Anabaptists typically located the spiritual Christ on earth, as within the true church, the corporate body of believers. Consequently, the rehearsal of the Supper served as a remembrance of Christ's suffering and death, "to announce it loudly and to be eternally thankful for it," but also served, as Balthasar Hubmaier underscored, as a communal pledge of love expressed by each member to the others, which obligates each to live in conformity to Christ for the others. The Supper was thus a form of uniting oneself with Christ yet also reaffirming oneself to the community's shared bonds of obligation and discipline, each person to and with the other believers.[126] Finally, while many Anabaptists could be characterized as Sacramentarians, often even eschewing the use of the word "sacrament" for the rites of baptism and the Supper, prominent Anabaptist theologians like Hubmaier, Pilgram Marpeck, and Menno Simons often referred to the communal oath

---

122. Zwingli, *An Exposition of the Faith*, LCC 24:258.

123. Ibid., LCC 24:259.

124. Gerrish, "Reformation and the Eucharist," 237; and Spinks, *Do This in Remembrance of Me*, 277.

125. Michael Sattler, from the proceedings of Sattler's trial, here cited in *The Legacy of Michael Sattler*, 71.

126. See Brewer, *A Pledge of Love*, esp. 50–66; and John D. Rempel, *The Lord's Supper in Anabaptism: A Study in the Christology of Balthasar Hubmaier, Pilgram Marpeck, and Dirk Philips*, Studies in Anabaptist and Mennonite History 33 (Scottdale, PA: Herald Press, 1993), esp. 52–57.

or pledge as the true "sacrament," while the corresponding loaf and cup were the sacramental signs of this congregational commitment.[127]

James F. White has observed that John Calvin sat on the privileged perch of a second-generation Reformer who could sagaciously appropriate the best and diminish the worst of the contributions of his predecessors.[128] This observation is perhaps nowhere truer than in Calvin's theological appropriation, nuancing, and systemization of a variety of Protestant theologies on the Eucharist, especially those of Luther and Zwingli. Calvin's interpretation of the Supper essentially carved a middle road between Luther's sacramental union and Zwingli's symbolic memorial. Key to Calvin's theology in general and the Supper in particular is his notion of the mystical union of Christ and the church as cohering with the perichoretic bonds of the Trinity.[129] In his commentary on Romans, Calvin wrote: "This is the purpose of the gospel, that Christ should become ours, and that we should be engrafted into his body."[130] He observed that the Word itself testified to this promise of union by which Christians have communion with Christ. But due to the foolishness of humanity, no one can receive Christ through the simple teaching and preaching of this Word. God then deigned "to attach to his Word a visible sign, by which he represents the substance of his promises, to confirm and fortify us, and to deliver us from all doubt and uncertainty."[131] Even from this brief summary, one may readily observe traces of both Luther's and Zwingli's influence. Yet unlike Zwingli, Calvin insisted that the sacrament does not contain mere signs but those that come to humanity as "a mystery so high and incomprehensible," which seals the consciences of the weak-minded to understand God's promise. And unlike Luther and the Catholics, he asserted that the elements are not signs that possess Christ corporeally or substantively, but God nevertheless

---

127. Marpeck wrote, e.g., "Thus you can see how both baptism and the Lord's Supper are called sacraments, namely, because both of them take place with a commitment and sanctification, which is actually what a sacrament is, for merely to plunge somebody into water or to baptize them is no sacrament. You must baptize in such a manner that the one who is baptized dies to his sins in a sincere way and in the power of a living faith in Christ. From henceforth, he commits himself to a new life, and only then is baptism a true sacrament, that is, when the content and action of baptism happens with the commitment to a holy covenant. It is the same way with the Lord's Supper." *The Writings of Pilgram Marpeck*, trans. and ed. William Klassen and Walter Klaassen (Scottdale, PA: Herald Press, 1978), 171–72.

128. White, *Sacraments*, 78.

129. See Michael S. Horton, "Union and Communion: Calvin's Theology of Word and Sacrament," in *International Journal of Systematic Theology* 11, no. 4 (October 2009): 399–401.

130. Calvin, *Commentary on the Epistle of Paul the Apostle to the Romans*, trans. and ed. John Owen (repr., Grand Rapids: Baker, 1996), 9; here via ibid., 400.

131. Calvin, *Short Treatise on the Holy Supper of Our Lord and Only Savior Jesus Christ*, in *Calvin: Theological Treatises*, trans. J. K. S. Reid, LCC 22:143–44; here via Johnson, *Sacraments and Worship*, 235.

adds reality to the symbol through the mysterious work of the Holy Spirit so that Christians may become "partakers of his substance."[132] For as long as Christ is outside of the human, God and that person remain separated and Christ's work on the cross is superfluous. Therefore, the Eucharist becomes the means, by the promise of Christ and the power of the Spirit, for humanity to enjoy all Christ's benefits.[133]

What Calvin claimed here only makes sense when one understands that Calvin concurred with Zwingli's idea that the bodily Christ remained in heaven but that, by the work of the Holy Spirit through the sacrament, the believer may be united with Christ even through these intervals of space. By hearing the words of institution and viewing the ensuing fraction of the bread, Christians can perceive and appropriate how the otherwise earthly signs may be used for a heavenly purpose.[134] Calvin wrote: "But greatly mistaken are those who conceive no presence of flesh in the Supper unless it lies in the bread. For they leave nothing to the secret working of the Spirit, which unites Christ himself to us."[135] The recipients of the Supper, then, do not have Christ brought down to them but instead may be mysteriously transported, in a sense, by the Spirit to the heavenly realm in order to partake of his body there. What Calvin articulated here is a kind of theosis (Greek *theōsis*), or divinization, through the spoken, visible reenactment of the spoken Word. Even Calvin conceded: "I shall not be ashamed to confess that it is a secret too lofty for either my mind to comprehend or my words to declare. And, to speak more plainly, I rather experience than understand it."[136] Through the earthly signs, which are the instruments of God's grace, the faithful may feed upon the flesh and blood of Christ "as if it penetrated into our bones and marrow," effecting a mystical union with Christ.[137]

With the vast array of Protestant eucharistic theologies, Thomas Cranmer ultimately was influenced by several of his Protestant theological predecessors. At the advent of open reforms of the Church of England following Henry VIII's death and Edward VI's accession, Cranmer manifested a eucharistic theology most similar to Luther's. Relatively conservative in its description, Cranmer maintained the real presence of Christ in the Supper without diminishing the substance of the bread and wine. This notion of Christ's corporeal but shared

132. Catechisms of the Church of Geneva, in *Calvin: Theological Treatises*, trans. J. K. S. Reid, LCC 22:137; here via White, *Sacraments*, 79.
133. Calvin, *Inst.* 3.1.1; here via Horton, "Union and Communion," 400.
134. Davis, *This Is My Body*, 70–71.
135. Calvin, *Inst.* 4.17.31; LCC 21:1403.
136. Calvin, *Inst.* 4.17.31–32; LCC 21:1403.
137. See Calvin, *Inst.* 4.17.10; LCC 21:1370; and Lee Palmer Wandel, *The Eucharist in the Reformation: Incarnation and Liturgy* (Cambridge: Cambridge University Press, 2006), 160.

physical presence Cranmer referred to as "true presence." But by 1547, Cranmer
gravitated from a conservative Lutheran understanding of the sacrament to a
theology more aligned with Calvin. In the 1548 Order of Communion, Cranmer described the consuming of the elements as one "spiritually" partaking
of Christ's body and blood. The 1549 Book of Common Prayer also subtly
reflected Cranmer's Reformed influences: the physical elements were understood as symbols of the accompanying reception of Christ's spiritual body
and blood.[138] Artfully yet intentionally ambiguously worded as a transitional
document,[139] the first English prayer book contained many prayers that have
remained mostly intact. For instance, the priest's words following the words
of institution read:

> Wherefore, O Lord and heavenly Father, according to the instruction of thy
> dearly beloved Son, our savior Jesus Christ, we thy humble servants do cel-
> ebrate, and make here before thy divine majesty, with these thy holy gifts, the
> *memory* which thy Son hath willed us to make, having *in remembrance* his
> blessed passion, mighty resurrection, and glorious ascension, rendering unto
> thee most hearty thanks for the innumerable *benefits* procured unto us by the
> same, entirely desiring thy Fatherly goodness, mercifully to accept this our
> *sacrifice* of praise and thanksgiving [etc.].[140]

Such passages could have been interpreted as supporting any number of theories of Christ's presence in the sacrament. Nevertheless, following the prayer
book's publication, Cranmer defended and further defined his own view of
the Supper by articulating that the human body consumes the common bread
and wine while the believing heart receives "the spiritual meat" of Christ's
celestial body.[141] At this later juncture, Cranmer's mature eucharistic theology
paralleled much of Calvin's project. Regardless, still much akin to Luther,
Cranmer maintained that the grace signified in the divinely ordained signs is
effected by each individual's faith in God's promise.[142]

---

138. James F. Turrell, "Anglican Theologies of the Eucharist," in Wandel, *Companion to
the Eucharist*, 140–42.

139. On this point, Turrell observes: "The 1549 prayer book therefore should not be read as
a reflection of Cranmer's own eucharistic theology, as much as the effort of a practical liturgist
to construct a transitional rite." Ibid., 141.

140. *First English Prayer Book*, 27–28, emphasis added.

141. Cranmer, "An Answer to a Crafty and Sophistical Cavillation Devised by Stephen Gar-
diner," in *Writings and Disputations of Thomas Cranmer, Archbishop of Canterbury, Martyr
1556, Relative to the Sacrament of the Lord's Supper*, ed. John Edmund Cox (Cambridge:
Cambridge University Press, 1844), 43; here via Turrell, "Theologies of the Eucharist," 143.

142. For further development of this theme, see Gordon P. Jeanes, *Signs of God's Promise:
Thomas Cranmer's Sacramental Theology and the Book of Common Prayer* (London: T&T
Clark, 2008), esp. 136–37.

A Contemporary Protestant Appropriation of the Eucharist

Of the writing of Protestant eucharistic theologies there is no end. Each of the theologies of the Reformers listed above has something compelling to consider regarding the Supper, not to mention Melanchthon, Bullinger, Leo Jud, Bucer, Oecolampadius, and Dirk Philips's contributions, whose own particular eucharistic thoughts were not expounded in this chapter. Amid the variegated notions of Christ's real or spiritual presence, bodily absence, sacramental union, memorial, congregational pledge of love, and mystical union, all the Reformers concurred that the notion of the elements transubstantiating into Christ, supported by the Aristotelian discrimination between an object's substance and accidents, was a construct unsupported by Scripture. Likewise the Reformers agreed that the Supper was not a sacrifice through which the properly ordained serve as a kind of conduit effecting the sacrament. Christ's work was instead accomplished at Calvary. Whether that grace is appropriated through the sacrament of the altar, and if so, how, remains their point of contention among themselves, and thus also among their theological descendants.

While contemporary theologians may debate the value of these respective contributions from the earliest of Protestant thinkers, it is undoubtedly true that a version of Zwingli's symbolic memorialism has won the day among the majority of Protestant laypeople. This has happened gradually, both as a consequence of the hegemony of free-church theology in the West, especially in America, even among laity in historically magisterial Protestant denominations, and by the simple virtue of modern Westerners being products of post-Enlightenment thought. Contemporary Christians eschew any suggestion of the supernatural in proximity to physical objects. The physical, instead, belongs to the world of science as something that can be observable, measurable, and ultimately controllable. Interpreting the sacramental elements as signs and symbols of the invisible (and therefore acceptably transcendent) is more compatible with the times. Society in general is filled with symbols, from branding in business, to national monuments and flags, to signs of status and success. What's more, because Christians have traditionally acknowledged the propitiatory work of Christ on behalf of humanity as a historic event, the modern comprehension of the Lord's Table is reduced to Christ's words that are often carved on the table's front: "This Do in Remembrance of Me" (Luke 22:19; 1 Cor. 11:24 KJV). The sacrament is apprehended as a memorial only.

Regardless, ministers whose traditions confess this eucharistic understanding should avoid the use of such language of "mere" symbolism. Symbols instead can be exceptionally powerful tokens. For example, no person would think twice about wiping dirty boots on an ordinary doormat. But if one were simply to add the words "Christ Is King" to the mat (for a word itself is a kind of symbol), many people of all faiths would think twice about tramping the mat with their muddy boots! The substance of the mat was not changed. Only symbols, which point beyond the thing itself, were added to it. Such is the power of the word when associated with the outward sign. Furthermore, the new trend, among free-church congregations, of administering the sacraments without the reading or reciting of the words of institution is inexcusable. Symbolic memorialism still advances the power of the Word as reframing common, earthly objects for uncommon, heavenly purposes. The sacrament of the Table can and should still be approached with the same dignity and reverence as that with which those who avow Christ's real presence approach it.

Despite its popularity, many theologians take issue with Zwingli's symbolic memorialism as a service that diminishes the sacrament as a means of grace. It is little wonder that most churches that have appropriated Zwingli's sacramental theology also serve communion rarely. Avoiding the pitfalls of Thomistic transubstantiation, Protestants instead need to recover a more robust understanding of and appreciation for the Eucharist as part and parcel of the regular worship of the church. Regardless of whether a congregation interprets Christ's presence spiritually or corporeally, worshipers often experience the Supper as a means of being drawn closer to God. This feeling may be more objective than the contemporary mind at first perceives. Calvin's understanding of the Supper is attractive to contemporary theologians along these lines in that his thought is often presented as the middle way between Luther's real presence and Zwingli's real absence. Moderation in the contemporary context has its own appeal. Likewise, Calvin allowed the elements to remain as signs without attempting to explain exactly how Christ is otherwise physically present since the latter notion seems to push the boundaries of the Christian imagination (especially now to post-Enlightenment people). Nevertheless, Calvin's view of humanity's mystical union being both the goal of the gospel in general and the Lord's Supper in particular is admittedly spiritually powerful, systematically consistent, and theologically attractive.

Notwithstanding its lingering questions regarding the corporeal nature of Christ in the elements and the Western mind's inexorable desire to return to Scholastic constructs in order to explain the mechanics of God's activity in a ritual, Martin Luther's eucharistic theology may yet serve both as a critique on theologically unhealthy Protestant practices of the Supper and as a model for providing greater significance and theological import to a rite instituted by Christ himself and practiced each time the early church gathered for worship.

Luther's concern about Zwingli's (and what would be Calvin's) attempt to disengage the body of Christ from Christ's spirit may be grounded in a more well-constructed Christology and resurrection theology. Perhaps Luther is correct in his critique that one should not consider Christ, as the firstborn of creation, in terms of Platonic dualisms by dividing his physicality from his spiritual presence. As N. T. Wright explains, since the time of Christ, the ancient Jews and the early Christians who followed them did not consider a "spirit" as something disembodied but embodied, not "non-physical" but the physical indwelt by the Spirit of God.[143] And if Christ, as the Resurrected One, now demonstrates through his own perpetual solidarity with humanity the essence of what will be humanity's own postresurrection corporeality, "that where I am, there you may be also" (John 14:3), it suggests that Christ's ubiquity should not limit his reality as merely disembodied: "Touch me and see; for a ghost does not have flesh and bones as you see that I have" (Luke 24:39).

Hence, it follows that Christ is either wholly absent from the meal—which simply serves to memorialize his onetime incarnation, and his words of institution are to be taken metaphorically—or Christ is wholly, corporeally present in the meal, just as he straightforwardly promised: "This is my body." The inner logic of the spiritual presence and bodily absence of the Son of God will simply not do. If Christ's corporeal ubiquity is the divine reality, Luther was also sagaciously reticent about explaining just how this came to be, other than by using illustrations of common objects that appear to take on two natures or by the use of biblical examples of Christ's postresurrection appearance that demonstrate his physicality and what N. T. Wright has termed "transphysicality"[144] (e.g., he ate fish and invited his disciples to touch him but still appeared and disappeared at will). Although this concept is beyond human comprehension and experience, that does not make Christ's corporeal ubiquity less plausible. It simply makes it divine.

Having recognized the strengths of Calvin's and particularly Luther's understanding of the Supper, it is also important to observe the contribution of the Anabaptist tradition to the eucharistic conversation. Although for the most part inheritors of Zwingli's symbolic understanding of the elements, the Anabaptists demonstrate better than any other Protestant group

143. N. T. Wright, *The Resurrection of the Son of God*, vol. 3 of *Christian Origins and the Question of God* (Minneapolis: Fortress, 2003), 348–50.
144. Wright explains: "The word 'transphysical'. . . puts a label on the demonstrable fact that the early Christians envisaged a body which was still robustly physical but also significantly different from the present one. If anything—since the main difference they seem to have envisaged is that the new body will not be corruptible—we might say not that it will be *less* physical, as though it were some kind of ghost or apparition, but more. 'Not unclothed, but more fully clothed.'" Ibid., 477–78; cf. 2 Cor. 5:4.

the sacramental import of the rite of the Eucharist to the maintenance of the local expression of Christ's body in the church. For the Anabaptists, the service of the altar rightly understood is not simply to be an exercise of individual piety. All too often the debate about Christ's presence in the contemporary context appears to pertain to the individual's own perception, experience, and benefit from the rite to the exclusion of the corporate nature of the ceremony. The Anabaptists instead underscored the ritual as not only a vertically reinvigorating service between the believer and Christ; they also stressed the consequential horizontal value of the ceremony for the local congregation itself as a community bound not only to God but also to one another because of their shared faith and pledged commitments. The communal nature of the Supper that the Anabaptists accentuated can be very helpful to an increasingly hyperindividualistic society that, unfortunately, often perceives the matters of faith to be a private experience. The common loaf and cup serve well to represent this collective spirit. Immediately before or following the Lord's Supper, it would then be appropriate for contemporary congregations to stand and say the Apostles' or Nicene Creed or repeat their church's historic covenant. But by missing this corporate emphasis, by failing to bolster the sense of genuine community that is fostered by design in the Lord's Supper, modern congregants may completely overlook the meaning of the church as a place of spiritual mutuality and accountability for each believer.

It is perhaps a hackneyed but nevertheless true statement that the Supper presents not a singular but a multilayered meaning. Regardless of one's own perspective on Christ's presence, any Christian thinker can appreciate the meaning of a common loaf and cup, the powerful gestures of breaking the bread and pouring the wine, not to mention the important parallels of the eucharistic rituals to the holy meals of the ancient Israelites. Surely the meal is also intended spiritually to affect each believer personally and also establish closer bonds of individuals to their respective communities of faith. This list of layered purposes could be extended for several paragraphs. That such is the case is undoubtedly by divine design. Humanity, even the Christian congregation, cannot fully comprehend and thus control the fullness of the Supper's meaning. Since this is so, if the Eucharist requires faith in believing what Christians can see through tangible signs pointing to something far more marvelous that they cannot see or touch in this life but believe nevertheless, perhaps both Luther and Calvin were ultimately correct in supplying the apt word "mystery" to describe the meaning and essence of the Supper, without attempting to develop a new philosophical construct to replace its medieval predecessor. Mysteries, by definition, cannot be explained but only accepted by faith. Calvin articulated this well:

Now here we ought to guard against two faults. First, we should not, by too little regard for the signs, divorce them from their mysteries, to which they are so to speak attached. Secondly, we should not, by extolling them immoderately, seem to obscure somewhat the mysteries themselves. . . . It is a secret too lofty for either my mind to comprehend or my words to declare[:] . . . He declares his flesh the food of my soul, his blood its drink. I offer my soul to him to be fed with such food. In his Sacred Supper he bids me to take, eat, and drink of his body and blood under the symbols of bread and wine. I do not doubt that he himself truly presents them, and that I receive them.[145]

145. Calvin, *Inst.* 4.17.5 and 32; LCC 21:1364 and 1404.

Conclusion

For ritual allows those who cannot will themselves out of the secular to perform the spiritual, as dancing allows the tongue-tied man a ceremony of love.

Andre Dubus

These and similar perplexing disputes and questions are raised for us by those who ascribe nothing to faith and everything to works and rituals, whereas we owe everything to faith alone and nothing to ritual.

Martin Luther

Architecture is theological. This is an obvious point to many, but perhaps is still surprising to others.[1] How churches arrange their worship spaces and furnishings often speaks volumes regarding their priorities. While a general critique of modern worship spaces is beyond the scope of this work, one observation is that Protestants have either reduced or hidden their sacramental fixtures. On Sundays in churches where communion is not served weekly, the table is often unthinkingly placed in the storage closet or a darkened corner, as if it were merely a functional shelf. The baptismal font is put away or the baptistery is shuttered or covered, such that worshipers do not have to be regularly mindful of them in reference to the pulpit and the proclamation of the Word in weekly worship. The sanctuary itself divulges the theological reality that, generation by generation, the sacraments have been insidiously reduced in Protestant worship.

1. See, e.g., James F. White, *Protestant Worship and Church Architecture: Theological and Historical Considerations* (Oxford: Oxford University Press, 1964).

It is telling that the Protestant Reformers often argued among themselves as much as against their Catholic counterparts regarding the sacraments. The sacraments were of great significance to each of them and to the respective traditions they helped establish. But the inheritors of these traditions, while benefiting from a new ecumenical peace, have lost their founders' sacramental passion. Philip Lee observes: "It is significant that in the doctrinal test so important to American fundamentalists for distinguishing between authentic Christianity and liberal heresy, the sacraments are never mentioned. . . . For most American Protestants, it is a neutral area, an extinct volcano, representing no threat to either side. American Protestantism has to a great degree become de-sacramentalized."[2] Protestant ministers still proclaim from the pulpit and laity from the pews many of the core theological tenets of their foreparents' faith. But baptism and Eucharist are sadly no longer integral to worship and Christian life. The present book attempts to address this vacuum by highlighting why Luther and his contemporaries considered the sacraments to be central to the faith.

Protestants simply have lost their sacramental heritage. Leonard Vander Zee astutely observes:

> There is a powerful open channel of communication between what we see, taste, touch and smell, and our feelings, our imagination, our mind and our heart. This is true spiritually as well as in every other area of our lives. In our worship and practice as Christians, the place where the world of the spirit, mind and heart meets the world of the senses is in the sacraments. And yet, precisely at this point, many Protestants have deep suspicions.[3]

Some traditions within Protestantism, arguably as a consequence of the Enlightenment, refuse to allow for the visible to be a means of grace because spiritual things, they reason, are only found in the invisible. And yet one wonders, just as Luther wondered in the presence of Zwingli: If this is true, what becomes of the incarnation of Christ? Why would Christians celebrate Christmas if the spiritual could not be conveyed through the physical? But if Christ is indeed the holy sacrament through whom believers receive redemption, cannot he establish sacramental signs for his followers today? Didn't he?

Conversely, certain Protestant traditions are so keen to recover a robust sacramentalism that they forget their Protestant moorings by arguing a mechanical ex opere operato as if it were the only option for perceiving God's

2. Philip J. Lee, *Against the Protestant Gnostics* (Oxford: Oxford University Press, 1993), 183.
3. Leonard J. Vander Zee, *Christ, Baptism and the Lord's Supper: Recovering the Sacraments for Evangelical Worship* (Downers Grove, IL: IVP Academic, 2004), 14.

work through the elements. Hopefully this book has underscored a rich heritage that Luther and other Reformers have provided for how Protestants can understand and utilize the sacraments and other ceremonies and still maintain their principles of sola scriptura and sola fide. Only by understanding the Protestant sacramental heritage can the church continue its reforms. That notion was this volume's penultimate point.

This book will eventually be shelved in university libraries as another tome on sacramental theology; yet with the exception of the last two chapters, the book's primary theme focused instead on what Protestants do *not* see as sacramental: ceremonies, many of them at least, that Protestants have continued to observe, but without clearly understanding why they practice them. Beyond the problem of the abating importance of the sacraments themselves, Protestants today are generally more reluctant than the original Reformers to utilize many of the church's nonsacramental practices because contemporaries erroneously reason that these ceremonies are no longer deemed sacramental and mistakenly subvert their significance. Undoubtedly there are numerous reasons for this reluctance and downgrade. American Protestants are generally products of a Puritan heritage, which shared a hesitancy regarding the ordinances in general. Furthermore, Protestantism in the New World is admittedly a conglomeration of various denominational emphases: just as many American Episcopalians and Presbyterians now ironically share the Anabaptist view of the free church and freedom of conscience and often the desire for the autonomy of the local church despite their episcopal or connectional polities, so too do many Protestant laypeople gravitate to a more Zwinglian notion of the sacraments as symbols and signs. Such ideas simply make more sense to the modern mind. To make the sacraments more than that, many are afraid, would be to place oneself and the church on a dangerous trajectory toward Catholic superstitions, bell ringing, transubstantiation, and spiritual "magic." This would be the case all the more regarding the other rites beyond baptism and the Supper, particularly those that Rome maintains as sacraments. If these ceremonies are not even recognized ordinances of their own tradition, why practice them at all?

And yet, "nonsacramental" does not necessarily mean superfluous. Having a positive understanding of ordination, marriage, or even anointing the sick does not make one a closet Catholic or even paleo-orthodox. As we have seen, Luther offered many constructive comments about most of the remaining five former sacraments. In his mind they simply were not biblically established means of grace. That is to say, Luther did not interpret Christ as specifically apportioning grace to be conveyed through a designated sign in the other five church practices. Regardless, such ceremonies can potentially serve significant ministries to the church and convey rich theological meanings to its members.

In a dinnertime conversation at the former cloister that became the Luther family home, the Reformer discussed the importance of such ceremonies with his guests: "Anybody who wants to attack ceremonies," Luther said, "no matter how insignificant they may be, must grasp his sword with both hands. He mustn't do like Erasmus, who laughs at them merely because they are silly. If you object that God is foolish, too, and prescribed such silly things as circumcision, the sacrifice of Isaac, etc., I must ask you: What if these silly things which you laugh at are pleasing to God?"[4] Such a rhetorical question should be repeated today. As Luther repeated later in this conversation: "Perhaps a ceremony will be pleasing to God. Why, then, do you oppose it?"[5]

Any reasonable Protestant would concur that there is at least good reason for these rites still to be practiced. Ordination serves a role of setting apart and commissioning a Christian to lead on behalf of the others; the ministry of pastoral care to the sick and dying has become expected by laity and is a hallmark role for clergy, deacons, and church officers. Marriage will continue to be a ceremony for Christians as a bond not only between a human couple but also among husband, wife, and God. For traditions that continue infant baptism, confirmation persists as an important and even necessary rite of appropriating the faith for oneself. Finally, because of the persistence of sin in the life of each Christian, the perpetual act of reconciling oneself to God through repentance must continue to be practiced. Protestants have long agreed with Luther that these five ceremonies do not possess both God's promise and a corresponding sign; they are therefore not sacraments. Yet Luther himself posited that many church ceremonies have a biblical or ecclesial purpose, and he retained most of these as important church practices. This, of course, does not mean that Luther should simply be granted sole authority for how Protestants today understand the sacraments. He is the starting point of the discussion, not its conclusion. But Luther's works were intended to advance a robust theological conversation among Protestants, not to close it. Luther himself declared that he did not condemn such rites as ecclesial ceremonies but still positively perceived them as usages.[6] "What if these silly things which you laugh at are pleasing to God?"[7] he asked.

In a deeper sense, no matter what a theologian or church tradition accepts in its categories of sacraments and church rites, all Christians should concede

4. Luther, Table Talk, LW 54:68–69.
5. LW 54:68.
6. LW 36:91.
7. LW 54:68.

Luther's point that "according to the usage of the Scriptures, [we] should have only one single sacrament."[8] Christ is the true means of grace, the epitome of a being both earthly and divine, whom God used and still uses to dispense salvific grace to the world. The incarnation of God is the event of salvation and the true sacrament. Just as with the sacramental signs, Christ's grace cannot be received mechanically but only by faith (John 3:14–16; Acts 16:31; Rom. 10:9, 13; Eph. 2:8). States Gottfried Krodel, "The church confesses [the incarnation] in its dogma; the church preaches it in the Word; the church possesses it as reality in the sacraments. Word and sacrament are therefore the two means by which the individual can participate in the divine revelation."[9] Luther connected pulpit and table as the *verbum audibile* (the heard Word) and the *verbum visibile* (the visible Word). These became Christ's prescribed means of grace for his objective, justifying work accomplished on the cross and from the grave.[10] The *verbum visibile* allowed those postincarnation followers of Christ a means to see, feel, and taste something of the gospel message. These rites then are "God's flannelgraph,"[11] portraying the gospel story in ways those with childlike understanding can comprehend.

While avoiding the pitfalls of mechanical ritualism, Protestants should not be too quick to divide the physical from the spiritual, tangible things from mystical experiences, and this world from God's divine presence. As Vander Zee writes: "Things matter because God created the world in Christ and is redeeming it in and through Christ. Creation matters because Christ is the one in whom and through whom all things were created and by whom 'all things hold together' (Col. 1:15–17)."[12] Christians cannot fully understand their Creator and the incarnate Redeemer without seeing the importance of God's use of the tangible. The One who combined the Word with mud and spittle to bring sight to the blind (John 9:2–7) can speak through the Word and common, earthly things to bring sight to this generation as well. Whether in a sacrament or an ecclesial ceremony, God may use "silly" things to accomplish his "foolish" work (cf. 1 Cor. 1:23). Let Luther ask this contemporary generation once again: "What if these silly things [i.e., ceremonies] which you laugh at are pleasing to God? . . . Why then do you oppose it?"[13]

8. LW 36:18.
9. Krodel, "Lord's Supper in the Theology of the Young Luther," 29.
10. See John T. Mueller, "Means of Grace," in *Lutheran Cyclopedia*, ed. Erwin L. Lueker (St. Louis: Concordia, 1954), 344–45.
11. Vander Zee, *Christ, Baptism and the Lord's Supper*, 68.
12. Ibid., 17.
13. LW 54:68.

Bibliography

The Ante-Nicene Fathers. Edited by Alexander Roberts and James Donaldson. 1885–87. 10 vols. Reprint, Peabody, MA: Hendrickson, 1994.

The Apostolic Fathers. Edited by Michael W. Holmes. Translated by J. B. Lightfoot and J. R. Harmer. 2nd ed. Grand Rapids: Baker, 1989.

Aristotle. *The Nicomachean Ethics.* Edited by Hugh Tredennick. Translated by J. A. K. Thomson. New York: Penguin, 1976.

Austin, Gerard. *Anointing with the Spirit: The Rite of Confirmation; The Use of Oil and Chrism.* New York: Pueblo, 1985.

Bagchi, David. "Luther and the Sacramentality of Penance." In *Retribution, Repentance, and Reconciliation: Papers Read at the 2002 Summer Meeting and the 2003 Winter Meeting of the Ecclesiastical History Society*, edited by Kate Cooper and Jeremy Gregory, 119–27. Woodbridge, Suffolk, UK: Boydell, 2004.

Balthasar, Hans Urs von, ed. *The Scandal of the Incarnation: Irenaeus against the Heresies.* San Francisco: Ignatius, 1990.

Barth, Hans-Martin. *The Theology of Martin Luther: A Critical Assessment.* Minneapolis: Fortress, 2013.

Bauerschmidt, John C. "The Godly Discipline of the Primitive Church." *Anglican Theological Review* 94, no. 4 (Fall 2012): 685–94.

Bayer, Oswald. *Martin Luther's Theology: A Contemporary Interpretation.* Translated by Thomas A. Trapp. Grand Rapids: Eerdmans, 2008.

Bede. *Commentary on the Acts of the Apostles.* Translated by Lawrence T. Martin. Kalamazoo, MI: Cistercian Publications, 1989.

Die Bekenntnisschriften der Evangelisch-lutherischen Kirche. 9th ed. Göttingen: Vandenhoeck & Ruprecht, 1982.

Bonaventure. *Commentary on the Sentences: Sacraments; Translation, Introduction, Notes.* Works of St. Bonaventure 27. Edited by Timothy R. LeCroy and Luke Davis Townsend. St. Bonaventure, NY: Franciscan Institute, 2014.

Bonhoeffer, Dietrich. *The Cost of Discipleship.* German, 1937. Translated by R. H. Fuller with some revision by Irmgard Booth. New York: Touchstone, 1995.

Brecht, Martin. *Martin Luther: The Preservation of the Church, 1532–1546.* Vol. 3. Minneapolis: Fortress, 1993.

Brewer, Brian C. *A Pledge of Love: The Anabaptist Sacramental Theology of Balthasar Hubmaier.* Milton Keynes, UK: Paternoster, 2012.

———. "Radicalizing Luther: How Balthasar Hubmaier (Mis)Read the Father of the Reformation." *Mennonite Quarterly Review* 84, no. 1 (January 2010): 33–53.

———. "To Defer and Not to Hasten: The Anabaptist and Baptist Appropriations of Tertullian's Baptismal Theology." *Harvard Theological Review*, no. 106 (July 2013): 287–308.

Brock, Sebastian P., and Michael Vasey, eds. *The Liturgical Portions of the Didascalia.* Grove Liturgical Study 29. Bramcote, Nottingham, UK: Grove Books, 1982.

Browe, Peter. *Die Eucharistie im Mittelalter: Liturgiehistorische Forschungen in Kulturwissenschaftlicher Absicht.* Münster: Lit Verlag, 2003.

Bucer, Martin. *Melanchthon and Bucer.* Edited by Wilhelm Pauck. Library of Christian Classics 19. Philadelphia: Westminster, 1969.

Bullinger, Heinrich. *Heinrich Bullingers Reformationsgeschichte.* Edited by Johann Jakob Hottinger and H. H. Vögeli. 3 vols. Frauenfeld: C. Beyel, 1838–40.

Burger, Christoph. "Volksfrömmigkeit in Deutschland um 1500 im Spiegel der Schriften des Johannes von Paltz OESA." In *Volksreligion im hohen und späten Mittelalter,* edited by Peter Dinzelbacher and Dieter R. Bauer, 307–27. Paderborn: Schöningh, 1990.

Burns, J. Patout, and Robin M. Jensen. *Christianity in Roman Africa: The Development of Its Practices and Beliefs.* Grand Rapids: Eerdmans, 2014.

Bysted, Ane L. *The Crusade Indulgence: Spiritual Rewards and the Theology of the Crusades, c. 1095–1216.* Leiden: Brill, 2015.

Calvin, John. *Commentaries on the Epistle of James.* In *Calvin's Commentaries,* vol. 22. Edinburgh: Calvin Translation Society; Grand Rapids: Baker, 1999.

———. *Commentary on the Epistle of Paul the Apostle to the Romans.* Translated and edited by John Owen. Reprint, Grand Rapids: Baker, 1996.

———. *Institutes of the Christian Religion* [*Inst.*]. Edited by John T. McNeill. Translated by Ford Lewis Battles. 2 vols. Library of Christian Classics 20–21. Philadelphia: Westminster, 1960.

Cantalamessa, Raniero, ed. *Easter in the Early Church: An Anthology of Jewish and Early Christian Texts.* Translated by James M. Quigley and Joseph T. Lienhard. Collegeville, MN: Liturgical Press, 1993.

Clarkson, John F., and Heinrich Denzinger, eds. "The Second Council of Lyons (1274)." In *The Church Teaches: Documents of the Church in English Translation*. St. Louis: B. Herder, 1955.

Clebsch, William A., and Charles R. Jaekle. *Pastoral Care in Historical Perspective: An Essay with Exhibits*. New York: Jason Aronson, 1964.

Connell, Martin F., trans. *Church and Worship in Fifth-Century Rome: The Letter of Innocent I to Decentius of Gubbio; Text with Introduction, Translation and Notes*. Cambridge: Grove Books, 2002.

Coolman, Boyd Taylor. *The Theology of Hugh of St. Victor: An Interpretation*. New York: Cambridge University Press, 2010.

Cranmer, Thomas. *Writings and Disputations of Thomas Cranmer, Relative to the Sacrament of the Lord's Supper*. Edited by John Edmund Cox. Cambridge: Cambridge University Press, 1844.

Cully, Kendig Brubaker. *Sacraments: A Language of Faith*. Philadelphia: Christian Education Press, 1961.

Cutrone, Emmanuel J. "Sacraments." In *Augustine through the Ages: An Encyclopedia*. Edited by Allan Fitzgerald. Grand Rapids: Eerdmans, 1999.

Cyril. *St. Cyril of Jerusalem's Lectures on the Christian Sacraments: The Procatechesis and the Five Mystagogical Catecheses*. Edited by F. L. Cross. London: SPCK, 1951.

Davis, Thomas J. *This Is My Body: The Presence of Christ in Reformation Thought*. Grand Rapids: Baker Academic, 2008.

Denzinger, Henry, and Adolf Schönmetzer [DS], eds. *Enchiridion symbolorum: Definitionum et declarationum de rebus fidei et morum*. 33rd ed. Freiburg im Breisgau: Herder, 1965.

Didache. In *The Apostolic Fathers*, edited by Michael W. Holmes, translated by J. B. Lightfoot and J. R. Harmer, 2nd ed., 149–58. Grand Rapids: Baker, 1989.

Didascalia Apostolorum: The Syriac Version Translated and Accompanied by the Verona Latin Fragments. Translated by R. Hugh Connolly. Oxford: Clarendon, 1969.

Dudley, Martin, and Geoffrey Rowell. *The Oil of Gladness: Anointing in the Christian Tradition*. Collegeville, MN: Liturgical Press, 1993.

Elwood, Christopher. *The Body Broken: The Calvinist Doctrine of the Eucharist and the Symbolization of Power in Sixteenth-Century France*. New York: Oxford University Press, 1999.

Erasmus, Desiderius. *The Praise of Folly*. Translated by C. H. Miller. New Haven: Yale University Press, 1979.

Erikson, Erik H. *Young Man Luther: A Study in Psychoanalysis and History*. New York: Norton, 1958.

Evans, Ernest. *Tertullian's Homily on Baptism*. London: SPCK, 1964.

Evans, G. R., ed. *A History of Pastoral Care*. London: Cassell, 2000.

Fassler, Margot Elsbeth. *Gothic Song: Victorine Sequences and Augustinian Reform in Twelfth-Century Paris.* Cambridge: Cambridge University Press, 1993.

Ferguson, Everett. *Baptism in the Early Church: History, Theology, and Liturgy in the First Five Centuries.* Grand Rapids: Eerdmans, 2009.

Ferguson, Everett, Michael P. McHugh, Frederick W. Norris, and David M. Scholer, eds. *Encyclopedia of Early Christianity.* New York: Garland, 1990.

The First English Prayer Book. Winchester, UK: John Hunt, 2008.

Fisher, John Douglas Close. *Christian Initiation: Confirmation Then and Now.* Chicago: Hillenbrand Books, 2005.

Fitzgerald, Allan D. "Penance." In *The Oxford Handbook of Early Christian Studies,* edited by Susan Ashbrook Harvey and David G. Hunter, 786–807. Oxford: Oxford University Press, 2008.

Forest, Jim. *Confession: Doorway to Forgiveness.* Maryknoll, NY: Orbis Books, 2002.

Foxe, John. *The Acts and Monuments of John Foxe.* Edited by Stephen Reed Cattley. Vol. 5. London: R. B. Seeley & W. Burnside, 1834.

Froehlich, Karlfried. "Luther on Vocation." In *Harvesting Martin Luther's Reflections on Theology, Ethics, and the Church,* edited by Timothy J. Wengert, 121–33. Grand Rapids: Eerdmans, 2004.

George, Timothy. *Reading Scripture with the Reformers.* Downers Grove, IL: IVP Academic, 2011.

Gerrish, B. A. *Thinking with the Church: Essays in Historical Theology.* Grand Rapids: Eerdmans, 2010.

Gibson, E. C. S., ed. *The First and Second Prayer-Books of King Edward the Sixth.* Everyman's Library 448. London: J. M. Dent & Sons, 1910.

Gilmore, Alec. *Christian Baptism: A Fresh Attempt to Understand the Rite in Terms of Scripture, History, and Theology.* London: Lutterworth, 1959.

Gordon, Bruce. *John Calvin.* New Haven: Yale University Press, 2009.

Greaves, Richard L. "The Ordination Controversy and the Spirit of Reform in Puritan England." *Journal of Ecclesiastical History* 21, no. 3 (July 1970): 225–41.

Grubbs, Judith Evans. *Law and Family in Late Antiquity: The Emperor Constantine's Marriage Legislation.* Oxford: Clarendon, 1995.

Gusmer, Charles W. *And You Visited Me: Sacramental Ministry to the Sick and the Dying.* New York: Pueblo, 1984.

Hallock, Frank H. "Third Century Teaching on Sin and Penance." *Anglican Theological Review* 4, no. 2 (October 1921): 128–42.

Hamm, Berndt. *The Early Luther: Stages in a Reformation Reorientation.* Grand Rapids: Eerdmans, 2014.

Hedley, John Cuthbert. *The Holy Eucharist.* London: Longmans, Green, 1907.

Hejzlar, Pavel. "John Calvin and the Cessation of Miraculous Healing." *Communio Viatorum* 49, no. 1 (2007): 31–77.

Hendrix, Scott H. "Luther on Marriage." In *Harvesting Martin Luther's Reflections on Theology, Ethics, and the Church*, edited by Timothy J. Wengert, 169–84. Grand Rapids: Eerdmans, 2004.

———. *Martin Luther: Visionary Reformer*. New Haven: Yale University Press, 2015.

———. *Recultivating the Vineyard: The Reformation Agendas of Christianization*. Louisville: Westminster John Knox, 2004.

Henry, Paul, and Henry Stebbing. *The Life and Times of John Calvin, the Great Reformer*. New York: Carter, 1859.

Hinson, E. Glenn. "Ordination in Christian History." *Review & Expositor* 78, no. 4 (Fall 1981): 485–96.

Horton, Michael S. "Union and Communion: Calvin's Theology of Word and Sacrament." *International Journal of Systematic Theology* 11, no. 4 (October 2009): 398–414.

Hubmaier, Balthasar. *Balthasar Hubmaier: Theologian of Anabaptism*. Edited and translated by H. Wayne Pipkin and John Howard Yoder. Scottdale, PA: Herald Press, 1989.

———. "A Christian Instruction." In "The Writings of Balthasar Hubmaier." Collected and photographed by W. O. Lewis. Translated by George Duiguid Davidson. Microfilm of typescript in Conrad Grebel College Library, Waterloo, ON, 1939.

Hugh of Saint Victor. "On the Sacraments of the Christian Faith I, 9." In *On the Sacraments of the Christian Faith (De sacramentis)* [*Sacr.*], translated by Roy J. Deferrari, 154–65. Cambridge, MA: Mediaeval Academy of America, 1951.

Jacobsen, Herbert K. "Martin Luther's Early Years: Did You Know?" *Christian History* 9, no. 2 (April 1992): 2.

Janz, Denis R. "Confirmation." In *The Oxford Encyclopedia of the Reformation*, edited by Hans J. Hillerbrand, 1:405–6. New York: Oxford University Press, 1996.

———, ed. *A Reformation Reader: Primary Texts with Introductions*. Minneapolis: Fortress, 1999. 2nd ed., 2008.

———. *The Westminster Handbook to Martin Luther*. Louisville: Westminster John Knox, 2010.

Jeanes, Gordon P. *Signs of God's Promise: Thomas Cranmer's Sacramental Theology and the Book of Common Prayer*. London: T&T Clark, 2008.

Jensen, Gordon A. "Luther and the Lord's Supper." In *The Oxford Handbook of Martin Luther's Theology*, edited by Robert Kolb, Irene Dingel, and L'ubormir Bàtka, chap. 3. Oxford: Oxford University Press, 2014.

Johnson, Maxwell E., ed. *Benedictine Daily Prayer: A Short Breviary*. Collegeville, MN: Liturgical Press, 2005.

———. *The Prayers of Sarapion of Thmuis: A Literary, Liturgical, and Theological Analysis*. Rome: Pontificio Istituto Orientale, 1995.

———. *The Rites of Christian Initiation*. Revised and expanded ed. Collegeville, MN: Liturgical Press, 2007.

———, ed. *Sacraments and Worship: The Sources of Christian Theology*. Louisville: Westminster John Knox, 2012.

Jungkuntz, Theodore R. *Confirmation and Charismata*. Eugene, OR: Wipf & Stock, 1997.

Karant-Nunn, Susan C. *The Reformation of Ritual: An Interpretation of Early Modern Germany*. New York: Routledge, 1997.

Karlstadt, Andreas. *The Eucharistic Pamphlets of Andreas Bodenstein von Karlstadt*. Translated and edited by Amy Nelson Burnett. Early Modern Studies 6. Kirksville, MO: Truman State University Press, 2011.

Kavanagh, Aidan. *Confirmation: Origins and Reform*. New York: Pueblo, 1988.

———. *The Shape of Baptism: The Rite of Christian Initiation*. 2nd printing. Collegeville, MN: Liturgical Press, 1991.

Kelling, Hans-Wilhelm. "Martin Luther: The First Forty Years in Remembrance of the 500th Anniversary of His Birth." *Brigham Young University Studies*, no. 23 (Spring 1983): 131–46.

Kelly, Liam. *Sacraments Revisited: What Do They Mean Today?* London: Darton, Longman & Todd, 1998.

Kidd, B. J., ed. *Documents Illustrative of the Continental Reformation*. Oxford: Clarendon, 1911. Reprint, 1961.

Klaassen, Walter, ed. *Anabaptism in Outline: Selected Primary Sources*. Scottdale, PA: Herald Press, 1981.

Klausnitzer, Wolfgang. "Ordination." In *The Oxford Encyclopedia of the Reformation*, edited by Hans J. Hillerbrand, 3:177–79. New York: Oxford University Press, 1996.

Kolb, Robert, and Timothy J. Wengert, eds. *The Book of Concord: The Confessions of the Evangelical Lutheran Church*. Translated by Charles P. Arand. Minneapolis: Fortress, 2000.

Krodel, Gottfried G. "The Lord's Supper in the Theology of the Young Luther." *Lutheran Quarterly* 13, no. 1 (1961): 19–33.

Lazareth, William H. "ELCA Lutherans and Luther on Heterosexual Marriage." *Lutheran Quarterly* 8, no. 3 (Autumn 1994): 235–68.

———. *Luther on the Christian Home: An Application of the Social Ethics of the Reformation*. Philadelphia: Muhlenberg, 1960.

Lee, Philip J. *Against the Protestant Gnostics*. Oxford: Oxford University Press, 1993.

Leeming, Bernard. *Principles of Sacramental Theology*. Westminster, MD: Newman, 1956. 2nd ed., London: Longmans, Green, 1960.

Leithart, Peter J. "Augustine's Visible Words." *First Things*, February 5, 2011. https://www.firstthings.com/blogs/leithart/2011/02/visible-words.

Leppin, Volker. "Martin Luther." In *A Companion to the Eucharist in the Reformation*, edited by Lee Palmer Wandel, 39–56. Leiden: Brill, 2014.

Leroux, Neil R. *Martin Luther as Comforter: Writings on Death*. Leiden: Brill, 2007.

Lindberg, Carter, ed. *The European Reformations Sourcebook*. Oxford: Blackwell, 2000.

———. "Sacraments." In *The Oxford Encyclopedia of the Reformation*, edited by Hans J. Hillerbrand, 3:463–67. New York: Oxford University Press, 1996.

Littell, Franklin H. *The Anabaptist View of the Church*. Boston: Starr King, 1958.

Lohse, Bernhard. *Martin Luther's Theology: Its Historical and Systematic Development*. Minneapolis: Fortress, 2011.

Lombard, Peter. "Four Books of Sentences: IV." In *Peter Lombard and the Sacramental System*, translated by Elizabeth Frances Rogers, 79–246. Oakland: University of California Libraries, 1917. Reprint, Merrick, NY: Richwood, 1976.

Lortz, Joseph. "Sakramentales Denken beim jungen Luther." In *Luther-Jahrbuch 1969*, edited by D. Franz Lau, 9–40. Hamburg: Friedrich Wittig, 1969.

Luther, Martin. *D. Martin Luthers Werke*. Kritische Gesamtausgabe (Weimarer Ausgabe [WA]). 73 vols. Weimar, 1883–2009.

———. *D. Martin Luthers Werke*. Kritische Gesamtausgabe. Briefwechsel [WA Br]. 18 vols. Weimar, 1930–85.

———. *D. Martin Luthers Werke*. Kritische Gesamtausgabe. Tischreden [WA Tr]. 6 vols. Weimar, 1912–21.

———. *Luther: Letters of Spiritual Counsel*. Translated and edited by Theodore G. Tappert. Library of Christian Classics 18. Philadelphia: Westminster, 1955.

———. Luther's Works [LW]. American Edition. 55 vols. Edited by Jaroslav Pelikan and Helmut T. Lehman. Philadelphia: Muhlenberg and Fortress; St. Louis: Concordia, 1955–86.

———. *Martin Luther: Selections from His Writings* [Dillenberger]. Edited by John Dillenberger. New York: Anchor, 1962.

———. *Martin Luther's Basic Theological Writings*. Edited by Timothy F. Lull. 2nd ed. Minneapolis: Fortress, 1989.

MacCulloch, Diarmaid. *Thomas Cranmer: A Life*. New Haven: Yale University Press, 1996.

Macy, Gary. "The Medieval Inheritance." In *A Companion to the Eucharist in the Reformation*, edited by Lee Palmer Wandel, 15–37. Leiden: Brill, 2014.

Malia, Linda M. *Healing Touch and Saving Word: Sacraments of Healing, Instruments of Grace*. Eugene, OR: Pickwick Publications, 2013.

Marpeck, Pilgram. *The Writings of Pilgram Marpeck*. Edited and translated by William Klassen and Walter Klaassen. Scottdale, PA: Herald Press, 1978.

Marshall, Peter. "Purgatory." In *The Westminster Handbook to Theologies of the Reformation*, edited by R. Ward Holder, 33. Louisville: Westminster John Knox, 2010.

Martos, Joseph. *Doors to the Sacred: A Historical Introduction to Sacraments in the Catholic Church*. Ligouri, MO: Ligouri Publications, 2001. Updated and enlarged, 2014.

Marty, Martin E. *Martin Luther: A Penguin Life*. New York: Lipper / Viking, 2004.

McBrien, Richard P. "The Sacraments of Healing: Penance and Anointing the Sick." In *A History of Pastoral Care*, edited by G. R. Evans, 400–413. London: Cassell, 2000.

McEachern, Alton H. *Set Apart for Service*. Nashville: Broadman, 1980.

McGrath, Alister E. *Christianity's Dangerous Idea: The Protestant Revolution; A History from the Sixteenth Century to the Twenty-First*. New York: HarperOne, 2007.

McLaughlin, R. Emmet. "Truth, Tradition and History: The Historiography of High/Late Medieval and Early Modern Penance." In *A New History of Penance*, edited by Abigail Firey, 19–72. Leiden: Brill, 2008.

Melanchthon, Philip. *Melanchthon and Bucer*. Edited by Wilhelm Pauck. Library of Christian Classics 19. Philadelphia, PA: Westminster, 1969.

Menno Simons. *The Complete Writings of Menno Simons*. Edited by J. C. Wenger. Scottdale, PA: Herald Press, 1956.

Migne, J.-P., ed. Patrologiae Cursus Completus. Paris: Garnier Frères, 1958.

Miller, Gregory J. "Sacraments." In *Westminster Handbook to the Theologies of the Reformation*, edited by R. Ward Holder, 141–42. Louisville: Westminster John Knox, 2010.

Mueller, John T. "Means of Grace." In *Lutheran Cyclopedia*, edited by Edwin L. Lueker, 344–45. St. Louis: Concordia, 1954.

Ngien, Dennis. *Luther as a Spiritual Adviser: The Interface of Theology and Piety in Luther's Devotional Writings*. Milton Keynes, UK: Paternoster, 2007.

The Nicene and Post-Nicene Fathers. First Series [NPNF¹]. Edited by Philip Schaff. 1886–89. 14 vols. Reprint, Peabody, MA: Hendrickson, 1995.

The Nicene and Post-Nicene Fathers. Second Series [NPNF²]. Edited by Philip Schaff and Henry Wace. 1890–1900. 14 vols. Reprint, Peabody, MA: Hendrickson, 1995.

Oberman, Heiko A. *Luther: Man between God and the Devil*. New Haven: Yale University Press, 2006.

Oechsli, Wilhelm, Eden Paul, and Cedar Paul. *History of Switzerland, 1499–1914*. Cambridge Historical Series. Cambridge: Cambridge University Press, 1922.

O'Malley, J. Stephen. "Probing the Demise and Recovery of Healing in Christianity." *Pneuma* 5, no. 1 (1983): 46–59.

Origen of Alexandria. *Commentarii in Epistulam ad Romanos. = Romerbriefkommentar*. Vol. 2 (books 3–4). Edited by Theresia Heither. Freiburg im Breisgau: Herder, 1992.

———. "Matthew, Sermon 85." Translated by Paul Jacquemont. In *The Eucharist of the Early Christians*, by Willy Rordorf et al. New York: Pueblo, 1978.

Osborne, Kenan B. *The Christian Sacraments of Initiation: Baptism, Confirmation, Eucharist.* New York: Paulist Press, 1987.

Palmer, Paul F., ed. *Sacraments and Forgiveness.* Vol. 2 of *Sources of Christian Theology.* Westminster, MD: Newman, 1959.

———, ed. *Sacraments and Worship: Liturgy and Doctrinal Development of Baptism, Confirmation, and Eucharist.* Vol. 1 of *Sources of Christian Theology.* London: Darton, Longman & Todd, 1957.

Parsons, Michael. *Reformation Marriage: The Husband and Wife Relationship in the Theology of Luther and Calvin.* Eugene, OR: Wipf & Stock, 2011.

Pecklers, Keith F. "Eucharist in Western Churches." In *The Cambridge Dictionary of Christianity*, edited by Daniel Patte, 388–89. Cambridge: Cambridge University Press, 2010.

Peters, Albrecht. *Commentary on Luther's Catechisms: Baptism and the Lord's Supper.* St. Louis: Concordia, 2012.

Pless, John T. "The Use and Misuse of Luther in Contemporary Debates on Homosexuality: A Look at Two Theologians." *Lutheran Forum*, Summer 2005, 50–57.

Porter, J. Roy. "Oil in the Old Testament." In *The Oil of Gladness: Anointing in the Christian Tradition*, edited by Martin Dudley and Geoffrey Rowell, 35–45. Collegeville, MN: Liturgical Press, 1993.

Potter, G. R. *Huldrych Zwingli.* New York: St. Martin's Press, 1977.

———. *Zwingli.* Cambridge: Cambridge University Press, 1976.

Puller, F. W. *The Anointing of the Sick in Scripture and Tradition, with Some Considerations on the Numbering of the Sacraments.* London: SPCK, 1910.

Reinis, Austra. *Reforming the Art of Dying: The* ars moriendi *in the German Reformation (1519–1528).* Burlington, VT: Ashgate, 2007.

Rempel, John D. *The Lord's Supper in Anabaptism: A Study in the Christology of Balthasar Hubmaier, Pilgram Marpeck, and Dirk Philips.* Studies in Anabaptist and Mennonite History 33. Scottdale, PA: Herald Press, 1993.

Rittgers, Ronald K. "How Luther's Engagement in Pastoral Care Shaped His Theology." In *The Oxford Handbook of Martin Luther's Theology*, edited by Robert Kolb, Irene Dingel, and L'ubormir Bàtka, chap. 33. Oxford: Oxford University Press, 2014.

———. *The Reformation of Suffering: Pastoral Theology and Lay Piety in Late Medieval and Early Modern Germany.* New York: Oxford University Press, 2012.

Rordorf, Wiley, and Raymond Johanny, eds. *The Eucharist of the Early Christians.* New York: Pueblo, 1978.

Rorem, Paul. *Hugh of Saint Victor.* Oxford: Oxford University Press, 2009.

Rufus, Musonius. *Musonius Rufus: The Roman Socrates.* Translated and edited by Cora E. Lutz. New Haven: Yale University Press, 1947.

Rummel, Erika. *Erasmus's Annotations on the New Testament: From Philologist to Theologian.* Toronto: University of Toronto Press, 1986.

Salat, Johannes [= Hans]. *Chronik der schweizerischen Reformation: Von deren Anfängen bis und mit Ao. 1534*. In *Archiv für die schweizerische Reformationsgeschichte* 1 (Freiburg im Breisgau: Herder, 1869): 1–427.

Sattler, Dorothea. "Sacrament." In *The Encyclopedia of Christianity*, edited by Erwin Fahlbusch and G. W. Bromiley, 4:791–800. Grand Rapids: Eerdmans, 2005.

Sattler, Michael. *The Legacy of Michael Sattler*. Translated and edited by John H. Yoder. Scottdale, PA: Herald Press, 1973.

Schaff, Philip, ed. *The Creeds of Christendom*. Vol. 3. Grand Rapids: Baker, 1969.

Schroder, H. J., ed. *Canons and Decrees of the Council of Trent*. Rockford, IL: Tan Books, 1978.

Schuler, Rhonda. "Confirmation." In *The Encyclopedia of Protestantism*, edited by Hans J. Hillerbrand, 1:824–33. New York: Routledge, 2004.

Scribner, Robert W. *Popular Culture and Popular Movements in Reformation Germany*. London: Hambledon, 1987.

Seeburg, Erich. *Luthers Theologie in ihren Gründzugen*. 2nd ed. Stuttgart: W. Kohlhammer, 1950.

Sources chrétiennes [SC]. Paris: Cerf, 1943–.

Spinks, Bryan D. *Do This in Remembrance of Me: The Eucharist from the Early Church to the Present Day*. Norwich, UK: SCM, 2013.

———. *Reformation and Modern Rituals and Theologies of Baptism: From Luther to Contemporary Practices*. Burlington, VT: Ashgate, 2006.

St. Amant, C. Penrose. "Sources of Baptist Views on Ordination." *Baptist History and Heritage* 23, no. 3 (July 1988): 3–15, 41.

Stayer, James M., Werner O. Packull, and Klaus Deppermann. "From Monogenesis to Polygenesis: The Historical Discussion of Anabaptist Origins." *Mennonite Quarterly Review* 49, no. 2 (April 1975): 83–121.

Steinmetz, David C. "The Council of Trent." In *The Cambridge Companion to Reformation Theology*, edited by David Bagchi and David C. Steinmetz, 233–47. Cambridge: Cambridge University Press, 2004.

Stephens, W. P. *The Theology of Huldrych Zwingli*. Oxford: Clarendon, 1986.

Stone, Darwell, trans. *A History of the Doctrine of the Holy Eucharist*. London: Longmans, Green, 1909.

Strohl, Jane E. "Luther on Marriage, Sexuality, and the Family." In *The Oxford Handbook of Martin Luther's Theology*, edited by Robert Kolb, Irene Dingel, and L'ubormir Bàtka, chap. 26. Oxford: Oxford University Press, 2014.

Sundberg, Walter. *Worship as Repentance: Lutheran Liturgical Traditions and Catholic Consensus*. Grand Rapids: Eerdmans, 2012.

Tanner, Norman P. *Decrees of the Ecumenical Councils: From Nicaea I to Vatican II*. Washington, DC: Georgetown University Press, 1990.

Tentler, Thomas. "Confession." In *The Oxford Encyclopedia of the Reformation*, edited by Hans J. Hillerbrand, 1:242–44. New York: Oxford University Press, 1996.

Tertullian. *Tertullian's Homily on Baptism*. Translated by Ernest Evans. London: SPCK, 1964.

Thomas à Kempis. *The Imitation of Christ*. Edited by Hal McElwaine Helms and Robert J. Edmondson. Brewster, MA: Paraclete, 2008.

Thomas Aquinas. *Summa theologiae*. Vols. 56–59. Edited by David Bourke, James J. Cunningham, William Barden, and Thomas Gilby. London: Blackfriars / McGraw-Hill, 1975.

———. *The "Summa theologica" of St. Thomas Aquinas*. Translated by Fathers of the English Dominican Province. 22 vols. in 20. London: Burns, Oates & Washbourne, 1911–32.

Torbet, Robert G. *The Baptist Ministry: Then and Now*. Philadelphia: Judson, 1953.

Tranvik, Mark D. "Baptism: Popular Practices." In *The Oxford Encyclopedia of the Reformation*, edited by Hans J. Hillerbrand, 1:115–16. New York: Oxford University Press, 1996.

Trigg, Jonathan D. *Baptism in the Theology of Martin Luther*. Leiden: Brill, 2001.

———. "Luther on Baptism and Penance." In *The Oxford Handbook of Martin Luther's Theology*, edited by Robert Kolb, Irene Dingel, and L'ubormir Bàtka, chap. 21. Oxford: Oxford University Press, 2014.

Turner, Paul. *Sources of Confirmation: From the Fathers through the Reformers*. Collegeville, MN: Liturgical Press, 1993.

Turrell, James F. "Anglican Theologies of the Eucharist." In *A Companion to the Eucharist in the Reformation*, edited by Lee Palmer Wandel, 139–58. Leiden: Brill, 2014.

Vander Zee, Leonard J. *Christ, Baptism and the Lord's Supper: Recovering the Sacraments for Evangelical Worship*. Downers Grove, IL: IVP Academic, 2004.

Waters, Brent. "Marriage." In *Oxford Handbook of Sacramental Theology*, edited by Hans Boersma and Matthew Levering, chap. 33. New York: Oxford University Press, 2015.

Watkins, Oscar D. *A History of Penance*. Vol. 1. New York: Burt Franklin, 1961.

Wenger, Mark R. "The Origins and Development of Anointing among Nineteenth-Century Mennonites." *Mennonite Quarterly Review*, no. 79 (January 2005): 19–50.

Wengert, Timothy J., ed. *The Pastoral Luther: Essays on Martin Luther's Practical Theology*. Grand Rapids: Lutheran Quarterly Books / Eerdmans, 2009.

Werbick, Jürgen. "Penance." In *Dictionary of the Reformation*, edited by Klaus Ganzer and Bruno Steimer, 239. New York: Crossroads, 2004.

Whitaker, E. C., and Maxwell E. Johnson, eds. *Documents of the Baptismal Liturgy*. 3rd ed. Collegeville, MN: Liturgical Press, 2003.

White, James F. *A Brief History of Christian Worship*. Nashville: Abingdon, 1993.

————, ed. *Documents of Christian Worship: Descriptive and Interpretive Sources*. Louisville: Westminster John Knox, 1992.

————. *Protestant Worship and Church Architecture: Theological and Historical Considerations*. Oxford: Oxford University Press, 1964.

————. *The Sacraments in Protestant Practice and Faith*. Nashville: Abingdon, 1999.

Wicks, Jared. "Fides sacramenti—Fides specialis: Luther's Development in 1518." *Gregorianum* 65, no. 1 (Rome: Pontificia Universitas Gregoriana, 1984): 53–87.

Williams, George Huntston. *The Radical Reformation*. 3rd ed. Sixteenth Century Essays & Studies 15. Kirksville, MO: Sixteenth Century Journal Publishers, 1992.

Wingren, Gustaf. *Luther on Vocation*. Philadelphia: Muhlenberg, 1957.

Witte, John. *From Sacrament to Contract: Marriage, Religion, and Law in the Western Tradition*. 2nd ed. Louisville: Westminster John Knox, 2012.

Witte, John, and Eliza Ellison. *Covenant Marriage in Comparative Perspective*. Grand Rapids: Eerdmans, 2005.

Wright, N. T. *The Resurrection of the Son of God*. Vol. 3 of *Christian Origins and the Question of God*. Minneapolis: Fortress, 2003.

Zeeden, Ernst Walter. *Faith and Act: The Survival of Medieval Ceremonies in the Lutheran Reformation*. St. Louis: Concordia, 2012.

Zwingli, Huldrych. *Commentary on True and False Religion*. Translated by Samuel Macauley Jackson and Clarence Nevin Heller. Durham, NC: Labyrinth, 1981.

————. *Zwingli and Bullinger: Selected Translations with Introductions and Notes*. Edited by G. W. Bromiley. Library of Christian Classics 24. Philadelphia: Westminster, 1953.

Subject Index

means of 5, 10, 12, 13, 14, 15, 24, 27, 30, 51,
57, 64, 127, 165, 170, 171, 183, 189, 210,
216, 222, 228, 229–30
and ordination 118–19, 127, 128, 129–30, 135
and penance 39, 46, 49–50, 54, 56, 57, 64, 65
and sacerdotalism 129–30, 135
sign of 13, 34, 176, 185, 186–87, 188, 216
testimony of 32
and works 65
Zwingli on 30, 78, 138, 210, 216, 222
Gregorian Reform Movement 199

Holy and Blessed Sacrament of Baptism, The
(Luther) 173
Holy orders. *See* ordination
homosexuality 41, 98, 99n51. *See also* sexuality
Hussites 119

indelible mark 7, 47, 75, 77, 113, 118, 119–20,
126–27n51, 128, 135, 199. *See also* character, sacramental; dignity; intrinsic power
indulgences 45, 46
initiation 69–70, 85, 164, 172, 185, 187. *See also*
baptism; confirmation
intrinsic power 16

Jesus Christ. *See also* union with Christ
and absolution 50
and anointing 140–41
and baptism 180
death of 202–3
and God 57
grace of 229–231
incarnation of 169, 206
and marriage 89
prayer of 72n18
presence in Lord's Supper of 194, 195–96,
197, 198, 200, 202, 205–6, 209–14, 216–17,
218–20, 221–23
and repentance 39
as second Adam 5
Jews 19, 86–89, 113, 140, 165, 223

laying on of hands 32, 66, 67, 68–69, 70, 74,
77, 79, 80, 81, 82, 84, 113–14, 116, 118, 135,
153, 161. *See also* confirmation
Letter to Polycarp (Ignatius) 90
Lollards 119
Lord's Supper
as atonement/sacrifice 197–98, 202–3, 205,
206, 209, 221
and baptism 193–94

in Catholic Church 192–93, 196, 200, 205, 215,
217
and church as communal 223–24
as consubstantiation 197
contemporary Protestant 220–25
as covenant 218n127
division in 192–93
in early church 192–95
and faith 201–2, 210, 215
and fanatics 209–11
and humility 201
and laity 199–200, 204, 208
Large Catechism on 215
and love 203, 208, 214, 217, 221
Luther on 200–215
Marburg Colloquy on 213–14
in Mass 197–99, 205, 207–9, 215
in Middle Ages 195–200
and ordination 129
and penance 54–55, 62
presence of Christ in 194, 195–96, 197, 198,
200, 202, 205–6, 209–14, 216–17, 218–20,
221–23
Protestant 215–20
Small Catechism on 214
and superstition 198–99
as symbolic 210, 221–22
as testament 202–3
as transubstantiation 197, 198, 205–6
and union with Christ 198, 205–6, 210, 213,
218, 219, 221, 222
and utraquism 200
in Western church 221, 222
and Word 210
love
and baptism 160, 169, 171
and extreme unction 139, 146
feast 116
and Lord's Supper 203, 208, 214, 217, 221
and marriage 17, 87, 89, 90, 94–95, 97
and penance 42, 49, 62, 57
pledge of 160, 217, 221
and sacraments 9, 23

Mansfeld 73, 137
Manual of York Use 108
Marburg 30, 213, 214
marriage. *See also* celibacy
and children 94, 101–2
contemporary Protestant 109–11
as covenant 88, 94, 95, 98, 107–8, 110–11
cultural origins of 86–88

in Middle Ages 18, 19
and ordination 114, 116, 122, 126, 133, 135
and penance 21, 29, 38, 41, 43, 45, 47, 50, 57,
  61, 63
and priesthood of all believers 29, 122
priesthood of all believers 2, 25, 29, 47, 50, 52,
  56, 63, 64, 110, 119–22, 124, 125, 131–34,
  150–51, 154
promise 24, 31, 26, 28, 74, 126–27, 203
purgatory 45, 46, 198, 203

reform 1–2
of baptism 172–87
of confirmation 70–82
of extreme unction 145–62
of marriage 93–105
and Ninety-Five Theses 20–21
of ordination 119–33
of penance 46–61
of sacraments 3–4, 21, 26–27, 37–38, 227–29
repentance 38–39, 40–41, 42–44, 47–49, 55, 58–
  59, 61, 63, 65. *See also* confession; penance

sacerdotalism 3, 15, 47, 56, 119, 120, 129, 135,
  141, 150, 174, 199
sacraments. *See* anointing the sick; baptism;
  character, sacramental; confirmation; effectiveness of sacraments; extreme unction;
  Lord's Supper; marriage; number of sacraments; ordination; penance; pledge; Word
  and sacrament
sacramentum 6–7, 106
salvation 3–4, 22, 24, 169–70
Satan. *See* devil
satisfaction 44–45
Scholasticism 10, 14–15, 17, 18, 19, 142–44,
  171, 200
sexuality 87, 88, 91, 94, 98–99
Shepherd of Hermas 41, 118
sign
and faith 9, 23–25, 27, 30, 31, 32, 173, 174
and genuine sacrament 11
operative 9, 10
outward 32
of a sacred reality 11
and symbol 29–30, 185
visible 53, 169
and word 25, 51, 169
simul justus et peccator 56, 174, 186, 190–91
sin 40–42, 168, 171, 174, 175, 186. *See also* forgiveness of sin
Smalcald Articles 215

sola fide 1, 27, 30, 31, 33, 49, 190, 229
sola gratia 1, 150
sola scriptura 1, 229
substance 16, 77
Summa theologiae (Aquinas) 14

Table Talk (Luther) 154
testament, Luther's notion of 28, 175, 176,
  202–4, 205, 207
Thirty-Nine Articles 33–34
*Treatise on the New Testament, That Is, the
  Holy Mass* (Luther) 202–3
two kingdoms 104

union with Christ 33, 63, 92, 94, 106, 108, 186
  198, 205–6, 210, 213, 218, 219, 221, 222
universal priesthood. *See* priesthood of all
  believers

visible word 8–9, 10, 32, 169
vocation 17, 91, 110, 113, 123–24, 126, 130, 134,
  154
vow 11, 20, 31, 80, 96–97, 98, 100, 102, 104,
  107, 108, 131, 187, 202. *See also* pledge
Vulgate 27n95, 42, 43, 48, 106

Waldensians 119, 179, 182n71
Waldshut 159
Wartburg 54, 96, 207
Western church. *See also* Catholic Church
baptism in 170, 172
and church and state 104
and confirmation 66–67, 69–70, 73
and extreme unction 139–40, 143, 144, 145,
  154
and Lord's Supper 221, 222
and marriage 86–87, 88, 90, 91–92, 107, 108
and *mystērion*/mystery 6, 35
number of sacraments in 13, 14, 19, 37, 51,
  73, 204
and ordination 113, 119, 121, 128, 129, 132
and penance 44, 46, 47, 59, 62
reform of 2, 3
and Scholasticism 17, 18
and science 64
Wittenberg 21, 54, 96, 137–38, 152, 154,
  156n71, 173n33, 178, 207, 208, 209, 214
Word and sacrament 28, 51, 123, 135

Zurich 29, 30, 33, 78, 106, 157
Zwickau 75
Zwickau prophets 178

Name Index